REPLANTING A SLAVE SOCIETY

JEFFERSONIAN AMERICA

Charlene M. Boyer Lewis, Annette Gordon-Reed, Peter S. Onuf,
Andrew J. O'Shaughnessy, and Robert G. Parkinson, Editors

REPLANTING A SLAVE SOCIETY

The Sugar and Cotton Revolutions in the Lower Mississippi Valley

Patrick Luck

University of Virginia Press

CHARLOTTESVILLE AND LONDON

University of Virginia Press
© 2022 by the Rector and Visitors of the University of Virginia
All rights reserved
Printed in the United States of America on acid-free paper

First published 2022

9 8 7 6 5 4 3 2 1

Library of Congress Cataloging-in-Publication Data
Names: Luck, Patrick, author.
Title: Replanting a slave society : the sugar and cotton revolutions in the lower Mississippi
 valley / Patrick Luck.
Other titles: Jeffersonian America.
Description: Charlottesville : University of Virginia Press, 2022. | Series: Jeffersonian
 America | Includes bibliographical references and index.
Identifiers: LCCN 2022019668 (print) | LCCN 2022019669 (ebook) |
 ISBN 9780813947815 (cloth ; alk. paper) | ISBN 9780813947822 (ebook)
Subjects: LCSH: Slavery—Louisiana—History—18th century. | Slavery—Louisiana—
 History—19th century. | Slavery—Mississippi—History—18th century. | Slavery—
 Mississippi—History—19th century. | Cotton manufacture—Louisiana—History. |
 Cotton manufacture—Mississippi—History. | Cotton growing—Louisiana—
 History. | Cotton growing—Mississippi—History. | Sugarcane industry—Louisiana—
 History. | Sugarcane industry—Mississippi—History. | Agricultural innovations—
 United States—History.
Classification: LCC E446 .L93 2022 (print) | LCC E446 (ebook) | DDC
 306.3/620976309033—dc23/eng/20220610
LC record available at https://lccn.loc.gov/2022019668
LC ebook record available at https://lccn.loc.gov/2022019669

Cover art: Sucrerie Bouligny et Cie., St. Charles (Bouligny and Company Sugar Refinery),
Father Joseph Michel Paret, 1859. (Fred B. Kniffen Cultural Resources Laboratory,
Department of Geography and Anthropology, Louisiana State University)

For Laura, Elizabeth, and Rachel

CONTENTS

ILLUSTRATIONS

ACKNOWLEDGMENTS

I am happy to finally be able to acknowledge the many people who made this book possible. I first began work on this project as a dissertation while a student in the department of history at Johns Hopkins University. I am greatly indebted for the completion of this project to my dissertation advisor, Michael Johnson. During my work on the dissertation, he encouraged me in this project and provided crucial and meticulous feedback throughout the research and writing process. He has also always been a model of careful scholarship that I have tried (hopefully with some success) to emulate. He is an excellent teacher and scholar, and I hope this book reflects what he has taught me.

I would also like to thank the faculty and graduate students in the department of history at Johns Hopkins University. The faculty provided superb training in the discipline of history. Many of the faculty and grad students read various pieces of my dissertation or works related to it over the years and gave valuable feedback. Philip Morgan and Mary Ryan provided constructive criticism of my dissertation that has vastly improved this book. I would also like to thank the members of the Nineteenth Century American History Seminar who made many thoughtful suggestions and criticisms, both large and small, on different pieces of my dissertation, so thank you to Ian Beamish, Rob Gamble, Katie Hemphill, Craig Hollander, Amy Isaacs-Koplowicz, Gabe Klehr, John Matsui, David Schley, and Jessica Ziparo. Many of your suggestions ended up in this book, greatly improving it.

Special thanks go to Jim Sidbury, my master's thesis advisor at the University of Texas at Austin. He guided me through my initial years as a graduate student when I knew that I wanted to study something about southern history and slavery but had little idea what that something was or how to go about studying it. The road to this project began when he suggested I look at some lists of enslaved people held by the Natchez Trace Collection. Little did I know that those lists would lead me to this project and book. Ever since, he has encouraged me in my continued pursuit of this project.

My colleagues both past and present at Florida Polytechnic University (only one of them a historian) have been supportive of this project. Amanda Bruce, Jim Dewey, Liz Kelly, Jenny Lee, and Wylie Lenz read and commented on parts of this book. Jim and Wylie, despite being an economist and English professor respectively, often served as willing sounding boards for ideas related to this project. Kate Bernard, Florida Poly's former librarian, worked heroically to overcome the limits of our exclusively digital library and find books and articles I needed to complete this project. Finally, I would like to thank the faculty and labor organizers who fought to unionize our faculty and bargain our first union contract. Many of you sacrificed a great deal to achieve this. The greater stability unionization provided at our new and non-tenure-granting university gave me the time and space to complete the work of transforming my dissertation into a book.

I have also presented pieces of this work in several venues where I benefited from many scholars' feedback. These venues include the Louisiana Historical Association's annual meetings; the American Historical Association's annual meeting; the Florida Conference of Historian's annual meetings; the Society for the Historians of the Early American Republic's annual meeting; Trans-American Crossings: Enslaved Migrations within the Americas and Their Impacts on Slave Cultures and Society (a conference cosponsored by Omohundro Institute of Early American History and Culture and the John Carter Brown Library); the Southern Forum on Agricultural, Rural, and Environmental History; the Social Science History Association annual meeting; the American Antiquarian Society's research brown bag; the University of Toulouse's Louisiana/Interculturality day; and the Columbus State University's history faculty research brown bag. At each of these events, I received feedback from panel commenters, fellow panelists, audience members, and colleagues that shaped and improved this work.

As is the case for all historians, I owe huge debts of gratitude to staff at several museums and archives. I was greatly aided by staff members at the Louisiana State Museum, the Louisiana Division of the New Orleans Public Library, the Hill Memorial Library at Louisiana State University, the Historic New Orleans Collection, the Louisiana Research Collection of the Howard-Tilton Memorial Library at Tulane University, the Briscoe Center for American History at the University of Texas at Austin, the Library of Congress, the National Archives, the American Antiquarian Society, and the Massachusetts Historical Society. I would especially like to thank the archivists in New Orleans who made me feel more than welcome even though many of the city's archives had just reopened after the difficult times following Katrina.

I would also like to thank several organizations that made my research financially possible. A fellowship from LSU Libraries Special Collections allowed me to spend several weeks researching in their collections. An award from the Dolph Briscoe Center for American History allowed me to spend several weeks researching in the indispensable Natchez Trace Collection. A fellowship from the American Antiquarian Society allowed me to spend a month researching in their invaluable newspaper collections. Johns Hopkins University's department of history provided research travel money that funded several of my shorter research trips. Finally, Florida Polytechnic University, besides providing me a permanent academic position that has allowed me to work on this book, provided funding for me to write and research during the early process of transforming my dissertation into a book. Florida Poly also provided funds to purchase books for my research and to hire a research assistant. That research assistant, Cynthia Wooldridge, provided crucial assistance in reorganizing some of my research databases into more accessible formats. Finally, Florida Poly provided funds to have the map in this book drawn. Thank you to Meghan Cohorst for doing such a great job drawing it.

I would like to thank Dick Holway, who first approached me about the possibility of publishing this book with the University of Virginia Press. I have also been fortunate to work with Nadine Zimmerli at the University of Virginia Press after Dick's retirement. She took command of the project and kept it on course, even after the Covid pandemic began.

In particular, she was crucial in helping me productively work through the reports by the two anonymous readers. Throughout our time working together, the very fact that she saw promise in this project helped get me to the finish line.

As my final expression of professional gratitude, I would like to thank the two anonymous readers of the manuscript, whose careful reading of and comments on the (overly long) manuscript dramatically improved its final form. They were both models of what peer review should be: sources of detailed, constructive criticism. I greatly appreciate their selfless work. I would especially like to thank the reader who read and commented on the manuscript twice, the second time in spring 2021, when everyone inside (and outside) higher education was groaning under the pressures of the pandemic. The positive contribution of the anonymous readers cannot be exaggerated.

My family has offered me support and encouragement throughout my work on this project, for which I am very grateful. My mother, Mary Gail Karkoska, read and copyedited my dissertation in the final weeks before its submission and encouraged me in the years since to get this book written and published. I would also like to acknowledge my deceased father, Mike Luck, whose own love of history sparked my interest in the subject as a child. I never would have produced this work without his inspiration. I wish he were here to see this book.

I would like to acknowledge my daughters, Rachel and Elizabeth. You're too young to really understand why I have spent so many hours and days locked away working and writing, but you respected my need for quiet and time . . . unless of course you had something pressing to tell me or a game you wanted to play. I know it was especially trying for you during the pandemic when we were all stuck together at home for many months, and I was unable to spend as much time with you as we would have liked. Thanks also to Elizabeth for not knowing that you never ask an author, in an exasperated tone of voice, "Are you ever going to finish that book?" It was always a helpful reminder to "finish that book," and I finally have.

Thanks above all to Laura Young, my wife and partner. She has been a model of support and patience throughout the years of research and writing and the long separations caused by my research trips. I was only able to complete this thanks to her support and love. I am especially thankful that she took on extra responsibilities taking care of the children when they were unable to go to school because of the pandemic. I could not have finished this book when I did without that support during a very challenging time. She always believed in my ability to complete this project, even when I did not, and for that I am grateful.

In the end, countless people made this book possible, many left unmentioned here. To those people, I also say thank you.

REPLANTING A SLAVE SOCIETY

INTRODUCTION

> Is not this the country for the slave holder? Do not the cli-
> mate, the soil and productions of this country furnish allure-
> ments to the application of your negroes on our lands?
> —An Emigrant from Maryland, *Daily National Intelligencer,*
> September 5, 1817

In the mid-1790s, slavery in the lower Mississippi valley seemed, to the region's elites, on the verge of collapse at worst, stagnation at best. In 1796, one elite Creole, Joseph de Pontalba informed his wife of alarming rumors that slavery would soon be abolished, either via a French takeover (the French had abolished slavery in their colonies two years before) or by the Spanish king, who supposedly hoped that by doing so he would reduce the threat of revolution. Pontalba did not welcome abolition. He worried that the rural economy would disintegrate as planters would be unable to afford to hire freed people because of the recent collapse of the region's two main export crops: tobacco and indigo.[1] Pontalba was typical of the region's enslavers and other elite residents who feared that the region might plunge into instability because of the French and Haitian Revolutions and because the local economy might never again prosper. Many enslavers came to so fear the region's enslaved people that they encouraged the Spanish government to temporarily halt the slave trade, a step taken in 1796.[2]

The tone in 1804, only eight years later, and immediately after the Louisiana Purchase, could not have been more different. The new American governor, William C. C. Claiborne, learned early in his tenure that the continuation of the slave trade (the Spanish had reopened it in 1800) was necessary if he hoped to quickly win local support for the American take-over. One of his informants wrote that "no Subject . . . [is] so interesting to the minds of the inhabitants . . . as that of the importation of brute Negroes from Africa."[3] Summing up what he had learned after several months in New Orleans, Claiborne reported to President Thomas Jefferson that "prohibiting the Importation of Slaves into Louisiana, will be viewed by the Citizens as a great Grievance; on this subject much irritation is manifested, and the general opinion seems to be, that the Territory cannot prosper without a great encrease [sic] of Negro's."[4] Much had changed between 1796, when enslavers asked that the slave trade close, and 1804, when enslavers demanded it stay open.

The eight years between 1796 and 1804 were part of a roughly three-decade period during which the colonized areas of the lower Mississippi valley experienced sudden and rapid changes in their economic, social, and political conditions. The lower Mississippi valley, as used in this book, encompasses the zone of colonization begun by the French in the river valley in the early 1700s, divided between the Spanish and British after the Seven Years' War, united again under the Spanish after the American Revolution and incorporated into the United States between 1798 and 1810. In the early 1780s, the lower Mississippi valley's colonized areas mostly hugged the Mississippi River between New Orleans and Natchez with smaller colonial outposts on the Red River and in southwest Louisiana. By 1811, the colonized areas had expanded throughout much of the modern state of Louisiana as well as the southwestern part of the modern state of Mississippi along and near the Mississippi River. This book largely begins along the stretch of the Mississippi River between New Orleans and Natchez but follows colonizers throughout the larger area (much of which was away from the Mississippi River).

During the period covered by this book, roughly 1783 to 1811, these colonies of the lower Mississippi valley lurched from an economic prosperity they had never seen before to economic, social, and political crisis and then to an even more boisterous and sturdy prosperity. At the same time, the region's colonies had gone from a marginal part of a declining Spanish empire to a (only ever notional) part of the French empire to, finally, the western anchor of the new American republic. Residents of the region must have felt a whiplash tinged with excitement (or more negative emotions for those sympathetic to revolution, critical of slavery, or enslaved) by the early 1800s. By the post–War of 1812 boom, enslavers, such as the one quoted in the epigraph, viewed the region as a stable slave society where they could expect to make bonanza profits via cotton, sugar, and slavery.

This situation sharply departed from the recent and even long-term colonial history of the region. From its founding in the late 1600s, the Louisiana colony, despite its founders' dreams of plantation wealth, had, from the point of view of its imperial owners, first France and then Spain, languished as an underpopulated backwater, mostly dependent on trade with Native Americans and a financial sinkhole for its imperial owners.[5] However, in the years after the American Revolution, Louisiana's agricultural economy had experienced a brief period of prosperity. Tobacco and indigo cultivation on farms and plantations began to dominate the economy and, alongside trade with American colonizers in the Ohio River valley, eclipsed the trade with Native Americans in economic importance.[6] Decades after initial colonization, the lower Mississippi valley's export-oriented agricultural economy seemed headed toward the prosperity envisioned by its founders.

However, this vision of the future fell apart suddenly in the early 1790s, less than a decade after it had begun. Crucially, the newly prosperous export-oriented agricultural economy collapsed due to government action, natural conditions, and international instability resulting from the warfare and revolutionary events roiling the Atlantic World.[7] At the same time, the colonial power structure faced increasing external and internal threats. Local displays of Jacobin sympathy led to the mobilization of the militia.[8] Spanish Louisiana faced threats of invasion by a foreign power or filibustering Anglo-Americans.[9] Fears of rebellion by the enslaved, perhaps in concert with radical whites, were widespread. These fears were seemingly confirmed by the 1795 Pointe Coupee Conspiracy, an alleged plot involving dozens of enslaved people and several free white men in Pointe Coupee Parish (just upriver from Baton Rouge on the Mississippi River) who had been inspired by revolutionary ideals to rise in rebellion against local enslavers.[10] As pointed out in the opening vignette, these crises led to a collapse of faith in the future of slavery in the lower Mississippi valley.

Ironically, even as these crises were calling into question the future of slavery, changes were occurring in the lower Mississippi valley that would, once consolidated, launch the region's enslavers to heights of power and prosperity well beyond anything they had dreamed possible in the late 1780s. In 1795, the same year as the Pointe Coupee Conspiracy, Étienne Boré successfully granulated sugar on his plantation outside New Orleans. That same year, John Barclay, a mechanic recently returned from a trip to the Carolinas and Georgia, built Natchez's first Eli Whitney–style saw gin and began to process short-staple cotton. While the region would have its ups and downs (from the point of view of many of its free residents; from the point of view of its enslaved people, it was mostly "downs" after 1795), in some ways there was no looking back after that year. Sugar, with its high technical and capital requirements, advanced steadily across the region over the coming decades while cotton, with its very low barriers for entry, exploded across it. By 1803, indigo and tobacco were niche products, while sugar and cotton were dual monarchs contending for the loyalty of cultivators.

The importance of the lower Mississippi valley's sugar and cotton revolutions was recognized when they happened and has been acknowledged as well by historians who have written about the region.[11] However, despite the widely acknowledged importance of these revolutions, they have typically been relegated to the background of other histories being written about the region rather than being the focus.[12] Often the crop revolutions are treated almost like natural economic processes that have no real need for analysis. Much of this tendency can be explained by the fact that historians of the region disproportionately focus their attention on New Orleans, with the rest of the region (where most residents lived) serving as background to New Orleans's admittedly fascinating and important story.[13] Considering the importance of the cotton and sugar revolutions to the region's and even New Orleans's histories, this oversight is a major gap in the region's history. This book aims to explain and analyze how these commodity revolutions were made and how they changed the direction of the region's urban and rural histories.

However, the implications of the sugar and cotton revolutions go beyond the lower Mississippi valley. The story of these revolutions is an example of the hemispheric process that saw a transition from "colonial" or "first" slavery to "second" slavery, the latter term referring to the revitalization and expansion of slavery in the Americas, particularly in Brazil,

Cuba, and the American South, even as slavery was being challenged by the revolutions roiling the Atlantic World in the late 1700s.[14] Typically, the United States' second slavery has been strongly associated (even to the point of conflation) with cotton. Edward Baptist, in his history of the cotton South and its role in the development of American capitalism, argues that the Haitian Revolution "sounded the knell for the first form of New World slavery" based in the sugar islands, where "productivity had depended on the continual resupply of captive workers ripped from the womb of Africa," opening America to "a Second Slavery exponentially greater in economic power than the first," a second slavery dependent on cotton cultivation.[15] Looked at from antebellum America, this claim is imminently reasonable. Cotton was the hegemonic commodity of the Deep South and the engine of much of antebellum America's economic development, and thus, to understand the second slavery of the antebellum Deep South, one must understand cotton.[16]

An elite resident of the lower Mississippi valley in 1800 or even 1815 would likely have found this focus on cotton puzzling. They would have known that, for many of the wealthiest residents of the region, the Haitian Revolution meant the adoption of sugar, not cotton. Sugar was so dominant in the imagination of many of the region's elites that in 1806 one pseudonymous commenter (likely the Irish-born sugar planter and merchant Daniel Clark) even went so far as to condescendingly claim that planters growing sugarcane were making "immense fortunes" while "the poorer classes equally find their account in the cultivation of Indigo, Rice and Cotton."[17] For many of the region's elites, sugar, not cotton, was central to the enslaved-labor-driven agricultural economy's revitalization during these early, formative years of the second slavery.

However, the story of the lower Mississippi valley's second slavery was more complicated than these elites recognized and pointed to a future where sugar would recede to the background of the story of the United States' second slavery (it would remain central to Cuba's second slavery).[18] The roots of the cotton-dominated second slavery were already present during the first decade of the 1800s. While some elites viewed cotton with condescension as a crop fit for "the poorer classes," the reality of its adoption was very different. Cotton had exploded across much of the region during the late 1790s as a source of profit for the region's farmers (defined as those who enslaved up to twenty people or did not rely on enslaved labor) and planters (defined by historians of American slavery as those who enslaved twenty or more people). Some of the region's wealthiest and most influential planters, including the French-born Pointe Coupee merchant, politician, and poet Julien Poydras and the Scottish-born Natchez scientist and explorer William Dunbar, cultivated cotton, typically because they lived outside of the region where sugar was viable. While sometimes in local competition (a competition sugar usually won), sugar and cotton were both integral to the enslaved-labor-driven and elite-benefiting development of the lower Mississippi valley, and both would continue to advance across the region well into the antebellum period.[19] In fact, as we shall see, in this early period, cotton often served as a means for small planters to accumulate profits to move into sugar production, subverting notions of cotton's preeminence. However, in the long run, cotton could be cultivated on more land in the Deep South, including in the lower Mississippi valley, meaning that it, and not sugar, would come to dominate the region's economy, while sugar would continue to dominate in the limited area where it could be grown.

As should be clear, the beginning of the second slavery in the lower Mississippi valley is an intertwined story of sugar and cotton and the elites who embraced their cultivation to overcome the severe crises that they faced in the early and middle 1790s. It is a story that blends the first and second slaveries, allowing no clear division to be drawn between the two, and suggests commonalities between the second slavery of the United States and that of other parts of the Americas, particularly the sugar-driven second slavery of Cuba. This transformative period brought together, often on neighboring or even the same plantation, sugar, produced during this period largely as it was on the sugar islands, and cotton, made profitable by the Industrial Revolution and the adoption of the new Eli Whitney–style cotton gins. In its first decade or so, this second slavery depended on the importation of enslaved Africans but soon began to intertwine that importation with the new and accelerating movement of "American slaves" (as they were often called in the region) from the Atlantic Coast. Finally, a diverse group of elites (planters, merchants, and government officials born in the region or immigrating from Europe, elsewhere in the United States, or the Caribbean) formed intertwining connections across the region, operating within a shared economic system centered on New Orleans and to a lesser extent Natchez that they were developing in response to internal and external pressures and opportunities. Ultimately, cotton would overshadow (but never snuff out) sugar. However, in these early years, elites utilized them both to remake the region and had little, if any, recognition that cotton would dominate the region's future. The creation and reality of the second slavery was far more complex than a narrow focus on cotton in the antebellum period would suggest.[20]

This book is about how regional elites made these intertwined cotton and sugar revolutions that would transform slavery in the lower Mississippi valley as part of the larger story of the transformation of American slavery. To do so, they adopted, adapted, and improved a variety of "technologies" to replant their slave society over the decade and a half following the crucial year of crisis and opportunity: 1795. To understand those changes, I employ an expansive but straightforward definition of technology. The economist W. Brian Arthur has defined technology as "a means to fulfill a human purpose" and "an assemblage of practices and components." This definition leads him to conclude that business organizations, legal systems, and contracts are all types of technologies.[21] Even more succinctly, the historian Christopher Tomlins calls technology "a means of making and making do" in his study of the law as a technology of colonization and social organization in colonial Anglo-America.[22] Looked at this way, we can see that much of what made second slavery in the lower Mississippi valley was the very human activity of people, in this case largely the region's elites, using various new and old technologies to remake their world more to their benefit and liking.

As Arthur's reference to technology as "an assemblage of practices and components" suggests, historians and philosophers of technology recognize that technologies are rarely stand-alone.[23] Rather they are implanted in technological systems of varying complexity and extent. These different systems interact with one another by necessity and often depend upon one another to operate effectively.[24] For example, even in the most apparently straightforward stories of technological adoption, such as with the

Eli Whitney–style saw gin, a whole technological system was developed around that technology so that it fit the needs of its adopters. For the cotton gin, this system included technologies to market short-staple cotton and manage enslaved labor on a cotton farm or plantation. In addition, cotton cultivation interacted with and was supported by other technological systems such as the law and the slave trades. Technological changes in the lower Mississippi valley created thick webs of technological interaction and interdependence that drove further technological adoption, adaptation, and innovation.

Using this definition of technology, we can see that the creation of the second slavery in the lower Mississippi valley revolved around the interaction of its residents with various technologies and, ultimately, their adoption, adaptation, and improvement of available technologies and the development of systems to make those technologies meet their needs. As Ada Ferrer has written about Cuban planters transitioning to their own second slavery at roughly the same time, lower Mississippi valley enslavers "calculated . . . and improvised."[25] Their actions were intentional but unplanned. Enslavers and allied elites only wanted to "save" slavery and make it profitable. As such, they looked at their world and searched for technologies they believed might make their slave society profitable, stable, and more to their liking. By adopting and adapting these technologies and the systems within which they were implanted, enslavers and allied elites transformed a colonial region in crisis into one that was stable, profitable, and working to their benefit. They used technologies to move out of the crises of the Age of Revolutions into the stable and profitable world of the second slavery.

This book will focus most of its attention on three technological systems employed by the region's enslavers and allied elites to remaster and replant their slave society: cotton cultivation, sugar production, and the international and "internal" slave trades. I focus on these three technologies because they were central to the region's transformation and most telling of how enslavers and allied elites interacted with their world. Adopting and mastering sugar and cotton gave the slave system the economic basis it had lost in the early 1790s. The rapidity of this adoption also suggests the flexibility of enslavers and their resiliency in the face of challenges. The slave trades provided the labor enslavers desired for their plantations and farms. While these trades were, to some degree, externally driven, this was not entirely the case. Planters and merchants from the region sought out these trades and adapted them to their own needs, often in strikingly creative ways. This was particularly true of the internal slave trade, which was a largely new way of obtaining enslaved labor that regional actors helped develop even as they were still importing enslaved Africans.

Other technologies were also used by elites to re-create the region. However, these other technologies were less central to the rapid transformation of the region's slave system in the fifteen years after 1795 and thus receive less attention in this book. For example, after the Louisiana Purchase, regional elites, in keeping with traditions in the Anglo-American world, demanded local political control.[26] Ironically, in Louisiana, those pushing for these "traditional" rights were largely francophones who had never had such direct local control. Once they had obtained the "technology" of local control, elites set to work rewriting laws. They drew sharper racial boundaries, imposed harsher slave codes, and decentralized law enforcement to local elites, especially in relationship to enslaved people.[27] Elites also demanded and sometimes received imperial and federal support for their system through adjustments to trade laws and regulations and protection from insiders and outsiders who might destabilize slavery. They were turning the "technology" of the state to their own ends. For example, while ultimately irrelevant to putting down the rebellion, enslavers must have welcomed the presence of US Army soldiers in the region during the 1811 German Coast Insurrection, the largest slave revolt every to occur in North America, and requested that US Army forces be permanently based in the region after the rebellion. Later, regional elites supported the aggressive use made of the US military by Andrew Jackson during and after the War of 1812 to eliminate threats to the expansion of slavery across the American South by subjugating Native Americans and invading Florida. Through the "technologies" of local control, the law, and the state, lower Mississippi valley elites were engaged in the process of turning their region from "a borderland to bordered land."[28]

In using various technologies to create a second slavery and a "bordered land," these elites were taking part in the broader process of consolidating and expanding slavery in North America. Historians of the

United States have long struggled to make sense of a country whose most prominent founders recognized the contradiction between slavery and their stated ideals and the fact that, by the antebellum period, the polity they had helped found was the largest and wealthiest slave society in the world. Recent works attempting to address this issue have transformed the narrative of slavery's expansion from a focus on arguments between the "founders" and the actions of the federal government to one built on more diverse and decentralized perspectives.[29] However, these studies still typically focus on resolving questions about the national history of the United States by examining politics and policy or sweeping expanses of time and space.

One historian of slavery's expansion calls the creation of the enslavers' republic "by default more than by design," although he recognizes that this is only true when looked at from the East.[30] Looked at from the West, the expansion of slavery was assuredly by design and desired by many, likely most, western enslavers and allied elites.[31] In the lower Mississippi valley, elites actively searched for technologies that might return slavery to profitability, and hence "rescue" slavery. Only sparse evidence survives in the lower Mississippi valley of hesitation or doubts about the region's direction on the part of the region's enslavers and other elites. Instead, they got down to the metaphorical work of remaking their society (the actual work was largely done by the enslaved), only rarely looking up to defend themselves from criticisms coming from easterners uncomfortable with the expansion of slavery (some of whom came to the region as government officials or migrants). Enslavers and their allies made their world the way it was, and the world they created largely matched their desires. They appear to have recognized little contradiction between their actions and the ideals of the United States (a polity they were not even a part of when they began to adopt cotton and sugar) and demonstrated little interest in debates about the morality of slavery's continuation or spread.[32] Overall, they appear to have been proud of what they had achieved and likely would have bristled at modern concerns about their actions. They certainly did in response to contemporary critics. One local commenter went so far as to mock the very notion of "liberty and equality" in a slave society, calling it a "damning heresy."[33]

Due to the crop revolutions and the resulting consolidation and expansion of slavery, the lower Mississippi valley was a very different place in 1811 than it had been in 1790: profitable for enslavers and merchants, apparently stable, and committed to the production of sugar and cotton by a large population of enslaved laborers working on an expanding number of ever larger plantations. One could be tempted to argue that these changes would inevitably lead to the "modern," "capitalist" Antebellum South of powerful and self-confident enslavers, who would in fifty years split the union rather than accept a federal government headed by the anti-slavery Republican Party.[34] Such an argument is tempting, considering the importance of explaining the Antebellum South's role in the coming of the Civil War. The story told in this book is clearly a part of that story, as the transformations in the lower Mississippi valley (and the Deep South more broadly) during the years before and after 1800 were necessary if not sufficient conditions for the coming of the Civil War. However, in 1811, the trends that would lead to the world of the Antebellum South and secession were still in their infancy and not yet fully consolidated. Many contingent steps remained to be traveled between this story and that story. Surely, lower Mississippi valley elites would have been surprised to discover the "end" of the story, a story that was not even about the country they lived in when the crop revolutions began; their goals in making the sugar and cotton revolutions were limited and local.

This book is largely about the lower Mississippi valley's elites and how those elites remade the lower Mississippi valley to their own benefit. This elite was a small group (likely never more than a few hundred individuals) who had the social, political, and economic capital to mold the world around them. They were the larger planters, such as the Illinois Creole sugar pioneer Étienne Boré and the Sottish-born cotton planter and improver William Dunbar; wealthier merchants, such as the French-born Julien Poydras and Irish-born Daniel Clark Jr.; and Spanish and American government officials, such as the Massachusetts-born Mississippi Territory governor Winthrop Sargent and the South Carolina planter and American general Wade Hampton. These individuals often fell into more than one of these categories. Most typical were merchants and government officials who also became planters, profiting from the commercial agricultural economy they had helped develop. For example, Poydras, Clark, Sargent, and Hampton all owned large plantations in the lower Mississippi valley. As should be apparent, these elites also came from a variety of backgrounds. They were Creoles born in the region, Anglo-Americans from throughout the United States, Europeans from much of western Europe, and immigrants and refugees from the Caribbean. Despite this diversity, these actors typically found a way to work together or at least in parallel to remake the region into a place where they could profit from enslaved-labor-driven agricultural development.

Of course, these elites were not alone in the region. Nonelite inhabitants were affected by and integral to the sugar and cotton revolutions. Most crucially, this profitable society was built upon the exploitation and brutalization of enslaved Africans and people of African descent. To make cotton cultivation and sugar production as profitable as possible, the region's free residents desired Black bodies to work on their farms and plantations. They demanded the reopening of the African slave trade and then helped develop the internal trade in "excess" enslaved people from the Upper South. At the same time, enslavers developed or adopted labor practices to facilitate the production of cotton and sugar and broke enslaved people to that production. To truly understand the slave society being remade in the lower Mississippi valley, we must recognize that the commodity revolutions proved extraordinarily disruptive and destructive to the lives of both the enslaved already living in the region and the thousands forcibly imported into it.[35] Still, despite the grim prospects they faced, enslaved people found ways to survive the region's sugar and cotton plantations; they subtly and not-so-subtly resisted their enslavers' demands, made lives for themselves, and created communities. Enslavers' actions and desires broadly shaped the world of the enslaved but, as was always the case, not entirely.

Nonelite free people were also part of the sugar and cotton revolutions. In some cases, they were discomforted by them due to sympathies with Atlantic revolutionary ideas and events or simply by the fact that a small elite were disproportionately benefiting from the regional transformations and accumulating power as a result. However, many nonelite free people benefited from the introduction of cotton and sugar. Cotton exploded across the region, ultimately being produced on farms and plantations of all sizes, from ones without a single enslaved laborer to ones with hundreds. Sugar was a more challenging crop for nonelites to produce. However, as we shall see, many of them found creative routes into sugar production. Many of these nonelite cotton and sugar producers improved their economic well-being, often working their way into the enslaving or even planting classes, crucial economic boundaries in a slave society. Other nonelite free people benefited more indirectly from the revolutions by finding employment as overseers, working as small-time merchants in New Orleans or Natchez, or finding other ways to benefit economically from the commodity revolutions.

While many nonelite free people benefited from cotton and sugar, some were more directly involved in making the region's second slavery. In Natchez, the mechanic John Barclay built the lower Mississippi valley's first Eli Whitney–style cotton gin, allowing the widespread adoption of short-staple cotton. Further downriver, in the countryside near New Orleans, the St. Domingue refugee sugar maker Antoine Morin provided indispensable expertise and experience to Boré in his effort to produce granulated sugar. Barclay and Morin were crucial actors in this moment of transformation. Other nonelite actors, including other mechanics and sugar makers, also played a part in the crop revolutions. Therefore, while this book is largely focused on a small group of elites, other groups do figure into the story of the lower Mississippi valley's sugar and cotton revolutions.

However, one group is almost wholly absent from this book: Native Americans. It is worth taking a moment to explain why. Native Americans were present within and on the margins of the region and important to its larger history. In fact, two Tunica women played a crucial role in the Pointe Coupee Conspiracy, alerting whites to its existence.[36] However, by the time discussed in this book, Native Americans had been largely dispossessed or marginalized in the core regions of the lower Mississippi valley that this book discusses. As a result, elites typically did not have to consider Native Americans in their plans as they pushed the region toward cotton cultivation and sugar production. Essentially, the expropriation of indigenous lands was not central to the contemporary story of the cotton and sugar revolutions in the lower Mississippi valley. That expropriation had already largely happened decades before. Native Americans were certainly affected by the sugar and cotton revolutions and the broader changes they wrought, often quite negatively. However, tracing that story is not the goal of this book.[37] Later, the expansion of cotton would increasingly focus on converting indigenous land, including Chickasaw land on the Mississippi River, into cotton land worked by enslaved laborers, and Native Americans would move to center stage of the story of second slavery as southern elites worked to convert their land into cotton plantations. However, those events occurred after the end of this story and mostly outside of the places this story is about.[38]

In summary, this book recasts our understanding of slavery in the lower Mississippi valley and in the Early Republic United States. First, it demonstrates the severity of the crisis enslavers faced in one part of the colonial world of the Americas during the Age of Revolutions. Pummeled by economic crises and imagined and real threats to their social control, enslavers began to imagine (and dread) a world without slavery or, at the very least, with a stagnant slave system. Second, and more importantly, it illustrates how those elites went about overcoming that crisis by remaking their society. In these relatively unpopulated and marginal colonies, enslavers and allied elites scrambled to save their slave society. They found technologies that allowed them to do so and adapted them to their own ends. Crucially, and in sharp contrast to elsewhere in the United States, the central agricultural innovation was not only cotton but also sugar, producing a second slavery that was in some ways like that of the Caribbean, but that was ultimately unique, intertwining within the region's slave society two very different crop systems that have often been segregated in the history of American slavery.

The book is organized in a mixed chronological and thematic fashion. The first and last chapters reside at the beginning and end of the story this book tells. The middle chapters focus on the technologies central to the remaking of the lower Mississippi valley's slave society. At points those chapters range beyond the temporal and geographic limitations of this book, bringing in evidence that illuminates aspects of the story that cannot otherwise be illuminated. Chapter 1 begins by giving a brief overview of the region's colonial history as background for understanding the events of the 1790s before moving on to a discussion of the economic collapse and political crises the region experienced during the early and mid-1790s. These crises are the key to understanding why the region's elites remade their society in such a rapid and fundamental fashion. Next the book moves on to its heart, the explanation of how the sugar and cotton revolutions were made and spread through the region. The introduction of the Eli Whitney saw gin into Natchez by John Barclay and its spread throughout the region alongside short-staple cotton production is examined in chapter 2. Chapter 3 discusses the granulation of sugar by Étienne Boré and the steady advance of sugar production in the area around New Orleans and beyond. Both of these chapters also look at the complex ways that cotton and sugar producers adopted, adapted, and improved the technologies that made up the technological systems of cotton cultivation and sugar production.

Chapter 4 focuses on the ways that the region's enslavers augmented their labor forces via the internal and international slave trades, two crucial technological systems in the replanting of the slave society. This chapter looks at the revitalized international slave trade and growing internal slave trade and how they operated alongside one another in the region with a particular eye to the replacement of the former with the latter. In the final chapter, I analyze the events leading up to and surrounding the 1811 German Coast Insurrection. This analysis suggests the ways that the region had fundamentally changed over the previous sixteen years. It was now a booming colonial society attracting thousands of white men looking to make money. However, it also had a large, restive, and diverse enslaved population whom many feared would one day rise, perhaps successfully, in rebellion. They did exactly that in 1811, sparking the largest slave revolt ever in North America. However, instead of shaking planters' confidence in the society they had remastered and replanted over the previous sixteen years, the rebellion and its results ratified it. Elites crushed the revolt in a matter of days and killed around one hundred enslaved people, often in brutal fashion, as a cautionary example to enslaved people who might consider violent resistance. They had faced the worst the people they enslaved and brutalized had to offer and prevailed. By 1811, the lower Mississippi valley's second slavery had been built by regional elites and, by all signs, was on a firm foundation of sugar, cotton, enslavement, and violence.

This book reveals a world of self-confident, nimble European and Euro-American enslavers and allied elites who successfully remade the lower Mississippi valley in a strikingly brief period of time from a stagnant backwater of European colonialism built on an anemic slave system they feared was facing an existential crisis into a dynamic and expansive slave society that would ultimately become a center of antebellum slavery and a prime example of the second slavery that was central to the history of modernizing New World slave systems in the 1800s. They did this by identifying technologies that would allow them to remake their slave society, adapting them to their local needs and building the systems around them necessary to make them successful. Their efforts were part of a larger process that revitalized slavery in the Americas and ultimately, if not inevitably, led to the Antebellum South that would split the nation over slavery.

1

THE CRISIS OF THE 1790s

People no longer care to own such precarious property [as slaves], as it is feared, and with good reason, that the contagious spirit of freedom prevailing outside might well spread out and get here.

—Joseph de Pontalba to Jeanne des Chappelles, April 30, 1796

In February 1796, Louisiana resident Jeanne Louise le Breton des Charmeaux des Chappelles, the wife of Joseph Xavier Delfau de Pontalba, left for Spain to join her aunt Céleste de Macarty Miró, the ailing widow of Esteban Rodriguez Miró, a former governor of Louisiana. While preparing to join his wife by disposing of all their property in Louisiana, Joseph de Pontalba wrote her a series of detailed, daily letters. These letters mostly survive for the period from February 24 to November 10, 1796. Pontalba and his wife were members of Louisiana's elite establishment. As such, he had access to a network of informants that kept him well apprised of happenings and rumors in the colony and throughout the francophone Atlantic World, happenings and rumors that he shared with his wife alongside more prosaic news.[1] Pontalba's letters portray a colony whose elite residents went about their daily lives of socializing and business but with the specter of political and economic crisis hanging over everything.

In the earliest surviving letter, Pontalba told his wife of several recent threats to the colonial elite. He wrote his wife of a "Monsieur Ergon" who had just been expelled from the colony because of his vocal sympathies with the French Republic as well as rumors that one of the people Ergon enslaved had been encouraging other enslaved people to repeat

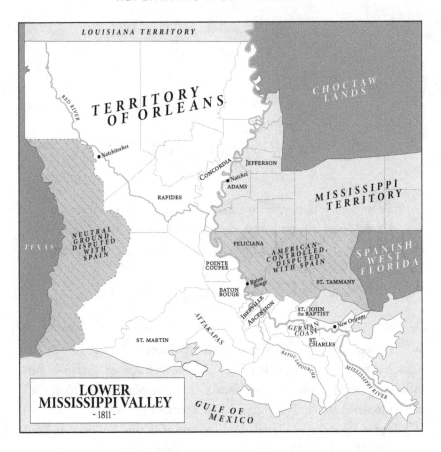

LOUISIANA TERRITORY

TERRITORY
OF ORLEANS

RED RIVER

Natchitoches

CHOCTAW
LANDS

CONCORDIA

JEFFERSON

Natchez
ADAMS

RAPIDES

MISSISSIPPI
TERRITORY

TEXAS

NEUTRAL
GROUND,
DISPUTED
WITH
SPAIN

FELICIANA

AMERICAN-
CONTROLLED,
DISPUTED
WITH SPAIN

SPANISH
WEST
FLORIDA

POINTE
COUPEE

Baton
Rouge

ST. TAMMANY

BATON
ROUGE

IBERVILLE
ASCENSION

ST. JOHN
the BAPTIST

New Orleans

ATTAKAPAS

GERMAN
COAST

ST.
CHARLES

ST. MARTIN

BAYOU LAFOURCHE

MISSISSIPPI RIVER

LOWER
MISSISSIPPI VALLEY
- 1811 -

GULF OF
MEXICO

"the disaster at St. Domingue" in Louisiana. He also informed her that a new plot had been uncovered at Pointe Coupee almost exactly a year after the unmasking of the 1795 Pointe Coupee Conspiracy. Finally, he wrote her that a slave ship had just been admitted into the colony but that "three free men of color and two black slaves, rightly suspected of having come from St. Domingue," had been detained. He had even heard that "one of the latter . . . held communications with all the blacks at the post and sang all the new patriotic songs."[2] This letter was rare, although not unique, in the degree to which it discussed dangers to the colony; most letters focused on Pontalba's longing for his absent family, business affairs, social life, and family news. Still, Pontalba wrote often of the dangers he saw all around him arising from the revolutions then raging in

France and St. Domingue (i.e., Haiti) as well as the open disaffection of Louisiana's enslaved people.

Beyond immediate worries about physical safety, Pontalba was most concerned about his inability to sell the people he enslaved. He complained often in his letters about the slave market, writing in one letter that "it is impossible to sell slaves." He related how one enslaved man, "a superb specimen of black, a good worker, young, and well behaved," was sold at auction for only four hundred piastres. Pontalba claimed that "at any other time he would have brought a thousand piasters" and that people wouldn't buy enslaved people because "people are uncertain as to what will be their fate."[3] This was indicative of Pontalba's fear that slavery would soon end either through the spread of the Haitian and French Revolutions to the province or as a preemptive move by the Spanish king. However, the problems in the market were also a result of economic conditions. Pontalba had less to say about these, possibly because he had already divested himself of his rural properties, agriculture being the economic area with the greatest problems. Yet hints of them do appear in his letters. For example, on March 17, he mentioned a petition being circulated in the countryside around New Orleans asking the king to delay debt payments.[4]

As Pontalba's letters indicate, the lower Mississippi valley's elites faced many challenges to their ability to control and profit from the region during the early and middle years of the 1790s. As another member of the local elite, the French-born planter, merchant, and poet Julien Poydras, wrote, "Everything turns against us. We make ourselves dizzy with deliberations [torn] awaiting the return of prosperity."[5] After an economic boom following the end of the American Revolution, the region's export-oriented agricultural economy had collapsed, placing immense pressures on indebted planters, farmers, and merchants. In addition, the region's residents were deeply affected by the revolutionary currents and international instability then spreading throughout the Atlantic World. Abroad, the French Revolutionary Wars loomed over the future of the former French, now Spanish colony. Closer to home, elites feared that French revolutionaries would infiltrate the colony, turning lower-class whites into wild-eyed sansculottes or lead Anglo-Americans in an assault on the colony, possibly sparking a slave revolt like the one then raging in St. Domingue. At the same time, some whites, enslaved people, and free people of color did look to the Atlantic's revolutionary events not with fear but hope, seeing them, perhaps, as an opportunity to create a more just and equal society.[6]

In the mid-1790s, the lower Mississippi valley's elites faced a deep crisis.[7] This crisis was both economic and political and was so severe as to cause some to believe that the colony's social order might be overthrown and slavery might soon end. In response, elites acted to protect their control and salvage slavery, while some whites and enslaved people acted to push the society into revolution. While the region's slave system and elite power structure would survive this challenge, understanding it is necessary to understand the context within which the region's rural economy and slave system would be remade over the course of just a few years in the mid-1790s. The crisis did not depose the colonial elites or free the enslaved, but it was the context within which enslavers and allied elites made the cotton and sugar revolutions.

For the broader context of the crisis of the 1790s, we first need to turn to the deeper and more immediate background of French and Spanish colonization of the lower Mississippi valley. The story of the French colonial period was one of a languishing colonial project, followed by a decade of rapid colonization, followed then by several decades of stagnation. While the French colonization of Louisiana had begun in 1699, two decades later the colony only had three hundred colonists. In 1717, the crown turned Louisiana over to Scottish financier John Law's Company of the Indies, hoping that it might be able to turn the colony around. In a bid to create a plantation colony that would be profitable, the company relocated the colony's center from Mobile to the Mississippi River, founding New Orleans, imported thousands of enslaved Africans, and gave large land concessions to elite colonists. As a result, by 1731 the colony had a large enslaved majority. During this period, the basic outline of the colony's economy was established. Colonists found that the most lucrative economic activities, besides the crucial trade with Native Americans, were indigo, tobacco, and lumber production. Indigo tended to be the staple of large planters, particularly those near New Orleans because of its large capital and labor requirements, while tobacco tended to be more popular upriver, where colonists often had less labor and capital.[8]

In 1729, the Natchez, after years of tensions with French colonists, attacked and destroyed the French settlement at Natchez, killing or capturing most of the colonists. This event, along with the expensive war between the Natchez and French that followed and the fact that Louisiana had yet to bring returns to the Company of the Indies, led the company to return the colony to the crown in 1731. The French crown had little interest in the marginal colony and largely ignored it for the next three decades, leading to the end of large-scale imports of enslaved Africans and European immigration. Over the next several decades, the colony was characterized by a stagnant population, an anemic economy dependent on the trade with Native Americans, and endemic smuggling.[9] This pause in colonization led to the creolization (i.e., made up of people born in Louisiana) of the enslaved population.[10]

In 1762, as part of the general settlement of the Seven Years' War, France transferred most of Louisiana to its Spanish ally. Spanish interest in Louisiana was fundamentally strategic. Spanish officials hoped that Louisiana would serve as a bulwark against Anglo-American encroachment that might threaten Spain's lucrative Mexican territories. These strategic concerns combined with the fact that the colony's white population never contained an appreciable number of Spaniards who might feel a patriotic connection to the empire deterred Spanish officials from actions that might lead to overt resistance by local elites and even led to policies that would have once been unimaginable in the Spanish empire. Despite an early attempt to force Louisiana into Spain's mercantile system, Spain allowed direct trade with France and its colonies after 1776. In addition, Spanish officials came up with a variety of schemes to encourage immigration, including of Anglo-American Protestants, to bolster the colony's population as a buffer against those same Anglo-Americans' new and aggressively expansive republic.[11] Local officials also tolerated activities that they often viewed as being in the colony's best interests but were not approved by Madrid. Most importantly, a contraband trade flourished along the Mississippi River border between Spanish Louisiana and

British West Florida, a colony organized out of Spanish and French territory east of the Mississippi River and transferred to the United Kingdom
at the end of the Seven Years' War. Even after Spain conquered British
West Florida during the American Revolution, smuggling, particularly by
the British and Anglo-Americans, continued and was typically tolerated
by Spanish officials, as it provided trade opportunities that legal trade
could not.[12]

Up to 1783 the European colonies in the region, Spanish Louisiana
and British West Florida, were still experiencing slow economic and demographic growth. However, the region was no longer an afterthought
in Europe's imperial competitions, even if it was not yet central to any
empire's strategic calculations. With the region divided between the
Spanish and British (who were succeeded by the United States), smuggling rife, and increasing Anglo-American penetration into the trans-
Appalachian West, the strategic importance of the Mississippi valley
became greater than ever before. As a region still lightly settled by colonial populations, bordered by powerful indigenous nations, and under
only loose imperial control, competition over access to land, waterways,
and trade routes would lead to decades of "intrigues" by colonists, Native Americans, and imperial officials who aimed for personal and imperial
advantage and control. These "intrigues" would create a constant uncertainty about the future of the region that would periodically wax and wane
through the end of the War of 1812 and even beyond.[13]

In the years after the American Revolution, when Spanish victories
over Britain on the Mississippi River and Gulf Coast reunited the region
under a single imperial power, Louisiana's colonial economy entered a
period of prosperity. This revitalization was, at least in part, a result of decisions made by Spanish officials in their continued efforts to create a self-
sustaining colony. For example, in 1776, the Spanish governor arranged a
deal whereby royal factories in Mexico agreed to purchase tobacco from
Louisiana, leading to a boom in tobacco production that peaked in the
late 1780s when the crown purchased Louisiana's entire tobacco crop. In
addition, planters continued to profit from indigo, which retained high
prices throughout the 1780s, and the production of timber products,
which were traded to the Caribbean or used locally. During these years,
the indigenous trade receded in importance and was increasingly replaced

by trade with Upper Louisiana (modern-day Missouri and Illinois) and the Anglo-American colonists flooding into the West. Spanish officials made various adjustments to trade policy vis-à-vis Anglo-Americans to take advantage of this trade and, ideally, encourage western separation from the United States. Ultimately, Spain agreed to open the Mississippi River to Anglo-American navigation in the 1795 Treaty of San Lorenzo (i.e., Pinckney's Treaty) and both licit and illicit trade by and with Anglo-Americans became increasingly important in New Orleans.[14]

This boom in the economy greatly increased the profits of farmers and planters while at the same time placing many of them further in debt as they purchased additional land, enslaved people, and equipment on credit to take advantage of the new opportunities. For example, when Daniel Clark, a merchant and planter, sold forty-three mostly African enslaved people in Natchez in 1787, they were all sold on credit with the money usually due at the end of the next year, or the year after.[15] As buying land and enslaved people on credit was a common practice throughout the region, the accumulation of debt would have been common, setting the stage for crisis should the region face economic challenges.

By the early 1790s, for the first time since the decade after the founding of New Orleans, the situation was promising for the region's elite planters and merchants. As one put it in 1792, "The present prosperous situation of our colony [lets] us forget [the] misfortunes we experienced when [we] suffered by fire [in 1788]. His Lordship, the Baron de Carondelet, our new Governor, uses every endeavor to [encourage] commerce, the arts, and agriculture. [Indigo], tobacco, rice, and cotton are inexhaustible sources of wealth."[16] As often happens, the anonymous letter writer was crowing about a boom that was already on its way to bust. By 1792, the factors that would push the colonial societies of the lower Mississippi valley into crisis were all already present.

The crises experienced by the colonial societies of the lower Mississippi valley in the mid-1790s arose from both internal and external sources, which then interacted in complex ways. The French and Haitian Revolutions and the wars spawned by both directly and indirectly threatened elite control in a region already characterized by intense imperial and colonial competition and conflict. Officials and elites feared that the ideas associated with each would infiltrate the region and cause un-rest and even rebellion among sympathetic whites and enslaved people. Locals also feared (or in some cases hoped) that the French would ei-ther invade the colony directly or send agents to raise an army of Anglo-Americans west of the Appalachians to descend the Mississippi River on New Orleans. The threat of Anglo-American filibusters was not new, but it was intensified when connected to a French Republic that had just validated enslaved people's hopes for freedom by abolishing slavery in the French colonial empire. The French Revolutionary Wars also af-fected the region as Spain first sided with the First Coalition against France and then, in 1796, with France. These changing international com-mitments remade Louisiana's trade relationships, shifting the bulk of it away from France and Spain as the British Navy cleared their merchant vessels from the sea and toward the Anglo-Americans, citizens of the only major trading power that remained neutral. In 1798, Louisiana officials recognized this new reality and formally opened New Orleans to trade with neutral vessels (effectively Anglo-American vessels) on the same terms as Spanish ones until peace or an order otherwise from the king.[17]

The 1790s saw several supposed revolutionary conspiracies and schemes against the Spanish government in Louisiana. Perhaps the most serious French threat to Louisiana, at least in the minds of Spanish officials, was the effort by Edmond Charles Genêt, the troublesome French minis-ter to the United States from early 1793 to early 1794, to raise an army of Kentuckians to descend on Louisiana.[18] While the conspiracy ultimately came to little, news of it reached Louisiana's governor Francisco Luis Héctor, barón de Carondelet, who responded by suggesting to Madrid an extensive program of fortification and militarization in Louisiana.[19] Carondelet also appealed directly to Louisiana's inhabitants by publish-ing a "Circulaire" in February 1794 that argued that the threat posed by Genêt was serious (the conspirators had been able to gather "a certain number of American brigands" and French refugees) and launched a short but full-throated attack on the French Revolution itself.[20] Carondelet as-sumed that the ideals of the revolution had made inroads into the prov-ince, unsurprisingly as he had felt it necessary to call the rural militia to New Orleans the previous fall to quell unrest caused by Jacobin agitators after news had reached the city that Spain had declared war on France.[21]

In the pamphlet, Carondelet spoke directly to these local sympathizers and admonished them to see the reality of the revolution and to reject it: "Finally open your eyes to the truth the most evident, and instructed by the murders, the fires, the devastation of France, and of its colonies." In another section, he scolded residents for having "let yourself be dazzled by the misleading hope of freedom, of equality." Carondelet understood that revolutionary ideals were very appealing to many. However, Carondelet argued that, despite their appeal, such ideals could only lead to their betrayal and destruction. He pointed out that, in France, "the liberty of the press, fundamental laws of the constitution, have been shamefully violated, and ruthlessly covered with blood by massacre of those who have written against the operations of the members of the convention or against Republican principles."[22]

Unsurprisingly for the governor of a colony with a large enslaved population (according to a 1785 Spanish census, 54 percent of the colony's population was enslaved) and reflecting elite fears that white revolutionaries might ally with the colony's enslaved population, he turned his attention to St. Domingue throughout the pamphlet.[23] He pointed out that the three "scoundrels" supposedly organizing the invasion force had come to the United States from St. Domingue. Carondelet argued that these "monsters" aimed to bring "looting, the loss of your properties; the massacre of your families; the repetition of all the disasters which have devastated St. Domingue," the final point a clear reference to a slave revolt. Carondelet continued that "the scenes of horror that they prepare, will without a doubt surpass all those which they have performed in St. Domingue." If residents allowed themselves to be divided by "the phantom of liberty," Louisiana would surely fall to revolutionary and servile violence and suffer the dreadful consequences. However, if they would only unite behind monarchical order, Carondelet would be "ready to march at your head . . . , and if you go on the field to the place that I will mark for you, I respond with the idea, brave inhabitants, that the enemy will not pass Nogales [a fort located north of modern Vicksburg, Mississippi]."[24]

Fears that revolutionary currents would upend the social structure of Louisiana were not limited to Carondelet. Pontalba, writing two years after the publication of the "Circulaire," believed that the French and Haitian Revolutions were direct threats to the colony's elites and wrote of their effects in his letters to his wife. He became particularly agitated after a French "corsair" docked in New Orleans in August 1796. Shortly after its arrival, he claimed that some of the ship's sailors "circulate all through the fields under cover of the night and do the reverse from advising the slaves to remain faithful to their masters."[25] A few days later he claimed that "the national cockades of the corsair ship . . . are beginning to make very unfortunate impressions upon our slaves" and that its sailors "roam about the fields and the taverns, and they keep talking to them of the injustice done them in holding them in slavery; they are being told that if they will it they can be freed from it, as has already happened in all the territories under the domination of France."[26]

Pontalba also shared rumors that a French takeover was imminent and that Louisianans were "expecting to see a Santonax or a Polverel [Léger-Félicité Sonthonax and Étienne Polverel, the two commissioners of the French Republic who had formally ended slavery in St. Domingue] come here, or some other type similar to the two who brought with them desolation, carnage, and unspeakable horrors to one of the finest colonies to be found in the entire world." Pontalba was concerned about how the enslaved reacted to these rumors: "Such news, already widespread, has caused our slaves to walk about with an air of victory."[27] A few days later, he mused further on the disasters that French rule would bring: "There is no doubt that lands will be left to grow wild since there will no longer be hands to cultivate them, even if the Blacks should be willing to work by renting themselves out, since the products of the cultivation of our soil are not high prices enough to warrant such expenses."[28]

Pontalba did not believe that that these threats were only coming from outside the province. In one letter, written while the "corsair" ship was in port, he told his wife of a rumor that a local Creole had admitted to another that he had fomented the conspiracy in Pointe Coupee the previous year and that he hoped to be appointed French consul to the United States, at which time he would "[explain] to the negroes exactly what were their rights." The Creole supposedly justified his position by arguing "that his duty to humanity came before any and all such things, and that the blacks were his compatriots as much as the white man."[29]

While many of the rumors Pontalba related to his wife were likely just that, rumors, he was not merely being paranoid in his fears about what enslaved people were learning about the revolutions. Just the year before he wrote the letters, the Pointe Coupee Conspiracy of 1795 had revealed that revolutionary ideas and knowledge of revolutionary events had in fact infiltrated the region's slave quarters and apparently inspired enslaved people to attempt to re-create the St. Domingue rebellion in Louisiana. As with most slave conspiracies, it is difficult to know what exactly happened at Pointe Coupee and just how serious a threat to the colony's elites the conspiracy was.[30] However, the story that the extensive Spanish investigation uncovered was alarming to elites and indicated, at the very least, enslaved people's familiarity with the revolutionary events and ideas roiling the Atlantic World.

Pointe Coupee is located just upriver and across the Mississippi River from Baton Rouge. At the time of the conspiracy, the parish was a relatively populous region with particularly large plantations and a large slave majority. The parish had had a slave majority since at least a 1766 census, when 58 percent of its population was enslaved. According to a 1785 census, taken ten years before the conspiracy, Pointe Coupee had 1,521 residents, of whom 68 percent were enslaved.[31] Between 1785 and 1795, the area's planters imported many, disproportionately male, enslaved Africans as part of the post–American Revolution economic boom. This had important implications for the dynamics of the conspiracy; Gwendolyn Midlo Hall has shown that the conspiracy was concentrated on particularly large, Africanized plantations with imbalanced sex ratios.[32] By 1795, Pointe Coupee's economy had been pushed into crisis by the collapse of indigo and tobacco, but its residents, with few other options, were still trying to make those staples work.[33]

According to the extensive records of the Spanish investigation of the conspiracy, discontent, centered on Poydras's plantation, had been bubbling for some time in early 1795. The investigation reported that the situation had come to a head in April when enslaved people began to discuss setting an actual date for revolt. Shortly after, several whites learned the details of the conspiracy from enslaved people and two Tunica women. In response, officials began arresting and interrogating enslaved people implicated in the plot. According to the investigation, a secondary plot was hatched toward the end of the month with the goals of attacking slave patrols, assassinating the local commander, and freeing those already arrested. The investigation also found that the plotters had planned to reenact St. Domingue, killing most of the whites, sparing the women in order to rape them (a standard trope in investigations of slave conspiracies), and freeing themselves. The Spanish investigation condemned thirty-six enslaved people to death and nineteen to prison. Governor Carondelet commuted several of the death sentences to imprisonment. In the end, twenty-three people were executed, fifteen in Pointe Coupee and the other eight at locations along the banks of the Mississippi to set an example to other potential conspirators.[34]

While serious enough in its own right, the Pointe Coupee Conspiracy was probably seen as even more threatening by local elites because the investigation had implicated several whites as having encouraged the enslaved. Unlike many slave conspiracies where unnamed whites were blamed but never identified, two whites were found guilty of conspiracy and sentenced to prison. Tellingly, both were accused of having expressed radical sentiments to enslaved people. One was a Walloon teacher named Joseph Bouyal, who lived on a local plantation. Enslaved people testified that he had kept them informed of the revolutions in France and St. Domingue. Some also claimed that he had told them that slavery would soon be abolished, although others added that he had encouraged them "to be patient because slavery would not last very long." The other white man sentenced to prison was George Rockenbourg, a tailor who claimed to be a German born in Philadelphia. Enslaved people testified that he had told them that the Spanish king had freed them but that the local commandant had refused to act on the order (another common slave conspiracy trope). Enslaved people also claimed Rockenbourg had been present at a meeting with several enslaved people and white *engages* (indentured servants), one of whom had said, "Why make petitions [for freedom]? There are letters asking if it would not be better for you to do like the *negres du* Cap" (i.e., the St. Domingue insurrectionaries of 1791). After this, Rockenbourg supposedly wrote a petition that was given an enslaved man who said to the others that "he would bring it to town when he went with his master, and if that failed they would kill all the whites."[35]

While we should be skeptical of the truth of any of the specific claims made during the high-stakes interrogations that occurred during the investigation, enslaved people's testimony shows that the enslaved were learning all kinds of rumors from travelers on the river and other sources. One slave commander (an enslaved person with managerial responsibilities) testified that some of the enslaved people on his plantation had informed him that a group of travelers on the river had told the enslaved people that if the French won the war they would be freed. Another enslaved person reported that the white leader of another group on the river asked them why they were sowing corn for their enslaver, as they would all be free soon.[36] Whether the conspiracy was as dangerous or extensive as the investigation concluded, the enslaved were learning about events in the Atlantic World from the rumors that were spreading throughout the colony along its waterways. At the very least, they had learned enough to tell believable stories about radical whites and enslaved people inspired by the French and Haitian Revolutions conspiring together against the region's elites.

Elites in the region reacted with alarm to the events at Pointe Coupee and the investigation's revelations. In a letter to his wife, written nearly a year after the conspiracy had been uncovered, Pontalba reflected on the events of 1795, illustrating the sense of doom that stalked the colony's elites. In it, he recalled the dangerous situation at the time "when our position in this colony was ever so critical; when we used only to go to bed armed to the teeth." According to Pontalba, the position was "critical" because "of the dreadful calamities of Saint Domingue, and of the germs of insurrection only too widespread among our own slaves." He continued that he "often thought, on my going to bed, of the means I would use to save you and my son, and of the tactics I would pursue if we happened to be attacked. I figured out by what exit and in what manner I would have you escape, while my own resistance would keep the scoundrels busy."[37]

Information the New Orleans Cabildo, a city council that also had some administrative responsibilities for the entire colony, received around the time of the revolt suggests general alarm among elite residents. In a meeting on April 25, 1795, after the conspiracy had been uncovered, Miguel Fortier, the colony's attorney general, reported "repeated warnings by word and in writing from prominent citizens of this Colony. . . . [that]

there is strong suspicion of revolt among the slaves."[38] Fortier included two letters from prominent local residents as examples of these fears. In one, a Mr. Fleurian warned that residents must "take every precaution imaginable, even more than actually needed" because while "the spark flared up at Pointe Coupee . . . the seat of the rebellion might be here!" He continued that a failure to act might make the threat "incurable."[39] In the other letter, Mr. Bringier, a planter, related his own discovery of enslaved people conspiring near his plantation. One night Bringier had happened upon two enslaved men on the levee conversing with another in a boat in the river. He overheard them making threats to various local residents and mentioning weapons. Bringier concluded his statement by arguing that "this incident proves that it is high time for taking prudent and wise measures to quell an uprising which would most certainly result in the loss of our settlement" and requested that Fortier "please employ all means in [his] power to secure that end."[40]

In response to such exhortations, the Spanish government acted vigorously to prevent the conspiracy from turning into an actual revolt and to prevent future revolts. Beyond immediate responses such as the movement of soldiers to Pointe Coupee and the arrest and prosecution of the accused, the government took several systemic actions to head off insurrection. Following up on earlier reforms that had attempted to head off a slave rebellion like that in St. Domingue, Governor Carondelet tried to further reform slavery by instituting new rules that aimed to restrict enslavers' power and autonomy. New regulations set maximum work hours, minimum ration levels, and Sundays as a day of rest. This ameliorative tendency reflected the belief amongst Spanish officials that abusive treatment by enslavers had been an important factor in the St. Domingue slave revolt. However, the regulations were not merely ameliorative; they also placed new restrictions on enslaved people, reflecting a belief that they also needed to be brought under greater control. The regulations banned gatherings of enslaved people from different plantations, required passes for enslaved people to move about, and banned their possession of horses and guns.[41]

In addition, to control the influx of possibly "dangerous" enslaved people, elites moved to cut off the slave trade into Louisiana, a move that would have been facilitated by the economic challenges that coincided with the political ones. This shift was first promoted by the Cabildo in the summer of 1795, indicating a level of support among local elites. At that time, the Cabildo urged the governor to ban the importation of all enslaved people who were not fresh from Africa (which had already been largely instituted) and to further ban new enslaved Africans as long as the French Revolutionary Wars continued.[42] A memorial presented to the Cabildo by the attorney general, Gabriel Fonvergne, on February 19, 1796, asked them to appeal to the governor to finally institute a ban on slave imports.[43] The governor instituted the ban shortly after this appeal, nearly a year after the first petition.[44] Writing several years later, in a description of Louisiana for the French government, Pontalba connected the ban to the conspiracy by writing that it was a response to the fact that "on hearing the news of the St. Domingo insurrection, the negroes made an attempt to follow that example." He also argued that the ban had "saved the colony" by allowing the white population to increase relative to the enslaved population.[45]

In perhaps the most striking evidence of how severe a shock Pointe Coupee and the surrounding crisis had been, Pontalba believed that the Spanish government might go to the extreme of abolishing slavery to preempt the threat of revolutionary insurrection. This belief was not merely the workings of a solitary, overheated imagination; he claimed that the idea originated from conversations with Governor Carondelet himself. In one letter, Pontalba informed his wife that the governor had told him that he "has strong reasons for his believe [sic] that within three or four months the King of Spain will have a schedule published granting general freedom to all the slaves in the colonies." Pontalba did not welcome emancipation by the king. He believed that such an act would ruin the colony.[46]

Despite Pontalba's fears, there is no evidence the king ever considered taking such a step.[47] In fact, while Spanish officials in the colony were concerned, even alarmed, by internal threats in the mid-1790s, it is not clear how seriously Spanish officials back in the metropole took those concerns. For example, those who have studied Spanish interest in returning Louisiana to France, an interest that first became apparent in 1795, typically point to Louisiana's expense (it was a financial sinkhole), indefensibility, and role in creating tensions with the United Kingdom and the United States as the most important reasons for that interest. In other words, external threats and the effect Louisiana had on Spain's relationships with other powers seem to have been much greater concerns for Spanish officials in Madrid than the internal dynamics of the colony. At the end of the day, Louisiana was never central to the Spanish imperial imagination, and when it no longer appeared to effectively serve its purpose as a buffer, many Spanish officials were prepared to abandon it. The role of slave resistance and revolutionary instability in this decision was likely minimal. In addition, even the role of the economic crisis was likely quite small or even nonexistent. Even the increasing prosperity of the late 1790s did not cause Spain to become more attached to the colony and did not appreciably lessen the cost of the colony, and it willingly parted with it in 1800.[48] In the end, slave resistance and revolutionary instability in Louisiana was largely a local story.

Regardless of how it was perceived in Madrid, the threat revealed (or symbolized) by the Pointe Coupee Conspiracy continued to worry local elites in coming years. Pontalba still pondered the threat a year after it was uncovered when he related the story of another slave insurrection scare on the German Coast (the present St. Charles and St. John the Baptist Parishes just upriver from New Orleans) during Easter week 1796, almost exactly a year after the Pointe Coupee uprising had supposedly been planned to take place. The scare led to the flight of white women and children to New Orleans, the cancellation of Easter services (for fear of a large gathering of enslaved people), and the arrest of several enslaved people. Supposedly they had planned to kill all of the whites in the neighborhood and then break into four bands, two advancing up the river on each bank and two down in order to seize all of the whites (a plan with striking parallels to what would actually happen fifteen years later on the German Coast).[49] While not explicitly connected to the Pointe Coupee event (Pontalba's musings about that scare appeared in letters written around the same time he learned about the new scare), its date and the fear it engendered suggests a connection in some minds.

Perhaps most telling for the collapse of local faith in slavery, Louisiana's slave market appears to have virtually ground to a halt in the mid-1790s. Throughout 1796, Pontalba connected the Pointe Coupee Conspiracy and the more general sense of instability related to the French and

Haitian Revolutions to his inability to sell the people he enslaved. For example, on April 30, 1796, he wrote his wife that "people no longer care to own such precarious property, as it is feared, and with good reason, that the contagious spirit of freedom prevailing outside might well spread out and get here." He further informed her that no matter how much he lowered his asking prices, he could not sell his remaining enslaved people.[50] Another Louisiana resident, Armand Duplantier, connected problems in the slave market explicitly to the Pointe Coupee Conspiracy. Duplantier, who was selling the estate of his deceased uncle, wrote in a letter to his brother that he had "successfully made the sale of slaves." He was thankful for this because "otherwise, there would have surely been a great deal of compromise due to an insurrection of Negroes that almost occurred last spring in this colony and that had to start at Pointe Coupee."[51] According to both Pontalba and Duplantier, enslavers were no longer as willing to purchase enslaved people in the aftermath of Pointe Coupee, indicating a loss of faith in the durability of slavery. Of course, while unmentioned by Pontalba and Duplantier, the economic collapse discussed below was also certainly a factor in this loss of faith.

A debate held in the Cabildo several years later shows that the fears raised by Pointe Coupee continued to haunt elite residents. In August 1800, the Cabildo debated whether the African slave trade should be reopened. During the debate, the Cabildo split evenly, six for and six against, on whether to support lifting the ban. The depth and intensity of opposition shows how long a shadow Pointe Coupee and the attendant challenges of the mid-1790s had cast. The opponents agreed that the danger emanating from "the French Islands" was far from over. Gabriel Fonvergne asserted that "the terrible experience in the French Santo Domingo forces us to continuously watch in order to avoid such catastrophe." In addition, almost all the opponents explicitly connected these dangers to Pointe Coupee. Pedro de la Roche pointed to "the revolt which was intented [*sic*] in Punta Cortada during the year of 1795, the inclination towards greater revolts, which is noted every day in the insolent anger of the slaves towards their own masters and other white people." Jayme Jorda warned that, at the time of the conspiracy, "If their number would have been larger in order to be able to dominate, who would say that we would not have been their victims and the very same cause and fears exists yet." For at least six members of the Cabildo, existential danger still stalked Louisiana's slave regime five years after the Pointe Coupee Conspiracy.[52]

Beyond the fears and hopes spawned by the revolutionary instability of the 1790s, the associated wars, and the very apparent discontent of the region's enslaved people as shown most clearly by the Pointe Coupee Conspiracy, the colonial societies of the lower Mississippi valley also experienced severe economic problems during this period. These economic problems were connected to the international context and fed the broader sense of crisis. First, the region's tobacco economy collapsed in the early 1790s. This economic disaster was a man-made one. Having spent the 1780s purchasing increasing amounts of Louisiana's tobacco crop to supply the Mexican market, the Spanish crown cut back its purchases in 1790 and 1791 due to oversupply in Mexico. In 1792, the crown terminated its purchases entirely. While locals could still trade tobacco to France and the French West Indies, this avenue was cut off the next year when Spain declared war on France. At the same time, more American tobacco, considered to be of higher quality, was reaching New Orleans, pushing Louisiana tobacco out of the local market.[53] Suddenly, Louisiana tobacco had no commercial outlet.

Tobacco cultivators recognized the disaster they faced. In 1791, Natchez planters, farmers, and merchants produced a memorial begging the king to return his purchase of tobacco to previous levels and prices.[54] The next year, Natchez governor Manuel Gayoso de Lemos discussed the negative repercussions of the new policy on tobacco in a report on Louisiana's defenses and local sympathies with the French Revolution and the United States. De Lemos pointed out that locals had been promised that "a more extensive commerce than that enjoyed now" would be offered in place of purchasing the tobacco crop. However, no new order had been forthcoming, causing Natchez's residents to be "in consternation, for they are ignorant as to what cultivation they should bend their efforts."[55]

As the tobacco market disintegrated, indigo production also collapsed. Indigo planters faced the twin problems of adverse natural conditions and low prices. Drought, overabundant rain, and frost heavily damaged crops between 1791 and 1793. In 1793 and 1794, a worm, probably aided by the dampness, damaged crops.[56] At the same time, many noted that indigo prices no longer brought the returns planters depended upon. For example, Pontalba learned in 1796 that his indigo crop from 1795 could not be sold.[57] In 1795, Julien Poydras repeatedly complained about indigo prices, noting that "the sale of my indigo in London was wretched."[58] In 1796, another planter noted that "indigo . . . is not worth much here."[59] Most likely these price depressions were a direct result of British encouragement of indigo production in India. Indigo production collapsed at the same time in South Carolina.[60]

After at least four seasons of crop failures and more of low prices, planters began to abandon indigo production in the mid-1790s. In 1803, Étienne Boré, a planter near New Orleans, recalled his constant battle against bad weather and insects as an indigo planter in the early 1790s, noting that "each year he accumulated losses which rapidly accelerated his complete ruin." By 1794 he had decided he could not win and abandoned indigo and began to search for a new crop.[61] While some planters continued to pursue the cultivation of indigo for several more years, Boré was far from alone in abandoning the crop. During the 1780s, annual indigo crops had averaged between 400,000 and 600,000 pounds. By 1801, the annual crop had fallen to only 80,000 pounds.[62]

With few alternative commodities to produce, cultivators faced a grim situation. In a series of memorials written during the early 1790s, Natchez district residents pointed out how they had taken on large debt to purchase enslaved people and agricultural tools and to construct the buildings necessary for tobacco production.[63] By the time the memorials were written, many of them could no longer pay their debts. The situation became so dire in Natchez that in 1795 its governor gave its residents debt relief until 1800, requiring them to pay only one-fifth of their outstanding debts each year between 1795 and 1800.[64] Pontalba reported that a similar idea was proposed in the areas around New Orleans in 1796, although if such a petition was ever presented to the government, it appears not to have been acted on.[65]

The letter book of Julien Poydras, a French indigo planter and merchant in the Pointe Coupee region, gives insight into how one elite individual experienced this economic crisis. This letter book includes mostly business letters written by Poydras between 1794 and 1800. During the early period covered by the letters, Poydras was residing in Philadelphia, having traveled there in the summer of 1794. He returned to Pointe Coupee in late 1795 or early 1796. Despite being far from home, Poydras experienced the travails that were damaging the economy back in Louisiana. In June 1795, he was "embarrassed" to tell a Mr. Duplantier (probably the Baton Rouge area planter Armand Duplantier) that Duplantier's indigo had "brought only 2,800 piastres or thereabouts" (apparently Poydras, in addition to marketing his own indigo, was acting as a factor while in Philadelphia).[66] In October 1795, while discussing the possibility that peace was imminent, Poydras shared with his correspondent that he estimated he had lost "100,000 piastres . . . due to the interruption of France's commerce."[67] In a later letter, he revealed that 40,000 of these piastres had been lost in France directly due to the revolution.[68]

Once he returned to Louisiana, his situation did not improve. He told one correspondent that due to the Pointe Coupee Conspiracy several of the people he enslaved had been hung, costing him twenty thousand piastres (this is the only comment I have uncovered from Poydras about the conspiracy, which is perhaps surprising, as it originated and was centered on his plantation). In the same letter he related that while he was gone, "the expenses were greater that [sic] the revenue of the plantation."[69] Another letter suggests that he was a victim of the natural conditions that had crippled the colony's indigo crop. His crop of indigo had been "growing slowly due to lack of rains." Even when it did rain, it "only rained by bursts after which the indigo always died."[70] His crop "has been lucky so far in escaping the 'death'" that had destroyed the crops of other planters. However, the crop was still "not so fine."[71] While some years his crop improved and prices were more reasonable, Poydras was never able to make indigo the profitable enterprise it had once been. By 1798, he would go so far as to inform a correspondent that "if that dye [indigo] does not sell, having no other means of making money, I shall be forced to abandon business until better times."[72]

In some letters his tone even verged on the apocalyptic, transforming his business challenges into personal, emotional, and moral ones. For example, in 1796 he wrote to his brother that "the aged soul is tired and withered by the reverses, troubles and cruel experiences of men: it becomes hardened and never smiles on idle dreams of fancy, which always disappear at the moment you believe you can catch them."[73] In another, apparently unsent, letter, he asked a correspondent a series of increasingly desperate questions about future business prospects.[74] Despite his reversals Poydras was one of the wealthiest men in the region, as his estimate that he had lost 100,000 piastres due to commercial interruptions shows. By 1810, long after the crisis had passed, he enslaved at least 122 people, the third most of any enslaver in Louisiana.[75] Other planters, farmers, and merchants, much less well off, must have been at least as deeply affected by the crisis as he was.

By the middle of the 1790s, Spanish Louisiana was in crisis. After decades of stagnation as a marginal colony at the periphery of empire, its colonial economy had experienced a boom in the late 1780s on the back of royal tobacco purchases, strong international demand for indigo, and increased trade opportunities resulting from Anglo-American colonization west of the Appalachians and liberalization of Spanish trade policy. This boom collapsed in the early 1790s. The tobacco economy fell apart as the Spanish crown removed government supports. The indigo economy collapsed due to bad weather, disease, and low prices. Trade also suffered as the wars that plagued the period made the carrying trade a dangerous business. Planters and farmers who had taken on debt to buy enslaved people and finance other aspects of their operations faced potential bankruptcy. Merchants, who had extended the credit, faced the prospect that many of their customers would not be able to repay them.

However, exacerbating this economic crisis were the international crises that flowed from the French and Haitian Revolutions. Local sympathy for the revolutions potentially challenged elite control while French and Anglo-American schemes and threats of invasion created a sense, for good or bad, that the colony would not long stay under Spanish control. The spread of revolutionary ideologies raised the specter, so frightening to elites, that lower-class whites and enslaved people might band together to upend society, bringing the Reign of Terror and the St. Domingue insurrection to the lower Mississippi valley. In April 1795, these fears seemed more than ratified as residents and Spanish officials in Pointe Coupee uncovered a biracial conspiracy fueled by rumors and revolutionary ideology. In the aftermath of Pointe Coupee, some planters began to fear that slavery was headed toward extinction. At the very least, many supported attempts by the Spanish government to get the region back under control, including the decision to stop the slave trade.

Many planters, farmers, and merchants despaired that Louisiana would ever again see the type of prosperity it had briefly experienced in the late 1780s after over half a century of stagnation. Little did they know that, much as the factors that had caused the bust had been present even as many boasted of the boom, processes were already beginning that would bring Louisiana a prosperity that would far surpass any that had come before. By the 1790s, the Industrial Revolution in the United Kingdom had created a surging demand for cotton in the Atlantic World, and the Haitian Revolution had opened a gaping hole in world sugar production. In 1795, residents of the lower Mississippi valley were already experimenting with the agricultural staples, cotton and sugar, that would replace the failed ones of the past. In addition, while far from forgotten, the instabilities that plagued the Atlantic World would recede in importance as the French Revolution's most radical phase ended and Haiti achieved independence without spreading its revolution abroad. By the time of the Louisiana Purchase in 1803, Louisiana's planters and merchants once again lorded over a profitable slave society built on exportable agricultural staples. They once again pursued the dream of wealth in a colonial world built on enslaved labor. However, any dreams that the enslaved had had that their freedom would result from the revolutionary ideals afloat in the Atlantic World were dashed. Rather than becoming a site of freedom for peoples of African descent, the lower Mississippi valley's planters, farmers, and merchants would adopt sugar and cotton and renovate their region into one of the wealthiest and most cruelly exploitative slave societies in the world, sucking in and exploiting increasing numbers of Africans and African Americans over the course of the 1800s.

2

MAKING THE COTTON REVOLUTION

We are all over head and ears in cotton.
—Julien Poydras to Cavalier and Petit, October 12, 1799

On September 10, 1795, four prominent residents of the Natchez district, including the Scottish-born planter and scientist William Dunbar, gathered at the request of the district's Spanish governor, Carlos de Grand-Pré, to observe the operation of a new machine recently built in the district. Gathering at the house of the Irish-born merchant and planter Daniel Clark (often referred to as "Sr." to differentiate him from his nephew, the New Orleans merchant and planter of the same name), the inspectors began their task on a sour note, pointing out that the "workmanship of this Machine is performed in a rude and imperfect manner." However, despite this bad first impression, once the machine was put into operation, they were impressed: "The Gin being set to work for the space of three quarters of an hour, did clean out in a neat, compleat and elegant manner eighteen pounds and three quarters of clean Cotton." They calculated that the completed gin should be able to produce 1,020 pounds of clean cotton in twelve hours. They concluded that "this invention will prove of infinite utility to this Province, and has very far surpassed our most sanguine expectations."[1]

Dunbar and company were witnessing the second public demonstration of the first Eli Whitney–style saw gin built in the lower Mississippi valley. The previous July, John Barclay, a Natchez resident who had just returned from a trip to the Carolinas and Georgia, had presented to Grand-Pré plans for "a new machine to clean cotton, that he had seen in operation in the state of Georgia." Encouraged by Grand-Pré, Barclay had spent the next several weeks building a gin at Clark's house. Once complete, those who witnessed it in operation believed it would revitalize the region's economy.[2]

The introduction of the new type of gin was a turning point in the region's history. After 1795, the gin spread rapidly throughout the region, allowing the widespread adoption of cotton cultivation. By the time of the Louisiana Purchase, only eight years later, cotton was the dominant commercial crop throughout much of the lower Mississippi valley. This rapid, even explosive, spread illustrates one of the most striking characteristics of cotton: relatively easy adoption by virtually any cultivator. Of the two new crops adopted in the 1790s, cotton was more widely grown, being adopted almost universally and rapidly in cotton country and often produced as well on smaller plantations and farms in sugar country, pointing to its future as the Deep South's dominant export crop. This sudden and extensive adoption was made possible by cotton's biological characteristics and hence the economics of the crop. It was also the result of planters, farmers, and merchants quickly recognizing the opportunities cotton offered and acting to take advantage of them. Government officials also played a role, encouraging cotton production, intermittently regulating it for the benefit of producers and providing legal access to Atlantic markets (or ignoring the smuggling that took place when the legal trade routes did not meet cotton cultivators' needs).

Despite their rapid, widespread, and successful adoption of cotton, cotton cultivators did not rest satisfied with having rescued their economy. Instead, they continued to work to improve the new technological system of cotton cultivation both to overcome production and marketing challenges and to improve the quality and quantity of the cotton yielded by their farms and plantations. They did this by adopting or adapting a variety of technologies including state regulation, technical improvements to the cotton gin and other cotton processing machinery, market mechanisms, cotton breeding, and new labor (i.e., slave) management tactics. In the end, the region's cotton received its most important endorsement: robust sales on Atlantic markets at a premium compared to short-staple cotton produced elsewhere. Ultimately, one is struck by the ability of cotton cultivators to successfully remake their economy over the course of only a few years by rapidly adopting a new technological system and then continuing to improve that system. However, one is also struck by the harsh labor management tactics employed on cotton plantations and farms and the way these tactics degraded the lives of the region's enslaved people. Enslavers' cotton profits were built on the brutal and carefully calibrated exploitation of the enslaved.[3]

The rapid spread of cotton across the lower Mississippi valley can be partly explained by the crop's biology. First, while cotton required an extended growing season, which makes it a southern crop, the growing season throughout the region was sufficiently long to allow its cultivation. This meant that a farmer or planter could grow cotton in any fertile soil in the entirety of the lower Mississippi valley. As one regional booster wrote, "All sugar lands are capable of yielding cotton, but all cotton lands will not yield sugar cane with any certainty."[4] Second, cotton processing capability could be concentrated with several cultivators using a single gin. Cotton is a hardy crop that does not need to be processed immediately after harvest. A cotton cultivator could store his cotton and, when convenient, transport it to another's gin and pay to have it processed. In addition, the processing capacity of gins was high enough that they could feasibly process the crops of multiple producers. "Public" cotton gins that were owned and operated by merchants became common in cotton regions. In practice, this availability of cotton processing capacity meant that any level of production could potentially be profitable, from a family farm with no enslaved people to a plantation with dozens of enslaved people.[5] Finally, cotton gins were relatively inexpensive if still out of reach of most farmers. For example, an 1803 estate inventory in Spanish West Florida valued a cotton gin at $250, a typical valuation and a fraction of the price of an enslaved man.[6] Together, these features of cotton (biological suitability throughout the region, publicly available processing equipment, and relative affordability of that equipment) facilitated the explosive expansion of cotton.

Despite its sudden and rapid spread in the years before and after 1800 and association with the region only during and after that period, cotton was not a new crop in the lower Mississippi valley in the mid-1790s.[7] In the early eighteenth century, at the beginning of French colonization, officials and settlers noted the ease with which cotton could be grown and hoped it would become an important export crop, a hope that did not come to pass.[8] Decades later, in 1776, only a few years after Spain took possession of the colony, Spanish colonel Francisco Bouligny, in a memorial to his superiors in Spain, discussed the products with the most potential in Louisiana. Among these, he included cotton, which he wrote was "of great usefulness" and that "its cultivation is easy." He claimed that locally grown cotton was "the best of any nation in the world" and that residents "pick cotton and remove its seeds with great ease." However, Bouligny also wrote that most of the cotton produced was for local, usually household, textile production rather than for export.[9] Prior to the 1790s, cotton was produced for local consumption but was not an important export commodity. Cotton's marginality arose, at least in part, from the lack of an effective way to clean short-staple cotton, the type of cotton that could be most effectively cultivated in the region. Cotton gins existed and were in use in Louisiana, but they were roller gins, a type of gin that effectively cleaned smooth seed sea-island cotton but when used to process fuzzy-seed short-staple cotton was extremely inefficient.[10]

The cotton revolution and the fateful association of the region with cotton began with the introduction of the Eli Whitney–style saw gin in 1795. The gin was the crucial piece of technology that made possible the profitable adoption of short-staple cotton. This type of gin used circular metal saws mounted on an axle to pull the cotton fiber away from the seed. They proved to be far more effective in cleaning the fuzzy-seed short-staple cotton than had roller gins.[11] As we have seen, John Barclay introduced the new gin design into the lower Mississippi valley after having learned about it in Georgia. While Barclay brought the necessary invention back to the region, his story is not one of a lone entrepreneur (or intellectual property thief, as Eli Whitney would have seen it) who bravely and singly built a new, innovative machine that changed everything. Rather, from start to finish, the building and propagation of the machine was a collaborative effort that included merchants, planters, farmers, Spanish officials, and, via their labor, enslaved people. Barclay's story illustrates how Natchez residents worked to overcome the crisis caused by the economic collapse of indigo and tobacco.

Upon his return from his trip east, Barclay went to Natchez's Spanish governor, Carlos de Grand-Pré, to request support for building a gin.

Grand-Pré apparently encouraged Barclay in his effort, which is unsurprising considering the Spanish policy of encouraging economic development in Spanish Louisiana to increase its viability as a bulwark against Anglo-American expansion, a policy undermined by the economic problems experienced since the collapse of the tobacco market. Grand-Pré had also mobilized the Natchez militia only a couple of months before in response to the Pointe Coupee Conspiracy.[12] As they evaluated the new device, Grand-Pré, Spanish officials, and Natchez enslavers likely had on their minds the conspiracy that had just been discovered downriver and revealed the precarity of their control over the enslaved. The future of the region was uncertain in this moment; the gin promised the possibility of ending that uncertainty to the benefit of elites.

After Grand-Pré's encouragement, Barclay moved into the house of Daniel Clark to construct the machine.[13] Clark was an important merchant and planter who was influential in the region. He had imported dozens of enslaved Africans into Natchez during the late 1780s tobacco boom.[14] In 1792, a Spanish census listed Clark as enslaving nineteen people, putting him among the twenty-five largest enslavers in the Natchez region.[15] Clark was also a major landholder. By 1795, he owned at least 3,650 arpents (a French measurement of land area that is slightly smaller than an acre) of land in the Natchez area as well as a valuable city lot in the town.[16] However, Clark was also, like many others, in financial trouble by 1795. We know he owned those 3,650 arpents only because in February 1795 he mortgaged them in favor of John Barclay, a Philadelphia merchant and presumably no relation to John Barclay of the gin, to secure a $15,000 debt.[17] The 1792 Spanish census gives a hint of why Clark was in financial trouble. In that year, his plantation had produced three thousand pounds of indigo, three thousand pounds of tobacco, and three hundred pounds of cotton (less than a single antebellum bale). As we have seen, the prospects for indigo and tobacco were already grim by 1792 and grimmer still by 1795.[18] Perhaps that potential financial embarrassment was why he was willing to house Barclay's attempt to build the gin.

While we do not know what the relationship was between the two men, Clark was probably assisting Barclay more than just in giving him a place to work. For example, to build the machine, Barclay would have needed access to various raw materials and finished iron parts. Perhaps

Clark financed Barclay's acquisition of these materials or even acquired them for Barclay in his role as a merchant. As an enslaver, he likely also provided enslaved labor to Barclay. He certainly saw his role in its construction as crucial, informing a correspondent during its construction, "I have done a great deal to bring this brat into the world, and if it succeeds shall put in a claim for my share of the honor."[19] Later he would get more than his "share of the honor" as he would be converted into the main mover of the gin's construction, with Barclay transformed into one of the people he enslaved or a random traveler.[20] Regardless of Clark's exact role in the construction, he probably saw the gin as a way out of his debt and the regional economic crisis.

Once he had completed the gin, Barclay continued to work to gain the support of local elites for its adoption by having it inspected by a group of local notables: John O'Connor, Lewis Alston, David Bradford, Leonard Marbury, and Daniel Clark himself. These individuals were, or would become, relatively prosperous members of the community owning land and enslaved people, being actively involved in the economic life of the region and holding government office.[21] It's also likely that, in the economic atmosphere of 1795, these men were in financial trouble and looking for a way out. They were impressed by Barclay's gin, writing to Governor Grand-Pré that "being present at the First Assay made by Mr Barclay Newly Constructed Machine for ginning Cotton, [we] found its Operation in separating the Seed from the cotton far beyond any thing of the kind that we have ever seen."[22] After the demonstration, Barclay asked the governor to "appoint intelligent and capable subjects to inspect [the gin]." The governor appointed the group discussed in the anecdote beginning this chapter, who concluded that "this invention will prove of infinite utility to this Province, and has very far surpassed our most sanguine expectations."[23] The elites of the province were impressed by Barclay's machine and saw it as the missing technology that would allow them to rehabilitate the local economy through the mass adoption of short-staple cotton cultivation, a crop they understood was lucrative and in high demand.

To bolster his bid for a patent or some form of compensation, Barclay presented Grand-Pré with a series of calculations that he argued demonstrated the machine's revolutionary capacity. According to Barclay, a single worker could cultivate five hundred pounds of clean cotton. A traditional roller gin would have taken thirty-four days to clean the cotton, since those machines could clean only fourteen or fifteen pounds per day. With the new gin, the work could be done in only half a day, saving an immense amount of time and labor. He calculated that, assuming two thousand laborers were available to cultivate cotton in the region and they all did so, this machine would save sixty-six thousand days of work or 24,750 pesos, assuming a day of labor was worth three reales (a reale was an eighth of a peso). The saw gin would allow a planter or farmer for the first time to commit to cotton and clean it entirely before the next growing season began.[24]

In his letter to Louisiana governor Carondelet that enclosed these documents on the new gin, Grand-Pré endorsed the view that the gin was the salvation of the region's economy. He claimed that residents "have not devoted themselves to the advantageous and easy cultivation of Cotton owing to the lack of a machine to clean it." He believed that the inhabitants would adopt the gin, "augment[ing] [Natchez's] riches." Grand-Pré forwarded and endorsed a request from Barclay for an exclusive privilege to build the new gins.[25] Carondelet agreed with Grand-Pré's assessment and ordered him to call the area's planters, farmers, and merchants together to decide what would be the best reward: a voluntary subscription or a reward from the government and exclusive franchise.[26] Grand-Pré convened such a meeting and four hundred inhabitants attended it, a sizable number since the Natchez area only had 938 adult white male residents according to a 1795 census. Grand-Pré left it to this conference to suggest what would be the best way to compensate Barclay. After meeting for two hours, the attendees presented him with a list of voluntary subscriptions amounting to fifteen hundred pesos. Those who chose to subscribe (not all attendees did) agreed to pay Barclay two pesos for each person they enslaved. This solution satisfied Barclay, who hoped that similar subscriptions could be taken up throughout Louisiana. However, Grand-Pré suggested to Carondelet an additional five-year exclusive franchise for Barclay during which each cultivator using a saw gin would pay Barclay five dollars.[27] Carondelet agreed to the franchise but ordered anyone who operated a saw gin to pay Barclay ten dollars, not five.[28] The Spanish government of Louisiana lunged at a chance to rehabilitate the province's economy and wished to reward the person who provided them with the tool to do so.

Upon his return to Natchez in 1795 Barclay had set to work introducing the new Eli Whitney–style saw gin into the area. To do so, he turned constructing the gin into a community project, enlisting at every step in the process notable members of local society (the Spanish governor, planters, farmers, and merchants) who could aid him in building, spreading, and profiting from the new machine. These individuals enthusiastically supported his endeavor, and once the gin was built, they judged it to be a groundbreaking technology that would, if adopted, revolutionize the local economy. The willingness of planters, farmers, and merchants to voluntarily contribute to Barclay, Daniel Clark's housing of him while he worked on the gin, and the support Spanish officials gave him at every step demonstrate that the region's rulers and free residents were looking for a solution to their economic crisis and saw the new machine as that solution.

Almost immediately after the successful demonstrations of Barclay's gin, locals began to construct and use saw gins, confirming the judgment of Barclay, Spanish officials, and early witnesses. Grand-Pré reported to Carondelet that Barclay arranged with several merchants to use his machine to clean cotton that they had in storage, suggesting that cultivators had begun to produce cotton beyond their means to process it even before the new gin had been introduced, once again showing the desperate search for a profitable crop, as well as the recognition that cotton might be that crop.[29] A few months later in response to others building gins, Barclay posted a handwritten "advertisement" meant to dispel a rumor that "the Gentlemen of Natchez District who lately erected the new Constructed Cotton Gins were to be Stoped from some prior Claim the Subscriber had for bringing the Model to the District." Rather, Barclay "acknowledge[d] the voluntary subscriptions" and "wishe[d] them all manner of Success" while offering to assist anyone who had built or planned to build a gin.[30] In another example of early saw gin construction in Natchez, George Cochran sued James McIntyre for his failure to pay Cochran eighty-one dollars owed for materials sold to McIntyre to build a saw gin.[31] Finally, when a Presbyterian missionary traveled to the region in the winter of 1800–1801, he claimed that cotton gins were ubiquitous: "Almost every farmer of considerable force has a horsegin on his farm."[32] This was only five years after Barclay had first demonstrated his gin. Planters and merchants jumped at the chance to own or at least use these new machines.

The new saw gins soon spread south into the rest of the lower Mississippi valley. Natchez served as a "hearth" for their production and spread. Unfortunately, the sources do not allow us to sketch with great specificity how and when they came to various areas. However, residents of New Orleans and its vicinity quickly learned about the new technology. While the news would have spread via word of mouth and letters that have been lost to us, wider knowledge also came from the colony's only newspaper, *Moniteur de la Louisiane*. While almost all the issues of the paper from the 1790s have been lost, several public announcements made by Governor Carondelet that were published in the paper during the fall of 1795 were republished in the *Louisiana Courier* in 1812. In one of the announcements, Carondelet mentioned the benefits cotton would receive from Barclay's machine: "The manufac[ture of] cottons, which the precious machine brought from Georgia by John Bar[clay], an inhabitant of Natchez, will ren[der] very saleable to the foreign merchants." Carondelet made this announcement on October 19, 1795, less than a month after Grand-Pré had written the letter originally informing him of the gin.[33] Many residents of the lower Mississippi valley learned quickly about the existence of the new technology.

Cotton cultivation spread as saw gins were established by planters, farmers, and merchants, either for their own or public use.[34] The example of Julien Poydras shows how saw gins spread beyond Natchez into the francophone parts of the lower Mississippi valley. Poydras, a planter and merchant in the francophone Pointe Coupee region, was by the mid-1790s in financial and emotional distress. During this period, he told one correspondent that "if that dye [indigo] does not sell, having no other means of making money, I shall be forced to abandon business until better times."[35] This letter was written in November 1798, fully three years after the introduction of the new gins to Natchez. While the switch to cotton was strikingly quick and widespread, it was by no means universal or instantaneous. In fact, Poydras's correspondence shows that William

Dunbar, who was one of the region's major producers of indigo seed, was still selling indigo seed at least as late as 1798, even though he was one of the first witnesses to the new gin and an early cotton adopter.[36]

By November 1798, Poydras was probably beginning to consider the adoption of cotton, driven by his financial problems. As he had contacts and business dealings with Natchez planters and merchants, he would have been aware of the changes taking place there. For example, he ruminated in an undated letter to Dunbar (probably written during the first half of 1798) about the advantages of cotton cultivation. In a discussion about what to do with an estate of which he was the executor, he asked Dunbar "if cotton is a more advantageous crop than indigo," adding, "which I do not believe," a surprising claim considering the observations of many of his contemporaries. He went on to muse about whether "cotton [can] not be made here with more advantage than at the Natchez being nearer the market and soil abundantly better."[37] Still, this was about another planter's estate and shows some hesitation as to whether a switch to cotton was prudent. However, the letters shows that, by 1798, he was pondering cotton.

Unfortunately, no letter survives showing definitively when or how Poydras made his decision to switch crops. However, he did so in time for the 1799 growing season. That year he only grew a small crop of indigo which "did not succeed." He also planted 150 arpents of cotton although he apparently had trouble harvesting it because of bad weather.[38] During the harvest, he wrote letters to three of his mercantile contacts in New Orleans pressing them for information on the price of cotton while continuing to ask about the indigo and rice markets. In another letter written a couple of months later, he expressed some trepidation about the price of cotton: "God help [the price] to stand up!"[39] Having undergone years of suffering at the hands of indigo, he was not yet convinced that cotton would be his salvation. Despite these reservations, he also described a region almost wholly divested of indigo and committed to cotton, a striking change from recent years. He evocatively wrote "we are all over head and ears in cotton." As for indigo, he had "made almost none myself and I am to receive very little or none at all of other people" (being a merchant as well as planter Poydras marketed other cultivators' crops).[40] Poydras recognized how different the 1799 growing season was from those of previous years.

To produce marketable clean cotton, Poydras needed processing equipment. In a letter written in December 1799, he told his correspondent that he was "constructing a superb double mill to gin the cotton, which they promised to complete in six weeks."[41] By the next spring, he informed the same correspondent that "one of my mills is working very well." He also related that his press would be ready by the next week.[42] To build this equipment, he capitalized on his contacts in Natchez. This mill had been built by "Perry," "the finest worker in the country." According to Poydras he had had the machine "especially made in Natchez."[43] While no letter explicitly says so, Poydras probably gained his contact with Perry through Dunbar, his main Natchez correspondent. In one letter in the summer of 1799, when, presumably, Poydras would have been arranging the construction of his gins and press, he discussed with Dunbar some mechanical items he was having constructed in Natchez "under your inspection."[44] Cotton was spreading along the banks of the Mississippi, through mercantile and personal connections that readily crossed cultural and linguistic barriers. In this case, they were also readily crossing imperial boundaries, as Poydras resided in Spanish Louisiana while Natchez was, by 1799, a part of the Mississippi Territory of the United States.

At least by the time of the Louisiana Purchase in 1803, cotton had become the primary export commodity of much of the lower Mississippi valley, being shipped out of the region to ports on the East Coast of the United States and in Europe, most importantly to Liverpool to feed Lancashire's voracious textile mills. A Presbyterian missionary visiting the Mississippi Territory in 1800–1801 observed that cotton was "now the staple commodity in the territory, and grows to great pe[r]fection."[45] Cotton was also king by 1801 in much of Spanish Louisiana. The area just under the line of demarcation between American and Spanish territory (the east–west border between the modern states of Mississippi and Louisiana) probably adopted cotton around the same time as Natchez. This area had been part of Natchez's hinterland before the transfer of Mississippi to the United States in 1798, and all the original witnesses to Barclay's gin resided in that region except for Daniel Clark.[46]

Poydras's observations show that cotton had spread across the river into the francophone regions of the Mississippi valley by at least 1799 but likely earlier. By 1803, cotton had spread even further afield. According to one report, at least twenty-four cotton gins were operating on the Red River, and cultivators there were producing around nine hundred thousand pounds of cotton per year.[47]

Export figures from Louisiana show a large increase in cotton production shortly before the Louisiana Purchase in 1803. For 1800, one document claims that Louisiana exported 305,289½ pounds of clean cotton. For 1801, the amount was 379,137 pounds. These were not particularly large amounts considering that the relatively uncolonized Red River region was said to produce nine hundred thousand pounds in 1803. The export figures suggest a large jump in production in 1802, with 2,161,498 pounds of clean cotton exported that year. However, at the same time, many other commodities experienced large jumps in export quantities, suggesting some factor other than production increases caused such large single-year increases, most likely an increase in licit trade following peace with Britain.[48]

In fact, as the Poydras letters suggest, the shift to cotton in Spanish Louisiana likely happened several years earlier. However, this shift was probably masked in export figures by large-scale smuggling out of New Orleans, a central feature of the region's economy since the beginning of colonization whenever legal trade routes failed to meet local needs. In this case, American trade privileges facilitated smuggling, often to Britain, the main consumer of cotton but at war with Spain and, thus, cut off from trading directly with Spanish Louisiana. After Pinckney's Treaty, signed in 1795, Americans had the right to the free navigation of the Mississippi River, and American producers west of the Appalachians could deposit their produce in New Orleans to wait for American ships to carry it away duty free. According to Evan Jones, an American merchant in New Orleans, this arrangement had bred widespread smuggling of cotton (as well as other goods) by 1801. Jones explained that American goods "deposited" in New Orleans were never inspected by Spanish customs officials, and thus merchants easily passed off Spanish cotton as American cotton. Merchants and planters also bribed Spanish officials to allow smuggling. As a result, Jones reported that "almost all the Cotton of Louisiana and the quantity is very considerable" was smuggled out of the province.[49] Merchants and planters were adept at finding the cracks in imperial regulations and prying them open, and, as they had for decades, Spanish officials, even those at the highest level, turned a blind eye, recognizing the crucial role cotton was playing in revitalizing the region's export economy. In any case, by 1802, at the very latest and almost certainly several years earlier, large areas of Spanish Louisiana were committed to producing cotton.

While increasingly the main staple of the Mississippi Territory and the rest of the upper reaches of the lower Mississippi valley (and the Red River and southwestern Louisiana), cotton was also produced as an adjunct crop further down the river, where sugar was coming to dominate. In this region, it was only one possible crop among several and was not universally produced. For example, an 1804 census of St. Charles Parish, the first parish upriver from New Orleans, found 123 working farms and plantations. Of these, eight produced cotton as their primary crop, five indigo, twenty-one sugar, and the rest provisions such as rice, corn, potatoes and peas. The eight cotton farms produced 128,000 pounds of cotton.[50] These farms' existence shows that cotton cultivation, while not dominant in the southern part of the region, had become an option there. By the time of the Louisiana Purchase, only eight years after Barclay built the first saw gin in Natchez, cotton had spread throughout the region as either the dominant market crop or one option among several.

While regional residents were open to (and in certain cases enthusiastic about) adopting new technologies as shown by their rapid adoption of the saw gin and cotton cultivation, they were discriminating as to which ones they embraced. Another technology, brought to the Natchez area twelve years after the gin, and which had a similar story of introduction, illustrates how regional residents evaluated new technologies and sometimes chose not to adopt them. In 1807, William Dunbar wrote to his Liverpool merchant contacts Green and Wainewright with the news that "one of our Backwoods Kentucky men has lately produced a model of a machine which separates the seed from the cotton, cards & spins all at one operation." It would produce "about 8 lib: [pounds] of thread in 10 hours, the thread is of a quality which would make common sheeting."[51] This description was probably of a machine, called the Columbian Spinster, invented and patented by John McBride of Washington, Mississippi Territory.

McBride placed a series of advertisements about his machine in Natchez newspapers in the fall of 1807. The first and lengthiest advertisement, published on August 22, offered the model of the machine and patent rights for sale. It also described a demonstration of the machine during which the machine had produced four pounds of thread in five and a half hours. The bottom of the advertisement included the names of thirteen men who had witnessed the test and certified the accuracy of McBride's description. This demonstration with witnesses suggests a parallel with the one undertaken by Barclay twelve years before when he had twice demonstrated his saw gin to local notables. The thirteen witnesses to McBride's device are somewhat difficult to trace. However, one Samuel L. Winston probably appears in the 1820 federal census as the enslaver of sixty people in Adams County, suggesting an elite group of planters and, perhaps, merchants.[52] Interestingly, Bennet Truly, who, as we shall see, had fled Natchez eleven years before to avoid arrest by the Spanish governor for attempting to fraudulently sell bad cotton, appeared as a witness.[53] Two other advertisements appeared after this one, one in September, the other in November. Both suggest that McBride had been unsuccessful in finding a buyer for the machine or patent. By the final advertisement, he was offering to sell permits to erect machines rather than the machine or patent.[54]

However, the story of the Columbian Spinster did not end there. John Rollins, a resident of Spanish West Florida, tried to introduce McBride's machine into that region but ultimately failed. John Rollins claimed to be the agent for John McBride (although it is not clear what exactly their relationship was) and petitioned the Spanish government to obtain permission to introduce the machine into Spanish West Florida but also to gain protection for the enterprise, as it would "accrue to the benefit of the cotton growers." In 1808, Rollins petitioned Spanish governor Grand-Pré, who had been intimately involved in the introduction of the saw gin, to allow him to address the citizens of the area and enlist subscriptions for its production. Grand-Pré allowed the appeal. Its results are unrecorded.

Still, Rollins was encouraged enough by the response to employ three men to construct a copy of McBride's machine.[55]

Unfortunately for Rollins, the three men were unable to build a working machine, leading to litigation. The case turned on Rollins's desire to confiscate the machine to have it inspected by arbitrators to find the problem and fix it and the refusal of the builders to turn it over. At its core, the dispute was over who was at fault for the failure. Rollins blamed it on poor workmanship, while the workmen blamed it on bad instructions. Regardless, the case continued past the end of the Spanish period and into the American era, producing more case records. Most interesting was a deposition taken from William Duvall, a planter in Baton Rouge Parish. He recollected seeing in 1807 in Mississippi "a spinning machine which he understood to Belong to John McBride and invented by him." He testified that it should not have taken three workmen more than two months to build such a machine.[56]

The parallels between the introduction of McBride's machine into Spanish West Florida and that of the Eli Whitney cotton gin over a decade before by Barclay are striking. Both were introduced on Governor Grand-Pré's watch. Each was built with an eye toward either a local monopoly or bounty. Finally, each machine worked, as attested to by William Dunbar in both cases. While the workmen in Spanish West Florida had been unable to re-create the machine successfully, people had seen the original machine in operation. Just because the machine they built had not worked well should not have precluded people attempting to build their own. As we shall see, the original cotton gins were constant problems for their users. They were often poorly built and, even when the workmanship was good, they did not work particularly well, producing substandard cleaned cotton. Still, locals virtually lunged at the chance to build cotton gins, whereas all evidence, from McBride's advertisements and the attempt to introduce the machine to Spanish West Florida, points to local curiosity about the McBride machine but little beyond that.

The fate of the McBride machines suggests that placing capital and labor into producing thread and textiles was just not appealing to local planters, farmers, and merchants. Had it been, a working machine was available for them to use. However, after Rollins's suit, the whole business vanished from the lower Mississippi valley. Apparently, locals saw no advantage in moving beyond cultivating, cleaning, and packing the cotton. They might express interest in the possibility but chose not to actually adopt the machine. The failure of locals to embrace thread or textile production did not arise from a hesitancy to employ machines or even industrial organization; they enthusiastically did the former in the case of the cotton gin and the latter in the case of sugar. When it came to thread and textile production, planters appear to have made an essentially rational calculation that reallocating their capital and labor into that industry did not make sense.[57] These individual decisions would have immense ramifications for the South's economic future, but, in the moment the decisions were made, locals would have had little sense of this fact.

Despite the widespread (and in some areas nearly universal) adoption of cotton, cotton cultivation was not a finished technological system but rather a work in progress. Throughout the first two decades of cotton cultivation in the lower Mississippi valley, cotton cultivators, often working with or encouraged by regional and extraregional merchants, searched for ways to overcome technological challenges posed by the new crop and to improve the various parts of the new technological system of cotton cultivation. These efforts touched every part of the system, from cultivation to processing to marketing. What we can say about any given part of this effort varies. In some areas, we can, in some detail, trace these efforts and how successful they appear to have been. In others, we can only catch glimpses of these efforts and can say little more than that they were made and that they appear to have paid off. In still others, we can only assume the efforts were being made by comparison with other times and places but can see little direct evidence of them in this time and place. Regardless, what evidence we do have illustrates that efforts to improve cotton production never ceased once the crop was adopted.

While cotton production in this period presented various challenges, those that were most commonly recorded occurred between the harvest and export, most crucially problems related to the new saw gins and the quality of clean cotton they produced. Many operators found saw gins challenging to operate. More commonly, the new gins did not work properly. In either case, the gins might damage the cotton, making it less useful to textile manufacturers and thus worth less. Even when early saw gins did work as designed, they often produced low-quality cotton. For example, in an 1801 letter from Liverpool to a Philadelphia merchant, the writer stated that the New Orleans cotton, although it "looks fair and is well cleaned," had "so essential a want of staple in it that it will only answer for twist."[58] Other observers pointed out that the machines themselves were incapable of producing cotton of the quality desired by British manufacturers.[59]

Other problems also commonly occurred in the period after the harvest. Cotton was often stored improperly, leading to its becoming wet and rotting or catching fire, a common occurrence that could lead to accusations of arson.[60] In addition, whether through incompetence or fraud, the bales in which cotton was packaged, shipped, and sold were often damaged or contained elements such as seeds and stems that made them weigh more than the actual cotton they contained.[61] These various problems, while not serious enough to stop the cotton revolution, were serious enough to lead to a variety of responses, as government officials, merchants, and cotton cultivators attempted to overcome, avoid, or at least manage them. In these responses, various actors attempted to add new technologies to the technological system of cotton cultivation or to improve technologies that were already part of that system.

An example of the early challenges cotton presented, as well as efforts to overcome them, came almost immediately in the history of the Natchez cotton industry. On May 19, 1796, about eight months after Barclay first demonstrated the gin to Governor Grand-Pré, Manuel Gayoso de Lemos, Grand-Pré's successor as governor of the Natchez district, learned that Benito Truly's cotton gin was not working properly. De Lemos ordered Truly to stop using his gin and sent Captains Stephen Minor and William Vousdan to inspect it. The two found the machine "somewhat battered" but easily fixable. The major problem, however, was that the machine's location was dirty and open on all sides, possibly damaging any cotton processed by the gin. Also, the operators of the machine were feeding too much cotton into it at once. In response to the report, de Lemos decreed that he would issue Truly a series of regulations for Truly to follow to avoid similar problems in the future. Up to this point, this was a simple case of an early adopter of the gin finding it challenging to use the machine effectively and of the Spanish government acting to protect the quality of cotton being sold out of the colony.[62]

However, the case did not end there. Late in the evening on the same day that de Lemos issued his proclamation, Minor reported that two planters had discovered that some of their cotton, ginned and packed by Benito Truly, was in a very bad state. The next day de Lemos and four inspectors examined the cotton. They discovered that some of the cotton had been ruined by water damage. They also found, mixed with the cotton, loose seeds and unginned cotton. Other sacks of cotton were damaged but possibly salvageable. The inspection did not end with Truly's cotton; cotton ginned and packed by Jesse Haspard and Richard Harrison was also inspected. The inspectors found that Haspard's cotton had seeds stuffed into the middle of the sacks and that most of the rest was unginned except for the cotton at the top. Much of Harrison's cotton was of very bad quality (likely meaning the staple was too short) and had been packed wet and was beginning to rot. Upon the completion of the examination, the inspectors concluded that the conduct of Truly, Harrison, and Haspard was "malicious, fraudulent, and prejudicial to the country."[63]

After the inspection, de Lemos ordered Truly's arrest. However, Truly had been forewarned and escaped from the territory to parts unknown, leaving behind his wife and property.[64] In response to the accusations against him, Richard Harrison petitioned the governor for clemency, arguing that de Lemos was "too good to punish ignorance for design and too just not to distinguish and apportion every punishment to the offence." Harrison's argument was, essentially, that he was incompetent, not criminal. The year before was "the first season he ever attempted making Cotton as a Crop." The cotton that had been condemned was bad because it was the "last packed in the Fall after the leaves and Snow had fallen and mixed with it." He claimed that he had not intended to sell it as "prime Cotton" but at a price "agreeable to its quality." In addition, the cotton had fallen into a creek while being transported to Natchez and then been left on an open boat for several days and exposed to rain. The fact that one of the bags he shipped had been good showed that he had not had "any malicious intent to injure the Staple of a Country by which I expect to subsist a numerous Family." In response, de Lemos decreed that Harrison was only liable for damages and any costs of justice and would not be prosecuted. De Lemos did caution Harrison "to not pack any cotton of bad quality" and that, if he were to do so, "he will be responsible [for] the results according to the regulation established on the date of May 24 for the conduct of proprietors of these Machines."[65]

During the first year after the adoption of the saw gin, Governor de Lemos had felt compelled to issue cotton gin regulations in response to severe problems with the quality of cotton being sold to merchants, in some cases problems that he concluded were the result of fraud. Government regulation was one technology that the Spanish and later American governments used to help overcome challenges in the processing and marketing stages of the cotton cultivation system. The motive behind creating formal regulations of the quality of cotton shipped out of the region was not to protect the merchants who purchased the cotton (although it would have that effect, and they welcomed such regulations) but rather to protect producers as a group and thus the economy of the district by ensuring that the cotton that was exported was either of high quality and properly packaged or, at the very least, clearly labeled if it was not. Those involved repeatedly referred to the need to protect the reputation of the region's cotton when explaining why regulation was necessary. In the investigation of Truly, de Lemos initially legitimated the investigation by pointing out that bad cotton could result in "notable damage to the inhabitants of this district, and discredit to the production of this soil." Later, after the "fraud" had been discovered, he stated that it was "prejudicial to the country" and demanded a remedy "more effective to cut off abuses of this nature and to accredit the industry of the commerce of Cotton that [is] so much advantage to this country."[66] To rescue the region, its cotton had to sell on international markets; a poor reputation could hinder that possibility.

The belief that cotton quality had to be regulated to protect the "reputation" of Natchez's producers continued into the American period, as residents expressed concern about the quality of local cotton and insisted on government action to protect that quality. For example, in 1799 the grand jury of Adams County presented a series of grievances to the territory's new American government that included the lack of cotton gin inspectors. Once again, government gin inspections were framed not so much as a means to protect the people purchasing the cotton but rather as a means to protect the reputation of the region's product: "The success and prosperity of this Country chiefly depends upon our particular care and attention to that valuable branch of agriculture and to prevent any frauds and neglects in preparing it for exportation."[67]

Winthrop Sargent, the Mississippi Territory's first governor, and the territory's judges (together tasked with creating the Mississippi Territory's first laws) responded to this request by passing "A Law to provide for the Inspection of Gins, Cotton Presses, and cotton intended for exportation from this Territory" that was intended to "promote the interests of this Territory; by establishing a foreign market, the good reputation of the staple of this country." Under the law, the governor was to appoint inspectors who would at regular intervals and in certain situations visit the gins of the territory. A gin operator who flaunted this regulation would be subject to severe fines.[68] Judging how rigorously the cotton inspection law was enforced or followed is virtually impossible. However, despite the evident desire for such regulation, this law was either repealed or fell into disuse by 1802, was reinstated either that year or the next, and then was again repealed or fell into disuse several years later, perhaps indicating that the enthusiasm for government regulation was more apparent than real.[69] An 1807 compendium of Mississippi Territory statutes lists no inspection law or other regulation of cotton gins.[70]

In the early years of cotton cultivation, the territory of Orleans never passed a law for inspecting either cotton or cotton gins. The only evidence that it was ever considered comes from a short passage in a speech territorial governor William Claiborne (formerly the governor of the Mississippi Territory) gave to the territorial legislature in 1806 in which he called for the legislature to pass a law for the inspection of cotton produced in the territory for export. The legislature never acted on the recommendation.[71] The failure to pass an inspection regime does not mean that there weren't problems associated with cotton production in Louisiana. The same complaints about fraudulent or negligent practices that occurred in Mississippi also occurred in Louisiana. In a letter published in the *Union* in 1804, a merchant "from a respectable merchant house in Liverpool" complained about the general state of the crop arriving from New Orleans. After writing that there was no need to comment on the poor quality of the 1802 crop given "the losses both in the value and reputation have been so widely and exclusively felt," he went on to note his "particular pleasure . . . to notice the great improvement in the cotton of this year." The biggest problem was no longer "false package," by which he appears to have meant the packing together of high and low quality cotton in such a way as to deceive the buyer about the overall quality of the cotton bale or the packing of trash such as seeds and twigs into the bales to increase their weight. Now the largest issue was that many of the bales shipped from the region contained dirt and leaves. The leaves were a particular problem because they were impossible to remove and destroyed the dye used in the manufacture of cloth.[72]

Louisiana cotton cultivators were in danger of damaging their reputation much as Natchez cotton cultivators had feared shoddy practices would damage theirs. Yet, no inspection law was ever passed by the legislature. Surviving records do not give an easy answer to why Louisianans never showed any interest in regulating cotton production. The local government also never passed a law on the inspection of sugar even though, as we shall see, complaints about its quality were also common. Perhaps the different reaction of Louisiana can be explained by the different structure of its economy. In Louisiana, mercantile activities, many unrelated to local production, were extremely important due to New Orleans's role in trans-Appalachian trade. Also, even though cotton was a local staple, it was not "the" local staple as it was in Mississippi. It always existed alongside sugar, lumber, rice, and other provisions produced for consumption in New Orleans. It's possible that the main reason for the different reaction was that cotton was just not central to Louisiana's economy, and thus the political will to institute a potentially expensive and intrusive inspection regime did not exist.

Regardless, government regulation does not seem to have been an acceptable technology for solving quality issues in Louisiana and stopped being acceptable in Mississippi after the first few years of cotton production. However, the problems of quality did not disappear. To address these ongoing problems, merchants and cotton cultivators developed private mechanisms. The exact mechanisms used shifted over the years. At first, merchants came to rely on planters' and gin operators' reputations for producing good (or bad) cleaned cotton. Distant merchants claimed that they could keep track of who was and was not producing high-quality cotton. In the letter published in the *Union* the Liverpool merchant claimed that his house "have had an opportunity of seeing most of the gin marks" from Mississippi. He then pointed out two gins that produced the best cotton. He claimed that he and his colleagues "have the cotton sorted in our warehouse by the different marks and by thus holding them up to particular observation, each gin-holder will eventually find both his character and interest seriously involved, and the name of a person whose cotton has been uniformly good will always have its due weight with a purchaser." Implicitly those whose cotton had not been "uniformly good" would find the price of their cotton affected.[73]

The merchant was laying out a means whereby gin operators could be rewarded for producing good cotton and punished for producing bad cotton or committing fraudulent practices. Tellingly his language suggests that he did not see this process as merely instrumental. He claimed that his inspections would not just be a judge of the quality of the gin owner's cotton but also of his "character." This shows how a planter or merchant's "reputation," so important for obtaining credit and, apparently, good prices for one's cotton, was seen to encompass the whole person and not just his economic activity. In a very real sense, a planter's cotton crop was part of who he was; a judgment of its quality was a judgment of him. "Reputation" was another type of technology, "a means to fulfill a human purpose" that became a part of the technological system of cotton cultivation.[74]

Considering that both their "character" and "interest" were at stake, planters and merchants took threats to their crops' (and by implication their personal) reputations seriously. A Monsieur Bringier, likely Marius Pons Bringier, published in the *Moniteur de la Louisiane* a defense against rumors that he had defrauded local merchants. According to Bringier, rumors had spread "in various plantations, from [illegible] New Orleans to Attakapas, [illegible] [that] one had seen in the cotton bales of Sieur Bringier all sorts of frauds" including bones and dirt. To defend himself from these accusations, Bringier published a certificate from the New Orleans merchant firm Chew and Relf, which had handled his cotton contracts with Daniel Clark. The firm confirmed that, while his cotton had not been of the quality they had hoped, it had also not been fraudulently packaged.[75]

Letters between William Dunbar and the Liverpool merchants Green and Wainewright illustrate one planter's management of his reputation. In an early letter, Dunbar wrote that he would "endeavour to improve the reputation you have procured for me," showing the very personal nature of the early cotton market.[76] Several years later, Dunbar found himself having to defend his cotton's reputation. Apparently, "the last Cotton sent ... had been found by some of the manufacturers not so fair as was expected," meaning that his "reputation had suffered a little on this account." Dunbar felt that this was enough of a threat to instruct his correspondents "to explain to those same manufacturers that they did not receive any cotton that year from my own plantation," as he had lost all of his in a fire. Rather, the cotton had come from a plantation he had just purchased and hence was not the result of his own efforts. He explained that he "was perhaps wrong to suffer my own name to be marked upon those bales." This season he would earn back his reputation: "My Cotton Gins being now in perfect order I am willing to stake my reputation upon the quality of the Cotton."[77] A Liverpool merchant traveling many years later through Mississippi seemed to confirm the reasonableness of Dunbar's concern with his cotton's quality by noting, after a visit with Dunbar's widow, that "with the superiority of the cotton from his plantation, our English cotton-spinners are well acquainted."[78] Apparently, English merchants and manufacturers took care to keep track of the provenance of the cotton they were purchasing in order to judge quality and reputation across years, and planters both worried about this reputation and worked to build and defend it.

Still, this system likely never worked perfectly, perhaps not even well. Complaints about quality and fraud continued throughout the early years of cotton production, and merchants might not have always paid as much attention as the Liverpool merchant quoted in the *Union,* especially as the region's population exploded (more than tripling between 1785 and 1810 and nearly doubling again between 1810 and 1820), gins proliferated (by 1803, the relatively uncolonized Red River had twenty-four gins operating on it), and cotton was shipped to a diversity of destinations in North America and Europe via hundreds of merchant houses (a study of the Liverpool cotton trade between 1770 and 1815 found hundreds of merchants involved in the trade [although most would not have dealt with lower Mississippi valley cotton] and high turnover in the individuals and firms involved).[79] With so many participants, the trade must have been becoming more impersonal. In fact, Dunbar was skeptical that merchants actually paid close attention to the reputation of every planter or gin. In the same letter where he defended his reputation, he also claimed that cotton he had classified as second quality was better than much that was being passed as first quality because "it appears to me that our Planters are growing more negligent, which is the fault of our merchants who do not make the due distinction[,] giving the same price for the bad as the good."[80]

Ultimately, other means were settled on to deal with quality issues. Merchants moved away from the personal reputation of planters and gins toward categorizing quality through personal inspection and then assigning prices to that quality through markets. In 1809, Dunbar suggested something like this was already happening by stating that he had classified his own cotton as second quality and that others were passing worse cotton as first quality.[81] One Liverpool cotton-trading firm was grading cotton in its weekly price circulars by 1805 and by 1811 had developed "a clear grading system of the major types of cotton."[82] By 1820 at the latest, grading had become formalized in New Orleans with cotton prices printed in Louisiana papers categorized as "prime" and "second."[83] In 1827, a New Orleans newspaper categorized cotton into six different quality categories in one section but in its price list by a combination of quality and geographic origin that produced eleven distinct categories.[84] The use of quality grading suggests that merchants had worked out a system of quality categorization that allowed them to come up with fair prices that cultivators and merchants could agree to (ideally, however, merchants and planters surely continued to argue over crop quality). By 1820, and likely much earlier, impersonal market forces replaced more personal concerns about reputation when marketing cotton crops. The exact mechanism for how this happened is not clear (although distant, particularly Liverpool merchants were crucial drivers of the transition). Still, merchants and cultivators had developed a technology that allowed cotton marketing to be streamlined, regularized, and somewhat depersonalized, moving beyond what was likely a cumbersome dependence on reputation.

While cultivators, merchants, and government officials were attempting to improve cotton quality through government regulation and market mechanisms, cultivators also worked to improve the quality and quantity of their crops through other means. The main tactics used were attempts to breed (or introduce) a more beneficial variety of cotton, improve the gins and other machinery used to process it, and institute new labor practices. While records from the period do not allow a detailed sketch of these methods or their degrees of success, they do show that people attempted to improve cotton cultivation for their own benefit via these methods.[85]

Throughout this period cotton cultivators worked to improve cotton-processing machinery. As we have seen, early saw gins often damaged the cotton or cut its staple too short. Planters experimented with ways to improve the machines or searched for information on mechanics who had done so. For example, territory of Orleans governor William Claiborne wrote to an unknown recipient soliciting aid in getting a patent awarded to a man who had invented "a Cotton machine upon a new and improved Plan."[86] Dunbar worked constantly to improve his gin. In 1806, he informed Green and Wainewright that he was "now completeing some improvements to the Cotton machine, by which it will be twice fanned and skreened & afterwards hand picked upon a moving web, which conducts the Cotton from the machine."[87] In another letter, he noted that some bad cotton he had sold was the product of a machine to which "the best improvements . . . had not yet been applied."[88] Notices also appeared in newspapers advertising improvements to cotton-processing machines. One, to "Cotton Planters and Cotton Repressers" and placed in the *Louisiana Courier* by the New Orleans agents of a Philadelphia mechanic, advertised a new patented cotton press that "for cheapness and expedition . . . will excel [*sic*] all Presses now in the United-States."[89] Another advertisement offered a patented "*Steam Engine,* of a very simple construction, of unlimited power" that, among other things, could be used in "Cotton-Gins."[90] The records do not allow a judgment on the results of these particular experiments. However, during the first two decades after the cotton revolution improvements were made to saw gins and other cotton processing equipment that augmented the quality of the cotton being shipped to textile manufacturers.[91]

Cotton cultivators also experimented with new varieties of cotton in the hopes they would increase cotton yields and quality.[92] For example, in October 1807 Dunbar informed his Liverpool merchant contacts Green and Wainewright that during the growing season then ending he had "made two small experiments of new Cotton, one is the nankin, which I find very good, the other is a species from Mexico which I think excellent." He sent to the merchants samples of each to have them examined by "your manufacturers" to find out "the prices which will be given for such cotton, or rather the proportion of value between this & our own good cotton."[93] The sample from Mexico had been brought by a neighbor from Mexico the year before.[94] By November 1810 Dunbar's estate (he had died the previous month) produced 454 bales of cotton of which 10 or 12 were Mexican cotton.[95] Other planters also began to experiment with the variety.[96] Such experimentation would pay off in the Petit Gulf (*Gusypium barbadense*) variety of cotton, developed by 1820 and dominant in the lower Mississippi valley in coming decades.[97] Over the long run, experiments with the biology of cotton yielded results that help explain the greater profitability of plantations in the lower Mississippi valley when compared to other cotton growing regions.[98] In the early 1800s, this success was still many years away, but the experimentation had begun.

Cultivation practices and labor (i.e., slave) management were other areas where cotton cultivators surely made efforts to increase the quality and quantity of their cotton. To begin with, planters, farmers, and enslaved people would have had to learn the process of cultivation. Enslavers also would have instituted new slave management tactics tailored to cotton. Like any other technology, cotton cultivation was a system of knowledge that needed to be learned, and there would have been a learning curve. Snippets of evidence for this process do survive. For example, Poydras wrote that Anglo-Americans' "negroes are better pickers than ours," implying that those enslaved people had acquired cotton-picking skills.[99] In addition, estimates of the amount of cotton a single enslaved person could cultivate doubled between 1795 and 1806, suggesting that the cultivation process had become more efficient over that decade.[100] We can also reasonably assume that planters and farmers experimented with different ways to cultivate the crop and manage labor, just as they experimented with other parts of the cotton system. Unfortunately, little evidence survives from the late 1700s or early 1800s from the region about the operation of and labor management on cotton plantations or farms. Therefore, we cannot say much about how labor was organized on an early cotton plantation or farm or what efforts were made to change those practices.

Records from later times and other places can give us a sense of how labor management likely worked, some insight into enslaved people's work lives, and what innovations might have taken place. Unfortunately, the earliest plantation records from the region reveal little beyond the basic rhythm of cotton cultivation and some basic facts about labor management. Planting tended to begin in March or April although preparatory work began earlier. Throughout the spring and summer, enslaved people tended cotton and other crops by harrowing, ditching, plowing, hoeing, and sometimes replanting crops ruined by late frosts or heavy rains. Generally, the cotton crop was picked beginning in late August with work ending as late as December.[101] On cotton plantations, enslaved people generally had Sundays off, and when they did work on Sundays, the work appears to have typically been both voluntary and compensated.[102] The practice of paying the enslaved for Sunday work was likely the norm in the lower Mississippi valley. The law in Spanish Louisiana required enslavers to pay enslaved people for work on Sunday, as did the first Black Code passed in the territory of Orleans.[103] Solomon Northup, in his memoir of his enslavement in Louisiana in the 1840s and 1850s, reported that work on Sunday was compensated.[104] With the possible exception of the Sunday pay, little of this is particularly surprising or insightful; these rhythms would likely have seemed familiar to a cotton planter or farmer in 1800 or 1860.

To get a better sense of how labor worked, the point of view of the enslaved is more revealing. Unfortunately, no firsthand accounts of agricultural labor in the lower Mississippi valley survive from the late 1700s or early 1800s, which is unsurprising, as slave narratives written about or during this period are rare. To get some sense of what this labor might have been like, we need to turn to two enslaved men who experienced cotton plantations at a different place or time. Accounts from Charles Ball, who was enslaved in cotton-growing regions of Georgia and South Carolina in the early 1800s, and from Solomon Northup, a free man kidnapped into slavery in Louisiana in the 1840s and 1850s, suggest how enslaved people experienced cotton cultivation. Both Ball and Northup agreed that cotton was particularly demanding and could be challenging for enslaved people who were new to it.[105] These arduous labor demands likely arose from cotton farmers' and planters' desire to produce as much revenue as possible from this particularly lucrative crop and to overcome bottlenecks in production: "growing the plants and harvesting the fibers," as Edward Baptist has put it. Enslavers drove enslaved people hard in the fields to increase the amounts of cotton cultivated and harvested to feed the voracious new gins and, more distantly, textile mills in order to produce greater revenues.[106] The tactics they developed to do this became crucial components of the cotton system.

Labor demands at harvest, associated with the "pushing system," made the greatest impression on those enslaved on cotton plantations and farms and was likely the most important labor innovation made by cotton cultivators. The "pushing system" involved the assignment of daily picking quotas to each enslaved person based on experience and skill. The system appears to have been common across the South, but the details of how it worked varied.[107] Northup recalled in his memoir *Twelve Years a Slave* that his last enslaver drove the enslaved to meet picking quotas that for many were virtually impossible. If someone failed to meet their quota, they were whipped. If someone exceeded their quota, then that quota was likely to be raised.[108] Ball recalled a similar system several decades earlier with picking quotas and punishment for failure to meet the quotas. The main difference was that Ball's overseer paid enslaved people for exceeding their quota rather than raising the quota.[109]

While the pushing system was particularly memorable, enslavers' harsh demands on cotton plantations and farms went well beyond the harvest to encompass the entire process of cultivation. Northup experienced a grueling work schedule throughout the cotton cultivation season in which "the hands are required to be in the cotton field as soon as it is light in the morning, and, with the exception of ten or fifteen minutes . . . , they are not permitted to be a moment idle until it is too dark to see."[110] Ball agreed that cotton was particularly hard on the enslaved. Unlike Northup, who had been born a free man and was kidnapped into slavery, Ball had a basis for comparison, as he had been brought up in

Maryland working in tobacco cultivation. A major theme in his auto-biography was that slavery on cotton plantations was far worse than on the farms and plantations in Maryland and Virginia. He saw this difference as being one of degree rather than kind: "The general features of slavery are the same everywhere; but the utmost rigour of the system is only to be met with on the cotton plantations of Carolina and Georgia."[111]

Perhaps because of his ability to make comparative judgments, Ball wrote much more than Northup on the unique cruelties of the cotton South. According to Ball, enslaved people in cotton regions were subject to greater discipline, more controls on movement, and greater work demands. For example, he claimed that enslaved people were rarely allowed off the plantation on Sundays and were not allowed to go to church. In addition, their needs were largely neglected by enslavers focused exclusively on profits. They were given less food and clothing than the enslaved were in the Chesapeake region and only very limited provision grounds (small plots of land enslaved people were allowed to use to grow food for their own consumption) to make up the difference. Ball did not see the labor itself as particularly demanding. The challenge was not to find enslaved people with "great bodily strength, but rather superior agility and wakefulness." However, Ball did argue that cotton, while not physically demanding, did demand a greater amount of work over the course of a year than did tobacco. According to Ball, enslaved people on cotton plantations spent more time cultivating cotton than enslaved people on tobacco plantations spent cultivating tobacco. While Ball never made the argument explicit, he probably meant to suggest that some of the harsh control features he experienced arose from the desire of cotton cultivators to keep enslaved people in the fields as much as possible.[112] Many enslaved people brought to the cotton South from regions that grew other commodities agreed with Ball that cotton plantations were particularly harsh.[113]

We have no way of knowing when enslavers in the lower Mississippi valley adopted the innovative labor tactics discussed by Northup and Ball, tactics that focused on keeping enslaved people in the fields longer, pushing them to harvest greater amounts of cotton and, ultimately, wringing as much exportable clean cotton out of their labor as possible. We do know that enslavers in Georgia at the same time under study here and enslavers in the lower Mississippi valley three decades later used such tactics. Most likely, at least some enslavers in the region were using the tactics during the early years of cotton cultivation. For example, cotton-picking books, harvest records that recorded the amount of cotton each enslaved person picked per day, were being kept in the region by the 1820s at the latest and likely were being used earlier. Cotton-picking books were likely used to facilitate the pushing system.[114]

The cruel labor demands placed on enslaved people and the systems used to enforce those demands (e.g., rewards, violence, and slave patrols) were technologies (much like improvements to cotton gins, new varieties of cotton, government regulation, or marketing techniques) developed or adapted by cotton cultivators to make the cotton cultivation system run as efficiently and profitably as possible for their own benefit. Humanity's penchant for innovation does not end with machines or marketing systems but can extend to innovating new ways to force more efficient labor out of other humans, in this case enslaved humans from Africa or of African descent. Enslavers made brutal exploitation a central component of the cotton technological system.

The key event that allowed the dominance of cotton in the upper parts of the lower Mississippi valley and its availability as an option in the lower parts was the introduction of the Eli Whitney–style saw gin by John Barclay into Natchez in 1795. Upon being introduced to this invention, the region's rulers, merchants, planters, and farmers immediately saw its potential benefits and jumped at the opportunity to grow a crop that would return them personally and the region more broadly to profitability. While cultivators and merchants were lucky in that Eli Whitney had invented the new gin as world cotton demand was surging, they also made their own luck by quickly adopting cotton and the gin and adopting, adapting, and improving these technologies and other technologies to develop a successful system of cotton cultivation. At least by the time of the Louisiana Purchase, the vast majority of the planters and farmers in the upper parts of the lower Mississippi valley were growing cotton as their main market staple, and many cultivators below that were also producing it, although as only one possible crop among several.

Even after cotton's triumph, residents continued to work to improve the cotton cultivation system and to overcome the challenges they faced at various stages in it. They attempted to find ways to police crop quality, a major problem in the early cotton industry. Initially, they attempted to use government regulation and personal reputation. However, over time, they developed a system of standardized "grading" by merchants for quality enforcement. At the same time, cultivators continued to seek out improvements to the gin and even the crop itself. All signs indicate that they succeeded, finding ways to improve both, thus increasing the quality and quantity of their crops. Finally, they adopted, adapted, and developed systems of slave management that were tailored to cotton cultivation, producing a notoriously harsh system of slavery on cotton plantations.

In only a few years, they had developed an effective technological system for cotton cultivation and marketing. As a result, cotton would prove to be a profitable crop that drove an economic boom that would continue (with ups and downs) throughout the first two decades of the nineteenth century. Cotton, at least in the upper reaches of the lower Mississippi valley, helped planters, farmers, and merchants to overcome the economic and political crises of the early 1790s. In the next chapter, we will see how the adoption of sugar production followed a narrative that was both strikingly similar in some respects but also tellingly divergent in others.

3

MAKING THE SUGAR REVOLUTION

All planters have decided to raise cane; they are sure to succeed, and its cultivation will certainly help greatly the enrichment of this province.

—Joseph de Pontalba to Jeanne de Chappelles, November 2, 1796

In 1806, an anonymous Louisianan (possibly the Irish-born planter,
land speculator, and merchant Daniel Clark Jr., who was the nephew
of the Daniel Clark, who had housed John Barclay while Barclay had built
the first Eli Whitney–style cotton gin) wrote a series of articles for the
Louisiana Gazette under the pseudonym "An American."[1] These articles
were classic "booster" texts, lauding the prospects for the agriculture and
economy of Louisiana to non-Louisianans. In the articles, the author laid
out the required capital investments to set up a sugar plantation, a cotton plantation, and even a yeoman's cotton farm in the lower Mississippi
valley while also detailing the profits of each. He even discussed the profits of corn and rice cultivation. However, the author wrote far more about
sugar than any of the other crops, explaining in detail its adoption and
its possible returns.[2]

The author focused on sugar because he wanted to boast about its
extraordinary profitability while allaying worries outsiders might have
about its unique challenges. He claimed that an enslaved person working
on a sugar plantation would return $350 per year to his enslaver, in con-
trast to $200 per year for an enslaved person working cotton. As for the
challenges of sugar, he admitted that many planters were initially hesitant
to plant sugar and were only convinced to grow it by the success of those
who had done so successfully and proven that tropical sugar could be

adapted to Louisiana's cooler environment. He even subverted his read-ers' expectations by pointing out that Louisianans had an immense ad-vantage over Caribbean sugar planters: enslaved people could use ploughs to plant sugarcane rather than laboriously digging trenches as was done in the Caribbean, allowing planters and even farmers with relatively few enslaved people to produce sugar.[3] The message was clear: come to Loui-siana, grow sugar, and become wealthy.

The booster's message was not wrong. Sugar was the more lucrative crop in the revitalization of the lower Mississippi valley's slave system. Sugar produced even greater excitement and higher profit margins than did cotton. While historians customarily think of the Deep South as the cotton kingdom, planters throughout the first half of the nineteenth century often preferred to grow sugar if they could, and planters were more likely to move from cotton to sugar than vice versa. In fact, during the early years of the sugar and cotton revolutions regional elites often acted as if sugar were the only crop worth growing, at least for elites. For example, the 1806 booster claimed that those growing sugarcane were making "immense fortunes" but that "the poorer classes equally find their account in the cultivation of Indigo, Rice and Cotton."[4] One wonders if Natchez cotton planter William Dunbar or Pointe Coupee cotton planter Julien Poydras (two of the largest enslavers in the region) would have taken kindly to being called the "poorer classes."

While sugar may have been lucrative, its adoption was not without its challenges. In contrast to cotton cultivators, who were adopting a techno-logical system built around a new device, sugar cultivators were adopting a technological system that had existed in a similar form for centuries.[5] As such, much of the efforts of sugar adopters were aimed at successfully importing this complex technological system and overcoming challenges in doing so, not in smoothing the rough edges of a new technology. While some challenges early sugar planters faced would have affected any adopter of sugar, others were particular to Louisiana, due to its nonideal climate for sugar production. As a result, most of the innovations adopted by Louisiana sugar planters were adopted as a means of adapting sugar to the region's environment.[6]

In the end, the inherent complexity of sugar production, the high capi-tal barriers to entry, and the challenges of adaptation made its adoption a far more difficult prospect than was that of cotton, as reflected in its slow advance across the region. Still, it did advance across the region and, by the time of the Louisiana Purchase, some of the largest and most lucrative plantations in the region produced sugar. Sugar planters' efforts successfully created a lucrative new industry that was crucial in rescuing the region's elites from crisis. However, this success came at an immense cost to the region's enslaved peoples, as they bore the brunt of this uniquely lucrative but also uniquely harsh productive activity. As had been the case on Brazilian and Caribbean sugar plantations, among the most important inputs into the sugar-making process were the bodies and lives of the enslaved.[7]

The biological characteristics of sugar structured how the sugar revolution unfolded. Throughout the lower Mississippi valley, frosts and freezes could happen in late fall and winter. Being vulnerable to destruction or damage from such frosts and freezes, sugar had a limited zone in the lower Mississippi valley where it could flourish. In southern parts of the region, frosts and freezes typically occurred late enough and were mild enough that planters had a long enough growing season to produce an acceptable crop. As a local booster put it, "Southern positions, mostly exempt from the severe black frost, must be resorted to in all cases, for the rearing of cane."[8] Contemporaries were unsure where exactly the northern limit of sugar lay, and much of the first few decades of the nineteenth century would see experimentation that pushed the crop further north.[9]

In addition, because sugarcane is a fragile crop that degrades quickly after harvest, especially in the subtropical environment of the lower Mississippi valley, it must be processed as quickly as possible. Before the advent of rapid and cheap transportation, sugarcane could not feasibly be moved to be processed at a distant location. Therefore, most sugar planters found it necessary to build expensive sugar mills. They also needed large labor forces to feed the sugar mill enough sugarcane to make it economically viable. In and of itself, these two inputs (the processing equipment and labor of enslaved people) meant that a large investment of capital was typically necessary to set up a sugar plantation.[10] Therefore, farmers and modest planters found it challenging to set up sugar farms and plantations. In addition, sugar planters in Louisiana rarely had the processing

capacity to handle more than their own crop. This meant that small operators were typically precluded from taking advantage of their neighbors' equipment to process sugarcane. These factors meant that sugar
was usually produced by large planters. These factors also meant that, in
addition to concerns about environmental suitability, sugar's spread was
limited by capital availability, meaning that more humble farmers typically stuck to other crops, and poorer regions rarely saw widespread sugar
production in the early 1800s. As a result, sugar did not explode across the
region as had cotton but instead slowly, if relentlessly, expanded.

While the sugar revolution began in the mid-1790s, sugar was not
new to the region, long having been grown in gardens.[11] Even decades
before the 1790s, residents and government officials were interested in
its potential as an export commodity. In 1776, Spanish colonel Francisco
Bouligny discussed sugar in a description of Louisiana, noting that it grew
easily. However, he was skeptical that it could ever be profitable due to the
region's cold winters, and he reported on an earlier, unsuccessful attempt
to produce granulated sugar under the French.[12] However, sugarcane continued to be grown in Louisiana, just not to produce granulated sugar. As
we shall see, Étienne Boré learned how to cultivate sugarcane from farmers who grew it to produce taffia (a kind of cheap rum).[13] In 1792, a letter
from an anonymous New Orleans resident published in a Philadelphia
newspaper claimed that "we shall soon be able to add—sugar plantations
from this place to BALISE."[14] Perhaps the writer was reacting to and saw
an opportunity in the collapse of the St. Domingue sugar industry during
the Haitian Revolution. Regardless, in the early 1790s sugarcane continued to be grown as a niche crop, and its potential was already on some
residents' minds even before the crisis.

Much as we know who built the first saw gin in the region, we know
who first successfully granulated sugar in the 1790s: Étienne Boré. While
some contemporary controversy existed about how much credit Boré de-
served for sparking the sugar revolution, the weight of evidence suggests
that he was, at the very least, the main motive force behind sugar's initial adoption. The best source for Boré's foray into sugar making comes
from a document he wrote in 1803. This account of his accomplishments
was extraordinarily self-serving: written in the third person, intended
to outline his heroic contribution to the local economy, with the aim of

convincing the French to reward him for his achievement. Despite its obvious biases, Boré's statement is credible and matches the accounts of other contemporary observers. However, while Boré wanted his narrative to secure his place as the heroic "father" of sugar, it also reveals that, much as with the adoption of the saw gin, the process of adopting sugar was far from the story of a lone visionary. At every step Boré worked with and learned from others.[15]

According to his account, Boré had become an indigo planter sometime in the 1770s. Despite the two-decade gap between his beginning indigo cultivation and his abandoning it, Boré had nothing good to say about the crop. He claimed that growing it was a constant battle that could not be won and that "each year he accumulated losses which rapidly accelerated his complete ruin." The situation reached a nadir when, in 1793 and 1794, much of the region's indigo rotted in the fields. In contrast to fellow indigo planter Julien Poydras, who did not turn to cotton until 1799, Boré began to look for a replacement crop in 1794. As part of this effort, he visited the plantation of a Canary Islander named Manuel Solis, who grew sugarcane to make taffia and observed his operation, identifying a number of deficiencies, including bad processing equipment and a lack of labor (i.e., enslaved people). Believing "that his position did not exhibit the same inconveniences" as those of Solis, Boré purchased cane for planting from another farmer.[16]

Besides learning the basics of sugarcane cultivation and acquiring seed cane, Boré needed to find an expert sugar maker, a master of the process of converting cane juice into granulated sugar. Boré found one in the person of Antoine Morin, "recently arrived from St. Domingue where he had acquired practical knowledge about the culture of the cane, and the manufacture of sugar." According to Boré, Morin had learned about Boré's intentions to attempt to produce sugar and responded by declaring that attempting to grow sugar in Louisiana was "reckless." One of Boré's friends encouraged Morin to visit Boré and convince him to give up his scheme. However, according to Boré, rather than Morin convincing Boré of sugar's demerits, Boré convinced Morin that, considering the economic crisis, sugar production had to be attempted. In the end, Morin offered his expertise in the making of sugar, and Boré jumped at the chance to employ him.[17]

According to Boré, his sugar crop that first year exceeded his and Morin's wildest hopes. To make his point, he related that Morin had accepted the proceeds from eight arpents of cane rather than a five-hundred-piastre salary for his first year's work. The sugar from the cane sold for one thousand piastres, far exceeding expectations. After this success, all the planters "who had so strongly criticized the enterprise of Boré" changed their tunes to congratulations and gratitude "for having procured to the cultivation of lower Louisiana and to the commerce a branch of product so precious."[18]

In his narrative, Boré had set out to prove that he was the founder of sugar production. Some planters had instead given the credit to Morin, who was, according to Boré, trying to obtain a reward either from the inhabitants through subscription or directly from the Spanish government. Boré claimed that had he not seen the advantages of sugar, regardless of whose skill had granulated the sugar, the commodity would never have been produced in the province.[19] The existence of this conflict in 1803 over who could gain credit for the introduction of sugar shows that residents of the region recognized the transformational nature of sugar production and that winning recognition for being the key figure in its adoption was worth fighting for. In addition, the conflict indicates, as did his relationship with Solis, that Boré was not nearly as alone in his efforts as he claimed. Without the prior work of small-scale cane farmers or Morin's expertise, he would not have been able to produce his first crop of refined sugar, at least not when he did.

Once Boré had granulated sugar, he worked to get other planters to do the same. Boré publicized his experiments and success with sugar. His account of how he came to work with Morin shows that his fellow planters were aware in 1794 of his attempt to produce sugar. In addition, once he had succeeded, he apparently shared the details of his sugar crop with any curious observer. During a visit to the region in 1796, French general Victor Collot resided for a time with Boré, and they discussed the details of Boré's sugar plantation.[20] Several years later, in 1803, Boré eagerly gave a tour of his plantation to French colonial commissioner Pierre Clément de Laussat and shared with him his sugar production figures.[21]

Government, whether Spanish or American, was not as directly involved in sugar's adoption as it had been with cotton, but it was also not entirely aloof. Spanish officials played no part in in Boré's experiment but did institute two policies intended to encourage production once Boré had succeeded, seeing sugar as a possible means to rescue the colony's economy. Sometime prior to 1798, when they opened Louisiana's trade to all neutral ships, they allowed the free exportation of Louisiana sugar on American ships.[22] In 1800, they reopened the African slave trade. Debates in the Cabildo prior to this decision show that it was primarily intended to supply sugar planters with enslaved labor.[23] The United States was also interested in encouraging sugar planting, and, after the Louisiana Purchase, the federal government gave in to local demands for enslaved people, reopening the internal slave trade (and indirectly the international trade through South Carolina) after initially cutting off both the international and internal slave trades.[24]

Other Spanish and American policies encouraged Louisiana sugar production but were not directly instituted for that purpose. For example, a Spanish law first instituted in the 1520s protected sugar planters' land and capital goods used to produce sugar (including enslaved people) from being seized to pay debts.[25] Louisiana sugar planters were aware of this law and invoked it in debt suits.[26] After the Louisiana Purchase, American sugar tariffs protected Louisiana sugar planters (who sold their sugar domestically) from foreign competition. However, these tariffs had first been passed in 1789 to raise revenue when the United States produced little sugar; the law was not intended as protectionist.[27] These various policies at the very least encouraged sugar planting by providing access to markets, labor, and indirect price supports.

In response to Boré's success and abetted by government policy, many planters adopted sugar. In March 1796, Pontalba noted that another planter was trying to granulate sugar.[28] Later that same year, Pontalba wrote his wife that "all planters have decided to raise cane; they are sure to succeed, and its cultivation will certainly help greatly the enrichment of this province."[29] Of course "all" planters were only those with access to the knowledge, labor, capital, and environment to produce sugar. However, Pontalba was witnessing a real and profound shift. Based on observations made the same year, General Collot claimed that "the cultivation which seems, at present, to be the most favorable in lower Louisiana is that of sugarcane."[30]

Boré claimed that between 1797 and 1803 seventy sugar mills were established in Louisiana.[31]

The number of sugar plantations in the region as of 1803 might seem small in a region that had tens of thousands of residents and thousands of plantations and farms (by 1810 the part of Louisiana under American control had at least 352 plantations with 20 or more enslaved people).[32] However, the small number is deceptive. Sugar, due to its high capital requirement, was already taking up a large amount of the capital and labor in the region around New Orleans. St. Charles Parish, the first parish on the Mississippi River above New Orleans, was probably the area, excepting rural Orleans Parish, most committed to sugar as of the Louisiana Purchase. An 1804 census gives a unique insight into the parish's economy, listing each household's agricultural production. Of 125 farms and plantations, 21 were producing sugar. These plantations were easily the largest. On average, they had forty-three enslaved people each, as compared to seven for the nonsugar plantations and farms. Together, they held around 42 percent of the parish's land and 55 percent of its enslaved people.[33] Most of the largest planters of St. Charles Parish had committed to sugar.

Export figures and estimates from the late Spanish period show the rapid increase in sugar production in this period. In 1801, Louisiana exported 1,333,330 pounds of sugar. That nearly doubled to 2,499,274 in 1802.[34] These figures should be treated with some skepticism, as they would not have included all the sugar being produced. As we have seen, smuggling was endemic in the region.[35] Also, sugar, unlike cotton, was consumed locally; "country sugar" (meaning sugar produced in Louisiana) was commonly advertised in Louisiana newspapers for local sale. Still, the figures indicate that, by the time of the Louisiana Purchase, the region was producing millions of pounds of granulated sugar.

In 1803, sugar production was largely concentrated in the area around New Orleans. Other areas that were part of the "sugar bowl" by 1860 probably had few if any sugar plantations as late as 1820. For example, the 1810 federal census reported that Attakapas County only produced forty-two thousand pounds of sugar, which, considering the average per plantation production in St. Charles in 1803 of fifty-five thousand pounds, could have been produced by a single sugar plantation.[36] Fifty years later, the four parishes carved out of Attakapas County produced nearly forty-one million pounds of sugar, many times more than was produced in all of Louisiana at the time of the Louisiana Purchase.[37] Iberville Parish, just below Baton Rouge, would go from having a single sugar mill in 1820 to producing nearly eleven million pounds of sugar in 1860.[38] Louisiana in the early 1800s was only at the beginning of a decades-long expansion of sugar.

Still, planters embraced sugar production, and sugar production sharply increased throughout this period. One historian has estimated that the amount of sugar shipped out of the region (which would not have captured regional consumption) quadrupled between 1802 and 1817, outpacing cotton exports, which increased by 3.5 times over the same period.[39] Within only a few years of Boré's first experiment, most of the largest planters in the region around New Orleans had adopted sugar production. Much as with cotton, planters recognized the promise of sugar and a surprisingly large number rapidly adopted the lucrative and yet capital-intensive and challenging crop.

Throughout the first two decades of sugar production in the lower Mississippi valley, sugar planters worked to adopt this complex and expensive technological system and adapt it to the less-than-ideal environment of the region. Perhaps the most basic yet central challenge sugar planters faced when adopting sugar was gaining access to the technical knowledge and skills necessary to process sugarcane into sugar. Unlike the knowledge needed to build one of the new cotton gins, this knowledge was not new (having been long understood in American sugar colonies and before that in the Old World) and had been mastered by many people in the Americas. Also, in contrast to the cotton gin, sugar making was not about gaining a technological object and learning how to operate and maintain it but rather about finding a person with expert knowledge with whom one would have an extended, often multi-year, relationship. On a sugar plantation, the expert sugar maker was a necessary and constant presence. He maintained the sugar house and ran its operations during the all-important grinding season, when the sugar was made from the harvested sugarcane. He was also sometimes involved in the cultivation of the crop and might even work as the plantation overseer.[40]

Initially expert sugar makers came from outside the region. Unsurprisingly, many of these early sugar makers came from the French Caribbean, set in motion by the Haitian Revolution and instabilities in the region more generally and attracted to a francophone region with long-standing connections to the French Caribbean. According to General Collot, Boré's St. Dominguan sugar maker Morin was the only expert in the colony when Collot visited in 1796 and was splitting his time between several sugar plantations.[41] Morin did not remain alone for long and was soon joined by other St. Dominguan sugar makers, who often placed newspaper advertisements looking for work.[42] One early observer of Louisiana's sugar industry claimed refugees from St. Domingue were the only sugar makers in the colony during the industry's early years, illustrating their importance to the early adoption of sugar.[43] However, experts from the French Caribbean were not the only ones to come to the region. For example, Irish-born Patricio Urriel, who had previously worked in Puerto Rico, was working as a sugar maker in Louisiana in 1802.[44]

After the industry had been established in Louisiana, locals inevitably learned the technology of sugar making, taught by imported experts. Perhaps unsurprisingly, this knowledge transfer is difficult to trace. In a rare extant example from 1800, Gil Eugenio Mabire sued his former employers, partners in a sugar plantation, François Mayronne and Jean Baptiste Degruis, for back pay and claimed that his employment contract included a stipulation that he would be paid one hundred pesos to teach another man to make sugar.[45]

Another group also learned (or brought with them) sugar making skills: the enslaved. Enslaved people listed as "sugar makers" appeared regularly in newspaper advertisements. Enslaved sugar makers were typically only sold when a plantation was being liquidated, suggesting that planters valued them and held on to them unless selling off their plantation. For example, in 1807, a planter "preparing to leave the country" offered for sale sixty-two people he enslaved, including "complete sugar makers."[46] Of thirty-two enslaved sugar makers appearing in documents contained in Gwendolyn Midlo Hall's Louisiana Slave Database, eighteen were listed with a putative origin. They were a diverse group. Seven were Louisiana Creoles (i.e., born in the region), eight were from Africa, two were from the Atlantic Coast of the United States, and one was from

St. Domingue.[47] The presence of only one Caribbean individual in this group illustrates that sugar making knowledge was being transferred in Louisiana.[48]

In addition to finding and employing sugar making experts, sugar planters had to set up the extensive processing facilities to convert raw sugarcane into granulated sugar. While indigo had had its own processing demands, the scale of sugar processing facilities went well beyond anything seen before in the region. A sugar plantation needed a sugar house that combined the mill used to grind the cane to expel the juice as well as the series of cauldrons used to boil the juice down to make granulated sugar. A sugar plantation also required a "drying shed," where sugar was stored while molasses drained off. Setting up these facilities properly required technical knowledge of the sugar-making process, meaning that sugar makers were often involved. One local observer claimed that outside sugar experts taught planters how to build sugar works. He also claimed that locals quickly mastered the knowledge.[49]

Finding certain capital goods needed to outfit these processing facilities presented a more sustained challenge in the early years of the industry. Iron parts often had to be manufactured elsewhere, particularly the large rollers used to grind the cane. The same was true of the large copper cauldrons used to boil the sugar. In the early years, planters often had a great deal of trouble obtaining these crucial items. Collot noted during his visit to Boré's plantation that the planter's sugar house contained "six boilers of unequal size, the only ones that Mr. Boré could get in the colony."[50] Some planters had trouble finding any cauldrons at all. Julien Poydras wrote to William Dunbar of Natchez in 1796 to procure sugar boilers for another contact. According to Poydras, his contact needed boilers as soon as possible because of "the risk he is running of losing his crop" without them. Poydras also shared that his contact had tried but failed to get boilers from Philadelphia.[51] At this early stage, a sugar planter could find himself in danger of not having the appropriate equipment to process his crop.

After these early years, outside suppliers met sugar planter demands, and the procurement of capital equipment became more routine. One observer of the industry noted that, by the time of the Louisiana Purchase, "the cauldron and other necessary utensils are now available locally, and in such quantity that the prices are modest."[52] Most new capital goods were supplied from outside the region, generally from the American East Coast, the United Kingdom, or France. For example, in 1809, the merchant house of Talcott and Bowers offered for sale "two sets of French sugar mill machinery."[53] In 1811, the merchant house of Fortier & Son offered "Excellent Cylinders for sugar houses, lately imported from Philadelphia."[54] Some manufacturers made regular business of supplying equipment for sugar planters. One Philadelphia manufacturer, Francis D'Acosta, placed regular advertisements in Louisiana offering his services to sugar makers. In the first advertisement he placed in 1809, D'Acosta asserted his experience and expertise by revealing that he had previously manufactured sugar works in Nantz for export to the French colonies.[55] After the first few years of difficulties, outside manufacturers began to fulfill the needs of local sugar planters.

The procurement of expert sugar knowledge and capital goods unique to sugar making were early challenges for anyone attempting to adopt sugar production anywhere. Louisiana's sugar producers did face one unique challenge: the region's very different climate than that of traditional sugar producing areas. Sugar, a tropical crop, was not tolerant of extremely cold weather, particularly freezes, which could damage or even destroy sugarcane. In addition, sugarcane cultivation in the tropics generally followed a growing season that extended well beyond a calendar year. In Louisiana, such an extended growing season was not possible because freezes usually occurred during the winter, and planters had to schedule the harvest to avoid these freezes. Typically, Louisiana planters had a nine- to ten-month window to cultivate sugarcane. This combination of a tropical crop with a colder climate struck observers of the industry. For example, one traveler was particularly surprised to see sugar houses, normally a tropical feature, operating during his visit while covered with snow:

> But what particularly interested me, and awakened all my attention, was the appearance of the sugar-houses enveloped up to the vent holes of their chimneys in a robe of snow, while the volcanoes of smoke that issue from them, formed in their dark clouds a striking contrast with its whiteness. The reflections this *coup d'oeil* inspired me with were of a nature to make me forget the rigor of the season. The culture of what belonging

peculiarly to the torrid zone, had acquired perfection, and was naturalized in a climate of sugar and snow.[56]

The sight of sugar houses covered in snow would have emphasized to the planters the precariousness of sugar cultivation.

Successfully adapting tropical sugar to subtropical Louisiana was one of the most important technological innovations made in the early Louisiana sugar industry. A very basic part of this was identifying where sugar could be grown. While ultimately the line south of which sugar could be profitably produced was drawn just north of Baton Rouge, in this early period, people were uncertain about sugar's viable extent. In 1819, a traveler to the region wrote that "impartial men admit that the frosts render sugar too precarious a crop to the northward of Gen. [Wade] Hampton's great estates" (located in Ascension Parish, about seventy-five miles north of New Orleans).[57] This claim was already being proven incorrect as sugar plantations had been founded in Iberville Parish and West Baton Rouge Parish, north of Ascension. These parishes would later become major sugar producers. In fact, during this period, planters far north of where sugar could be profitably produced experimented with it, hoping to join the revolution. For example, in 1820, a plantation in Natchitoches was advertised in a New Orleans newspaper as having a sugar house although no sugar would be produced in the parish by 1860.[58] The sugar revolution, unlike the cotton one, involved an experimentation with and expansion of range that took place over decades.

The initial years of production must have involved experimentation with sugarcane cultivation, considering the need to find the best schedule for cultivating this tropical crop in a subtropical environment. This experimentation likely built on knowledge already developed by the farmers who grew cane to produce syrup and taffia. Pontalba claimed that planters, early on, had experimented with a work schedule that they found wanting and "now, it is worked over as it is being gradually cut, some being left standing until the first or the second frost, without suffering any damage from it; it is then cut and left on the spot, being merely protected with a layer of bagasse; it is preserved in that way, without ever souring, until it becomes possible to crush it."[59] By 1796, only two years after Boré had first experimented with sugar, planters had developed an effective approach to sugar production in subtropical Louisiana whereby they planted the cane in February and harvested and ground the cane in November and December.

Despite planters' mastery of the production calendar, the shortened growing season continued to have negative effects on sugar production. Due to a lack of labor, planters were often unable to harvest all the cane before a freeze ruined it. For example, Collot wrote that Boré's small enslaved labor force by West Indian standards (he only had forty enslaved people working his sugarcane) meant that "a great part of his canes was left to rot in the field."[60] This problem was not quickly overcome. The booster writing in 1806 pointed out that sugar planters "can plant and cultivate more than they can afterwards cut and secure." To cope, planters attempted to hire or purchase additional enslaved people during the harvest.[61]

The shortened season also harmed the quality of sugar produced in Louisiana or at least made it difficult to produce high-quality sugar. In 1796, Collot noted that, due to the shortened growing season, Boré's cane was harvested and refined into sugar before it had properly ripened, meaning that the cane contained too much moisture and was difficult to crystallize.[62] James Pitot, a French-born New Orleans merchant, agreed, claiming that, because of the short growing season, sugar makers in Louisiana could not get away with the carelessness in production that was possible in the West Indies.[63] People outside the region had also noticed these problems. In 1804 a Baltimore merchant wrote his factor in New Orleans to complain about a shipment from New Orleans in which "the quality of the sugar chiefly proceed[s] so bad" that had he not gotten a waver on the duties; "It would have been a most ruinous voyage." The merchant suggested that Louisiana sugar had at best a mixed reputation: "I will repeat to you that bad New Orleans sugar not be sold at this market," as "they are always running and they say have every bad quality."[64]

Unsurprisingly, Louisianans worried that their sugar would get a bad reputation, making it harder for them to market it to distant buyers. In his discussion of low-quality Louisiana sugar, Pitot noted that "five years of experience [had] not irrevocably fixed the opinion of commerce in [Louisiana sugar's] favor" and that "if . . . the cultivation was ever abandoned, it will be because of not having avoided the mistakes to which

I have just referred."[65] Unlike with cotton, little evidence has survived of attempts to police quality via regulation, reputation, or market pressures. No public pressure to regulate sugar production arose in Louisiana (which is in keeping with the lack of interest in government regulation of cotton production in Louisiana). Also, at least as of the late 1820s, quality grading for sugar was not included in newspaper price lists (in sharp contrast to cotton, which was graded, often in intricate ways, by then), suggesting that formal quality grading was absent.[66]

Despite this lack of evidence, reputation and market pressures surely enforced quality standards. An example from 1805 suggests that such tools were on the minds of at least some Louisiana sugar planters. In that year, Baltimore merchants accused Louisiana sugar planters of building heavier sugar hogsheads to defraud merchants, effectively selling wood as sugar.[67] Boré responded that the real problem was poor quality sugar that was "*melting at sea*," not fraud. He asked Baltimore merchants to publicly shame any planter who had defrauded them and encouraged Louisiana planters to make better sugar and clearly mark their barrels, the latter to allow for the tracking of who did and did not make quality sugar (a striking parallel to how cotton purchasers supposedly tracked cotton quality). Boré turned the Baltimore merchants' accusation of fraud into an argument for reputation-based policing of sugar quality.[68]

However, the Baltimore merchants had preemptively rejected a reputation-based solution as unrealistic considering the large volume of trade in Baltimore.[69] Their solution was impersonal and collective. They planned to form an association to increase the tare (the assumed weight of the hogshead that was deducted from the total weight to determine the amount of sugar inside) on Louisiana sugar hogsheads, punishing all Louisiana sugar planters. They also claimed that "associations to the same, are forming, in Boston, New-York and Philadelphia," the other major outlets for Louisiana sugar.[70] While this example from 1805 suggests that sugar planters were concerned about their reputations and that market pressures encouraged attention to quality and efforts to improve it, little other direct evidence for these concerns and pressures has survived.

Better documented were efforts to identify sugarcane varieties that were better suited to Louisiana's climate. From the earliest years of the sugar industry, planters experimented with different varieties of cane that might be better adapted to the region's climate. In 1796, Collot discussed experiments in the Caribbean with other cane varieties, "the sugar cane of Batavia" and "Otaheite" that might be better suited to Louisiana's climate. He argued Otaheite cane could provide a major advantage to Louisiana because it ripened in ten to fourteen months, much more quickly than did other varieties.[71] Soon after, planters began to experiment with Otaheite cane. In 1803, Laussat found several planters, including Boré, growing small amounts of it. Laussat wrote that Boré had already found the advantage of Otaheite cane's shorter growing cycle, suggesting that 1803 was not the first year Boré had cultivated it.[72] Otaheite cane would become a major factor in Louisiana sugarcane production during these early years before being replaced by a new variety (ribbon cane) in the late 1810s and 1820s.[73]

While sugar planters focused most of their efforts on importing an already mature technology and adapting it to their subtropical environment, they did adopt one crucial yet simple innovation that gave them an advantage over Caribbean sugar planters. Due to the soil in Louisiana, planters were able to plow to prepare the ground for sugarcane planting. The use of plows was in marked contrast to the method generally used for planting in the Caribbean, where enslaved people dug holes by hand, a laborious process. Plows allowed Louisiana planters to grow sugar with many fewer enslaved people than was the case in the Caribbean. The 1806 booster argued that "the same number of negroes required to plant, tend, and boil the produce of two hundred acres of cane would scarce be sufficient in a year to dig the holes to plant it in Jamaica."[74] The relative ease of planting alongside the threat of freezes created the production bottlenecks at harvest. However, had the planters been forced to have the enslaved dig holes to plant sugar, the take-off of sugar production might have been greatly hampered, as they might not have been able to plant enough sugar with their relatively small labor forces to make production worthwhile. The simple technology of the plow provided immense advantages.

While learning the sugar process and adapting it to Louisiana presented challenges for aspiring sugar planters, the most persistent barrier to sugar production for most Louisianans was that of accumulating the necessary capital and credit to acquire the goods, land, and labor necessary to set up a sugar plantation. The structure of entry into sugar was quite different from that of cotton, which virtually anyone with access to land could profitably grow due to broad access to cotton gins. In contrast, sugar refineries were usually used only for the crop of their owner and operator. Small producers could not usually piggyback on their richer neighbors' capital investments to enter sugar planting, meaning that sugar planting was generally dominated by larger planters. Such was the case in St. Charles Parish. In 1804, only one-third of the parish's sugar plantations had fifty or more enslaved people. Yet those plantations produced nearly 60 percent of the parish's sugar.[75] Later, as sugar plantations spread to other parts of Louisiana, they tended to be large. For example, the 1820 federal census returns for Iberville Parish mentions that the parish had only one sugar mill. This mill was owned and operated by Joseph Erwin, who enslaved 194 people according to the census, by far the most of any Iberville planter (the next largest planter enslaved 56 people).[76]

These larger plantations were typical, as aspiring sugar planter had to make a very large investment to gain adequate land, goods, and labor to run what was considered a reasonably sized sugar plantation. The 1806 anonymous booster laid out the capital requirements for establishing a sugar plantation from scratch. He took as his parameters the purchase of an eight-hundred-acre plantation, sixty enslaved people, and the necessary stock of oxen and horses. He estimated that the sixty enslaved people would cost $500 each, costing $30,000. The necessary livestock would cost $4,000. The cost of the land would vary. If one wished to buy a plantation near New Orleans "with dwelling and out houses, sugar works in complete repair, and the crop planted . . . paying a fourth part cash, and the balance in one, two and three years," it would cost $50,000, giving a total cost for the plantation of $84,000. One could save money by purchasing land or plantation further from the city, cutting the cost of setting up a sugar plantation to as low as $58,000. In contrast to these large sums for sugar plantations, the author estimated that one could set up "a cotton establishment on a middling scale" in Mississippi or Orleans Territory with thirty enslaved people for "only" $21,000. According to the writer's own numbers, even a sixty-slave cotton plantation would cost, at most, $33,000, $25,000 less than the cheapest sugar plantation.[77]

The booster's vision of planters setting up from scratch did not match the actual process followed by many and perhaps even most early sugar planters. Many sugar planters, especially the earliest ones like Boré, did not have to come up with the full amount to set up or purchase a plantation, since they owned land, enslaved people, and livestock (Boré pointed to his relatively large enslaved labor force as why he might succeed in his experiment). However, even they had to find the capital or credit to purchase seed cane, set up sugar works, and, often, purchase additional enslaved labor. Of course, new sugar planters, of whom there were quite a few, did have to come up with the money all at once or finance a sugar plantation through credit. As a result, sugar planting was largely, although not exclusively, the reserve of already established planters or newcomers with access to capital and credit.

While in theory one could purchase or set up a plantation using ready money, in this cash-poor society, this was usually not possible. Therefore, credit was an indispensable part of becoming a sugar planter, and it is worth explaining how aspiring sugar planters acquired that credit. However, the ways sugar and cotton producers accessed credit were not substantially distinct, so, while the focus here is on sugar planters, most of this discussion also applies to cotton cultivators (and other economic actors in the region), who also used credit as a matter of course.

In the lower Mississippi valley during the early 1800s, credit was mostly accessed via traditional means such as book debts with merchants, personal loans, and mortgages on enslaved people or land. However, banks did first make their appearance during this period as a new, although relatively minor, source of credit. As we shall see, most planters, merchants, and farmers accessed multiple sources of credit at once and often juggled these debts for years, making it difficult to point to a direct connection between a particular debt and entering sugar planting. For most elites, credit was a complex system involving many different moving parts.

Merchants were likely the most important source of credit for planters, especially elite ones, many of whom were themselves or had started as merchants. These merchants were implanted in broader international credit networks that, usually indirectly in this period, provided credit for planters. While it might seem logical to separate cotton and sugar mercantile and credit networks, this is not possible, as merchants were not yet specialized in one crop or the other. Instead, they used their local and extraregional connections to market what goods they could for profit. A merchant or merchant house might regularly handle cotton and sugar crops for farmers and planters, often shipping the crops on the same ship. Therefore, sugar and cotton planters often dealt with the same merchants and received credit from them.

The economic activities of planters and merchants were deeply entangled, and the credit extended by merchants to planters was typically part of complex commercial relationships, and not one-time loans. During the early 1800s, most planters sold their crops via consignment, meaning the planter would ship the crop to a merchant, typically based in New Orleans or Natchez, who would then sell the crop for the planter, usually at a distant port on the East Coast or in Europe; charge a commission; and handle remittances, insurance, and other services. Only rarely did merchants buy crops directly from planters. New Orleans merchants themselves often consigned sugar and cotton that had been consigned to them with merchant houses in distant ports, creating a chain of commercial dependence, all lubricated by credit.[78]

Merchants commonly offered credit to consignors, whether other merchants or planters. These debts and credits were typically treated as book debts and only settled periodically. Credit was offered by advancing goods (including enslaved people) or making a personal loan to a planter, who would then (in theory) pay back the amounts in the staples shipped out of the region. An example of such a credit relationship was between the sugar and cotton planter and slave trader Joseph Erwin and the New Orleans firm William Kenner and Company. In 1818, the firm informed him that "the proceeds of your Crops will fall very far short of your wants here." To cover the shortfall, they asked for "remittance from the proceeds of your negroes to ease your payments" (presumably a reference to the enslaved people he had just imported from the Chesapeake and sold in Natchez). They also drew on his account $100 for each hogshead of his sugar they had shipped to New York.[79]

Planters and merchants also accessed credit through advances paid (or noted in accounts) by merchants who handled the crops they consigned to them. For example, New Orleans merchant firms and particularly large planters were even able to receive advances from two-thirds to three-fourths of the probable proceeds of the sales of the goods they consigned to merchants in the northeastern United States and Europe. The Natchez cotton planter William Dunbar received an $8,000 advance on $12,000 worth of cotton he shipped to London. Such advances typically came at a cost (commissions on consignments with advances were 6 percent versus 2.5 percent for those without) but provided ready access to liquid funds that planters and merchants often needed.[80] These advances, of course, also placed the borrower further into debt. As in these examples, merchants often acted like banks for planters, advancing them money or goods and paying their debts. These credit relationship between planters and merchants often lasted for years, with planters finding it difficult, if not impossible, to ever get out of debt. These relationships were also fundamental to how commodity agriculture operated in the region and were a central part of how large planters were able to muster the capital necessary to grow sugar.

Other traditional sources of credit assisted entry into sugar planting. The purchase of enslaved people on short credit was standard.[81] For example, in the late 1780s Daniel Clark Sr. sold forty-three Africans in Natchez on credit, mostly on the terms of one or two years.[82] Credit was also given when enslaved people already in the region were sold. For example, when the estate of François St. Amand was auctioned off, its "about" eighty enslaved people were offered on credit terms of two payments, the first at one year and the second at two, standard terms for enslaved people sold at estate auctions.[83]

Credit was also typically given when plantations and farms were sold (sometimes with the resident enslaved labor force included). An analysis of 310 plantations and farms offered for sale in advertisements appearing in Louisiana newspapers between 1802 and 1820 shows the ubiquity of credit in the local economy. This analysis shows that, of the 188 advertisements (62 percent of all plantations or farms offered) that gave some information about the terms of the sale, only three (2 percent of those with terms) stated that no credit would be given. Another 27 (14 percent of those with terms) gave vague terms but ones that implied that credit would be offered. The remaining 84 percent of those with terms gave detailed credit arrangements that the seller was offering. Only forty

(21 percent of those with terms) asked for any amount of cash down, typically a fixed amount or a proportion of the sale price.[84] The sale of enslaved people and land on credit allowed individuals to enter planting or expand their enslaved labor force without ready cash.

While mortgages on lands and enslaved people sold and loans from merchants were probably the most common types of debt planters and farmers used to gain access to capital and were far from new, in the early nineteenth century a new, institutional source of credit became available in the region: banks. Immediately after the Louisiana Purchase, elites began to charter the region's first banks or bank branches. The first bank founded was the Louisiana Bank, followed shortly by a branch of the Bank of the United States.[85] Three more banks opened during the 1810s in Louisiana.[86] In Mississippi, the Bank of Mississippi opened in 1809.[87] The rapid foundation of banks after the Louisiana Purchase illustrates how residents were open to (for them) new and innovative financial institutions and instruments, an openness that would continue into the antebellum period, albeit tempered at times by financial panics.[88]

A newspaper article written to support the Louisiana Bank explained the advantages of such an institution. The article's authors argued that cultivators would be the most advantaged by the bank, as it would increase the money supply, allowing full value payments for crops, and allow more regular and dependable credit relationships between merchants and planters.[89] The way planters (and merchants) would access the bank's capital was by lodging debt notes drawn up by themselves or someone else with the bank. While they generally would not get face value for the note, this would give them access to cash at better terms than would otherwise be the case. For example, when the sugar planter Armand Duplantier declared bankruptcy in 1811, he owed $2,640 to two banks for notes lodged with them.[90] Access to cash to meet short-term obligations was a constant headache for any member of the cash-poor society of the late eighteenth and early nineteenth centuries. Banks were a means by which planters (and merchants) gained access to cash, which was necessary for keeping any business establishment, such as a plantation, operating.

Through these various credit sources elites could accumulate strikingly large amounts of debt. The example of Jean Baptiste Riviere, a Frenchman and New Orleans merchant, shows how one member of the mercantile elite leveraged his reputation into gaining the credit to start a sugar plantation (and then go bankrupt).[91] In 1799, Riviere bought a large plantation eleven miles below New Orleans with thirty-two enslaved people for $36,000. He paid $15,000 down, with the remaining $21,000 to be paid in three annual installments due in 1801, 1802, and 1803.[92] In 1803, Riviere advertised the plantation for sale. In the years since the purchase, he had expanded the plantation's capital goods and labor force. It now had "a vast field" planted in sugarcane. The sugar works were described in almost loving detail. They were of "the greatest solidity, extent, beauty and convenience." As the works were described as new and in good condition, Riviere had probably instituted sugar production on the plantation. The plantation now had fifty "heads of slaves" rather than the thirty-four enslaved people with whom it had been purchased.[93]

Riviere was selling the plantation because he could not make payments on his debts and had failed to make the annual payments on the plantation. In 1801, his first installment on the plantation was extended at interest. At a meeting of his creditors in November 1803, those creditors agreed to a further delay of the payments on the plantation.[94] Fortunately for historians, if not for his creditors, Riviere's bankruptcy dragged on for nearly a decade, apparently because the plantation could not be liquidated at an acceptable price, in and of itself showing the difficulty locals had in accruing the capital and credit necessary to purchase such an extensive estate. At the bankruptcy auction of the estate, the plantation was actually sold back to Riviere, since no one else was willing to offer an acceptable bid.[95] Even after this forbearance, Riviere was unable to make the payments.[96] According to an account from 1806, Riviere's debts amounted to $67,779. His debts included the $21,000 owed on the plantation (he had never made a single payment) and nearly $10,000 in other unspecified mortgages. He also owed $38,019 in unsecured debts, in part to other merchants. Unfortunately, as was typical for such debts, the reasons for them are unspecified.[97] However, what is clear is that Riviere, presumably through his status as an elite member of local society and a merchant, had been able to amass the large amount of credit necessary to obtain the capital, land, and labor to setup a sugar plantation.

Several different credit opportunities existed in the lower Mississippi valley for the prospective or extant planter: purchasing mortgaged land

and enslaved people, merchant credit, and bank loans. Still, as suggested by the Riviere example, one generally had to belong to one of several elite groups (the local planter class, the merchant class in New Orleans, Spanish officials, or elite Anglo-Americans with credit and reputation accrued through plantation or mercantile success outside the region) to have any hope to access credit at the levels necessary to set up a large plantation or build a large enslaved labor force. As such, credit networks, unsurprisingly, tended to reinforce social and economic status. Lower Mississippi valley elites in 1810 or 1820 were typically, although not universally, from elite backgrounds. This was particularly true of sugar planters, given the large capital requirements for sugar production.

Still, despite these very real and steep capital barriers to sugar planting that only elites could hope to overcome via credit, some individuals who did not have immediate and easy access to large amounts of capital or credit developed alternative tactics to move into sugar production. One common route to sugar planting was through the accumulation of capital (and credit) through the successful production over many years of the other products grown in the region. Planters could choose to produce other marketable crops such as cotton, foodstuff, and lumber and use the profits they netted to boost themselves into the world of sugar planting. The 1806 booster laid out a plan in his article for a planter "if not a man of large fortune" to boost himself up to sugar via cotton cultivation and enslaved labor.[98] David Rees, a planter in Attakapas County, followed a similar path to the one laid out by the booster. Having settled in the region shortly after the Louisiana Purchase, he grew cotton (and foodstuffs) exclusively until the mid-1820s when he began to grow sugar. By 1831, he had built a sugar house and produced sugar as his main cash crop.[99]

Another common tactic to overcome limited capital was the formation of formal partnerships with other cultivators or merchants to pool resources. Such arrangements were not unique to sugar plantations. Partnerships were also used to set up cotton plantations and cotton gins.[100] Still, partnerships appear to have been particularly common among sugar cultivators and was an effective way to overcome financial limitations and pool managerial responsibilities. For example, on November 22, 1799, Guillaume Desk, a resident of rural Orleans Parish, entered a partnership with Pierre Berguine to grow sugarcane together until the end of the sugar harvest in 1800. The former provided eight enslaved people and the plantation, and the latter provided twenty enslaved people and management.[101] In another example, an advertisement in the *Louisiana Courier* offered a plantation to be "sold on a liberal credit, or a part thereof would be exchanged with a person possessing 30 or 40 good field negroes, and who would undertake to establish and manage the same as a sugar estate, in joint concern with the proprietor."[102] The provision of land in return for access to enslaved labor was often a feature of such partnerships.

Other cultivators entered sugar production by sharing processing equipment or using the excess productive capacity of sugar planters' sugar mills without forming formal partnerships, going against the dominant perception in the region of how sugar plantations operated. A probable example of this kind of activity can be found in an anonymous account book of a plantation's production between 1814 and 1828. The account keeper, focused on cotton cultivation, periodically sold raw cane, granulated sugar, and molasses. The latter two could only have been produced in a sugar house, which the account keeper almost certainly did not own, meaning that he was using someone else's to process his sugarcane.[103] After David Rees constructed his sugar house in 1830, he periodically processed the cane of his neighbors in addition to his own.[104] Cultivators could sometimes take advantage of a neighbor's processing equipment to produce sugar. Still, this was probably never a major part of the local economy. Considering the constant labor shortages, planters were typically racing against the clock to finish their own crops and would not have had the resources to process someone else's.

As a result of these tactics and the use of the plow for planting, enslavers with surprisingly small enslaved labor forces found ways to produce sugar. For example, many of the twenty-one sugar farms and plantations in St. Charles Parish in 1804 had relatively few enslaved people. Eleven enslaved more than forty people (still few by Caribbean standards). Six enslaved between twenty and forty people. Most surprisingly, four enslaved fewer than twenty people. One enslaved only eleven people.[105] A Maryland migrant to Louisiana in 1816 claimed that even smaller enslaved labor forces were used to produce sugar. In a description of the production of several "plantations" in Attakapas, he mentioned farmers producing small amounts of sugar with only two, three, and even four "hands."[106] Despite these examples, the Louisiana sugar industry was always dominated by larger plantations and became more consolidated as the years progressed.

Labor management and practices were another crucial area where sugar planters learned, adapted, and likely innovated. As with labor management on cotton farms and plantations detailed information about this process is thin for the lower Mississippi valley during the early years of sugar production. Still, the information that does exist shows that planters instituted practices that, while far from new on sugar plantations, diverged from previous norms in the region. They instituted semi-industrial work practices (e.g., shift work and managerial hierarchies) and demanded far greater and more demanding labor from those they enslaved than was the case on plantations growing other crops. They also molded enslaved labor forces that they believed better met their labor needs. The way planters structured, organized, and formed their enslaved labor forces was a technology crucial to the successful adoption of sugar.

Some of the labor practices adopted by sugar planters were likely introduced by their sugar makers. These Caribbean immigrants would have been familiar with labor organization on Caribbean sugar plantations. Much as they had directed the building of the first sugar processing establishments, they likely taught aspiring sugar planters the complex gang labor practices and managerial hierarchies common in the Caribbean. Still, even in the Caribbean, labor management was neither uniform nor unchanging. As Justin Roberts points out, "Gang labor was not a static form of organization" but varied over time and location, including between plantations.[107] In the lower Mississippi valley, planters would have adapted Caribbean practices to their existing practices, very different environmental conditions, and much smaller enslaved labor forces. Unfortunately, the details of these local adaptations are difficult to excavate. For example, while gang labor was almost certainly the norm on Louisiana sugar plantations, only very limited evidence for it survives from this early period.[108] Still, we can give an overview of some aspects of labor practices that suggest that sugar labor was distinct from, and much harsher than, other forms of rural labor in the region.

As even sugar planters recognized, a central fact of sugar production was that the labor practices they adopted and enforced were exceptionally harsh. As one article describing Louisiana that appeared in a Washington, DC, newspaper put it, "A gang dwindles away on a sugar estate, while it increases on a cotton plantation, the labor of the former being extremely severe and the privations great."[109] A traveler to the region reported that a cotton planter told him that he would grow sugar (and reap the larger profits) except that "having no children, he was more content to live [by cultivating cotton] than by wearing out himself and his Negroes."[110] This sentiment, that sugar consumed the enslaved, was repeated again and again in descriptions of the region and has been confirmed by modern historians.[111]

While evidence from other regions and Louisiana during the antebellum period suggests that various points in sugar's production process led to its reputation for being particularly hard on the enslaved, observers of the early Louisiana sugar industry almost exclusively focused on the harvest when discussing sugar planters' labor demands. The harvest, called the grinding season, was a frenetic time. As has already been discussed, the very biological nature of the crop created intense pressures regardless of where sugar was grown. However, in Louisiana, sugar planters also pushed enslaved people to get their crops harvested and processed before the unpredictable freezes. The pressures to finish the grinding season quickly were immense. To do so, planters adopted and developed intensely demanding, grueling, and exploitative labor practices during the harvest period.[112] Like cotton, sugar had a major production bottleneck, and planters drove enslaved people to get as much sugar successfully through the bottleneck of grinding as possible.

The French colonial commissioner Laussat described an early Louisiana sugar plantation during the grinding season. He chose to describe the labor organization of an enslaver he saw as particularly benevolent, Jean-Noël Destréhan. Destréhan, according to Laussat, treated the people he enslaved particularly well, supplying each enslaved person "his own little plot" to cultivate and buying "clothes and such other articles as the slaves needed wholesale and resold them to the slaves without making a profit." Destréhan also organized labor during the harvest to maximize each enslaved person's work while minimizing their strain. Destréhan divided workers into "watches" that "relieved each other every six hours." Laussat also claimed that "during the grinding, the Negroes grew fat because the master paid the food bill as long as they worked in the refinery." Other enslavers were much more severe in their labor demands; "other sugar mills worked their slaves without stop for twelve to twenty-four hours." He also noted that enslaved people on other plantations were much more likely to escape during the grinding season.[113] Regardless of whether we want to accept that Destréhan was driven by a desire to be benevolent, he still implemented labor methods on his plantation that he believed would most effectively extract work from the people he enslaved. According to Laussat, other planters implemented labor methods to achieve a similar result but without the pretense of benevolence.

Unsurprisingly, considering the paucity of slave narratives from the early 1800s, no firsthand account survives from an enslaved person working on a sugar plantation during this period. However, we can turn to Solomon Northup to understand the labor demands of sugar in a later period, which were likely similar. Northup was often hired out to various sugar plantations during the harvest. While starting in the fields cutting cane, Northup was soon transferred to the sugar house, where he was made a driver, given a whip, and told "to use it upon any one who was caught standing idle." He also wrote that "if I failed to obey them to the letter, there was another one for my own back." Northup described the sugar house as almost a hell in which "the grinding and boiling does not cease day and night." One of his main tasks, beyond discipline, was to maintain the timing of the necessary shift work by calling shift changes. He wrote that he "had no regular periods of rest, and could never snatch but a few moments of sleep at a time." As described by Northup, sugar production, during the grinding season, had a semi-industrial character with a constantly operating "factory," timed shifts, managerial hierarchy, and grueling work periods.[114]

As with cotton, no detailed planter-kept work logs exist for the early years of sugar production in Louisiana. However, work logs kept by that Attakapas planter David Rees give insight into changes that happened after a planter switched to sugar from another crop, in his case cotton. Rees switched to sugar in the late 1820s, and his plantation journal reflected escalating demands on the people he enslaved. One of the more basic, but still telling, facts from his journal is that, after he adopted sugar, he began to keep it year-round. While growing cotton he had not done so, typically omitting the end of the year. This fact alone suggests the dramatic escalation of work expectations on a sugar plantation. The work required during the grinding season gives the details of this escalation. During the first year he produced sugar, Rees recorded each "grinding," the distinct periods during which the sugar house was in operation, which alternated with the harvesting of sugarcane. The grindings began at odd hours, any time between midnight and eleven in the morning. The average amount of time these grindings lasted was about twenty-three hours, with the shortest one lasting eight hours and the longest lasting a grueling forty-six hours. This forty-six-hour grinding also contained a notation that appeared nowhere else: "with an intermission of 4 or 5 hours." From this, one can assume that the "grindings" generally went on without a break until they were finished.[115]

Another major change on Rees's plantation was that Sunday work became far more common, especially during the grinding season. Whereas while a cotton planter, Rees had rarely worked enslaved people on Sunday, and when he did only a small fraction of the people he enslaved worked, once he began producing sugar, Sunday work during the harvest became common, with enslaved people working on well over half of all Sundays in November and December during 1832, 1833, and 1834. Considering the immense pressures to harvest and process the crops, one can speculate that this work was likely involuntary. This was the case when Northup worked on sugar plantations in the 1840s and 1850s. While these new demands must have fallen heavily on the enslaved, Rees continued to pay them for Sunday work. Northup was paid as well, a practice he viewed as the norm.[116]

A crucial aspect of the harsh labor system instituted by sugar planters was managerial hierarchy and control. Enslaved managers, known as drivers in English or *commandeurs* in French were the norm on sugar plantations, with Laussat noting that "there exists an organized hierarchy of drivers, chiefs, and overseers, always whip in hand."[117] When a sugar plantation was inventoried in St. Charles Parish, if the recorder bothered to record the enslaved people's jobs, plantations typically had drivers. Drivers were appraised at high values in these inventories, relatively old (around forty), and typically listed first in the inventory of enslaved people, suggesting their status and leadership role on the plantation.[118] Besides management, drivers could also be used by enslavers to practice a divide and conquer strategy by establishing a separate privileged class of enslaved people. A cotton planter in the lower Mississippi valley who used drivers claimed this was their main purpose.[119] Considering the more complex operations of a sugar plantation, the managerial role of drivers on those plantations was likely more important. Their high appraisal values and age suggest they were not merely individuals raised up to divide the slave community.

Drivers were not the only enslaved people given managerial roles. As Northup's experience in the sugar house shows, planters made more informal use of enslaved people for managerial tasks. Northup also described how during the harvest field workers were placed into teams of three harvesters with a "lead hand" in charge.[120] In the Caribbean, structures on sugar plantations could be quite complex with multiple gangs and enslaved managers of varying ranks all overseen by white managers.[121] How fully these sorts of complex structures transferred to early Louisiana sugar plantations is unclear. Most likely they did not because of the much smaller enslaved labor forces. Still, managerial hierarchies including enslaved managers, even if more truncated than in the Caribbean, appear to have been the norm.

A final aspect of sugar plantation labor management was their molding of labor forces planters believed were necessary on sugar plantations. This aspect of the sugar technological complex would have immense repercussions for the lives of enslaved people who ended up on sugar plantations. Put simply, sugar planters wanted young men. The 1806 booster had priced enslaved workers for a sugar plantation at $500 because they were "Prime Negroes" but those for a cotton plantation at only $400 because the latter were "slaves of different sexes and ages."[122] Sugar planters wanted labor, so they used and bought the enslaved people available to them. Early on, this was enslaved Africans. Later this was "American slaves" (i.e., slaves from the anglophone parts of the United States). In and of itself, this created certain structures to the labor forces on plantations (i.e., a high proportion of males among enslaved Africans imported through the slave trade meant very masculine slave forces). However, they also put their preferences into practice, disproportionately buying young men. In the German Coast, the sugar-growing region that included St. Charles Parish, enslaved adults of all major origins (Creole, African, and American) appearing in estate inventories between 1800 and 1820 were more likely to be male than was the case elsewhere in Louisiana. For example, during the first decade of the 1800s, estate inventories in the German Coast listed 3.1 African men for each African woman, whereas inventories in the rest of Louisiana listed 2.1 African men for each African woman.[123] By 1820, St. Charles Parish had 1.75 enslaved adult men for each enslaved adult woman. In contrast, Feliciana Parish, a cotton parish with a rapidly growing enslaved population, had a nearly balanced adult sex ratio.[124] Throughout the antebellum period, sugar regions had disproportionately large numbers of enslaved adult men fed by a specialized branch of the internal slave trade that delivered young men to sugar plantations.[125]

Planters' molding of masculine enslaved labor forces meant that enslaved people in sugar regions lived in a world of young men, typically brought from elsewhere, whether Africa or the Chesapeake.[126] The disproportions between men and women in the sugar regions of Louisiana as well as the harsh labor demands enslavers made on the enslaved had a negative effect on family formation and the reproduction of the enslaved population. Planters and other observers noticed these negative effects. For example, in 1817 a writer claimed, "A gang dwindles away on a sugar estate, while it increases on a cotton plantation, the labor of the former being extremely severe and the privations great."[127]

Demographic data illustrates these negative realities. By the 1820 census, sugar regions of the lower Mississippi valley had abnormally small numbers of children. In St. Charles Parish, the ratios of children under the age of fourteen to women between the ages of fourteen and forty-four was 0.97. By contrast, further upriver, in solidly cotton country, the ratios tended to be much higher, suggesting an enslaved population that was more successfully reproducing itself. In Feliciana Parish, the ratio was 1.50. As a comparison, the entire enslaved population of Virginia had a ratio of 2.05 in 1820.[128] These small numbers of children were the result of the challenges of family formation and the adverse effects work on a sugar plantation had on the health and well-being of enslaved people.[129]

Women on sugar plantations were less fertile and saw more of their children die than was the case on other plantations.[130]

It is worth taking a moment to stop and consider further the disastrous effects of sugar on enslaved people's lives. Sugar regions had large sex imbalances and few children, the former hampering family formation and the latter suggesting an unhealthy population. Strikingly, these shifts happened rapidly in a region once significant numbers of planters began to grow sugar, suggesting that it was an inherent aspect of the technological system as practiced by enslavers in the Americas. For example, in the early 1800s, St. Tammany Parish, across Lake Pontchartrain from Orleans Parish, had a period of several decades when sugar was produced in the parish (by 1860 none was).[131] While sugarcane was already being grown there by the 1810s, the true revolution took off in the 1820s.[132] One effect of this was the sudden formation of very large plantations in the parish. In 1820, only 23 percent of enslaved people in the parish were enslaved on plantations with twenty or more people. The largest plantation had twenty-nine enslaved people.[133] By 1830, 58 percent of enslaved people were enslaved on plantations with twenty or more people. The largest plantation now had 155 enslaved people.[134]

The demographic effects of sugar planters moving into the region on the parish's slave communities were disastrous. In the enslaved population, the male-to-female ratio in 1820 had been 1.13. In 1830, the ratio had increased to 1.53. Some of the new, larger plantations were essentially male-dominated work camps. One had seventy-seven enslaved people, of whom only four (5 percent) were female and only six (8 percent) were under the age of ten. St. Tammany had a relatively large number of enslaved children in 1820. Thirty-eight percent of the enslaved people in St. Tammany were under the age of fourteen (compared to 23 percent in St. Charles Parish, a sugar parish, and 40 percent in Feliciana Parish, a cotton parish). By 1830, St. Tammany now had strikingly few enslaved children. Only 22 percent of its enslaved population was under the age of ten (compared to 17 percent in St. Charles Parish and 31 percent in West Feliciana Parish, Feliciana Parish having been split into East and West Feliciana Parish).[135] Sugar was like a cancer spreading across the landscape of the early nineteenth-century lower Mississippi valley. Over decades, planters spread it from plantation to plantation and from parish to parish in a rolling sugar revolution. Wherever they brought it, the cancer of sugar consumed enslaved people and converted them into profits and wealth for the sugar planters.

After the introduction of sugar, planters adopted and developed labor practices tailored to the new crop, including semi-industrial practices and intense labor demands. These practices were extremely harsh yet effective in achieving the planters' goal of profit. Much as with the unique labor demands of cotton, those implemented by sugar planters, no matter how harsh, cruel, and even deadly, were a part of the technological system of sugar production and, at least according to planters, necessary for the profitable adoption of that system. In fact, much of the experience of an enslaved person on a Louisiana sugar plantation would have looked familiar to an enslaved person on a sugar plantation in Barbados or Cuba, just as the process for making sugar would have looked familiar to a sugar maker from those islands. Methodical and calibrated cruelty was part and parcel of Atlantic sugar production.

While aided by a favorable international climate (the collapse of St. Domingue sugar production), the adoption of sugar came about through the decisions and actions of actors within the lower Mississippi valley. Also, much as with cotton, we know when and how sugar was adopted. Spurred on by the crisis created by the collapse of tobacco and indigo, the planter Étienne Boré decided to attempt to produce granulated sugar. With the aid of the knowledge of small sugarcane farmers and the St. Domingue migrant Morin, he succeeded. After his success, other planters quickly followed suit, leading to the creation of dozens of sugar plantations. While not as universal as the adoption of cotton, the adoption of sugar occurred on plantations that were some of the largest and most lucrative in the region. Sugar also continued to spread throughout the region, creating a decades-long rolling revolution very different from the near instantaneous cotton revolution.

To adopt sugar, planters did a great deal of technological work. Most crucially, they gained access to knowledge about a technological system long known in the Americas and the means to adopt that system, most crucially by identifying and hiring sugar makers and obtaining necessary capital goods. During the first few years, they faced challenges in doing so, but, by the Louisiana Purchase, had largely overcome those challenges. Most innovatively, sugar planters adapted sugar to their relatively cool environment, finding a cultivation schedule and harvesting process that worked in the region and identifying and adopting a variety of sugarcane, Otaheite, better adapted to their shorter growing season. They also adapted sugar to their smaller labor forces and lower capital availability via a variety of different tactics. Finally, they adopted and adapted regimented and harsh labor management practices typical of Caribbean sugar plantations and built masculine labor forces they believed were necessary to produce sugar. Together, these practices and labor force structures produced brutal lives for those enslaved on sugar plantations.

Sugar proved to be a profitable crop that mostly benefited the region's largest planters and, alongside the more widely adopted cotton, helped to drive the region's agricultural commodity boom. As cotton had been elsewhere, in the lower reaches of the lower Mississippi valley, sugar was a major factor in the receding of the economic and political crises of the 1790s. It was also a central factor in implanting a notoriously harsh slave system in the region, a system implemented and embraced by profit-hungry enslavers. In the next chapter, we will turn to the final crucial technological systems adopted and adapted by planters to rescue their plantation dreams from the crisis of the mid-1790s: the international and internal slave trades. The former was far from new in the region but experienced a renaissance in the years following the cotton and sugar revolutions and followed new pathways opened by changes in regional sovereignty. The latter was a technological system built to feed the insatiable hunger for labor of the sugar and cotton cultivators of the lower Mississippi valley by relocating "excess" enslaved people from other slave societies in the United States to the expanding slave society of the region. This trade would become a central feature of antebellum slavery and severely disrupt the lives of countless enslaved people over the next several decades.

4

REMAKING THE SLAVE TRADES

You will ask, what do they want with so many negroes, the answer is, to make more Money—again, you will ask what do they want with so much Money. The answer is to buy more Negroes—

—John Mills to Gilbert Jackson, May 19, 1807

In the spring of 1818, several articles appeared in American newspapers describing a ring that was smuggling enslaved people out of New Jersey to ship to New Orleans. At the time, it was illegal to transport an enslaved person out of the state without their express consent. According to the various articles published about this ring, the smugglers were "respectable" men who colluded with local officials (who were also their relatives) to forge the enslaved people's consents. The leader of the ring was Charles Morgan, a planter in Louisiana with family in New Jersey.[1] It is unclear exactly how many people Morgan smuggled to New Orleans.[2] However, in an article published in a New Orleans newspaper in July 1818, the author claimed that Charles Morgan was to thank for "the copiousness of the present supply [of slaves]." He continued that "*Jersey* negroes appear to be peculiarly adapted to this market" and looked forward to "large importations in future."[3]

In response to these stories, Morgan published a self-justificatory letter claiming, incredibly, that the people he smuggled were going to New Orleans willingly. According to his defense, he purchased them in New Jersey due to serendipity. Morgan asserted that his original plan had been to travel to Virginia with $45,000 to purchase enslaved people, a common venture for lower Mississippi valley planters. He was only in New Jersey to visit relatives and while there had discovered the availability of cheap en-slaved people.[4] According to one newspaper article, Morgan was indicted on sixteen counts of "taking people of colour from [New Jersey] contrary to law," although it is unclear whether he was ever tried.[5] Thirty-six of the enslaved people were impounded in New Orleans, leading, according to the newspapers, to a trial and decision in favor of Morgan.[6] Two years later, Morgan was resident on a plantation in Pointe Coupee Parish, hav-ing expanded his enslaved labor force from twenty-four people in 1810 to eighty-four people in 1820.[7] Presumably some of those eighty-four people had been smuggled from New Jersey. Morgan and his confederates were willing to bend and probably break the law to provide enslaved labor to the lower Mississippi valley. Locals appreciated their efforts.

While we might not normally think of New Jersey as a source of en-slaved labor for the lower Mississippi valley, Morgan's actions as well as the reaction to them in the lower Mississippi valley are unsurprising as, following the sugar and cotton revolutions, the lower Mississippi valley's residents hungered for more enslaved labor. In 1800, Louisiana's governor the Marquis de Casa Calvo wrote that "this Province can not be self sup-porting without negroes" and warned that a failure to import enslaved people "will let the Colony be ruined."[8] In 1804, the newly installed American governor of the territory of Orleans William C. C. Claiborne reported to Thomas Jefferson that "the general opinion seems to be, that the Territory cannot prosper without a great encrease [sic] of Negro's."[9] In the years before and after the Louisiana Purchase, lower Mississippi valley merchants and enslavers were importing thousands of people from wherever they could get them.

The slave trades that delivered those enslaved people were complex technological systems connecting actors throughout the Atlantic basin and beyond in webs of interdependence. The international slave trade was particularly extensive and complex, connecting European merchants, Af-rican merchants and political leaders, American enslavers and merchants, and other distant actors such as Indian (South Asian) textile producers.[10] The internal slave trade connected merchants and enslavers elsewhere in the United States with merchants and enslavers in the lower Missis-sippi valley. Much more extensively than did the cotton and sugar tech-nological systems (which themselves depended on extraregional actors), the slave trades depended on the actions of and interactions between individuals outside the region who could not always be directly influenced by lower Mississippi valley residents. Much of the system they depended on to supply the enslaved labor they so desired was beyond their control or even knowledge.

However, regional residents were not merely passive recipients of enslaved people brought to the region. They were actively involved in directing the trades toward their region via their Atlantic connections (in the same way those Atlantic connections facilitated the marketing of cotton and sugar crops). This was particularly, although not exclusively, true of the internal slave trade, a system being developed by actors throughout the United States. Likely because of the proximity of supply as well as this trade's largely unstructured form in this period, lower Mississippi valley merchants and enslavers sought out the internal slave trade and directed "American slaves" or "English slaves" (as they were often called in Louisiana; they will be referred to as enslaved Americans in this book to differentiate them from enslaved Africans, Creoles, and Caribbean Creoles) to the region.[11] The New Jersey smuggling case is an example of this dynamic. Morgan made use of his contacts to take advantage of an available (if illicit) supply of enslaved labor that was largely untapped.

As should be clear, the international and internal slave trades were, in crucial ways, distinct. However, during this period the strong differentiation between the internal and international slave trades that we impose were likely neither as clear nor as important to lower Mississippi valley elites. They wanted labor to profit from sugar and cotton, and they used the connections they had throughout the Atlantic World to procure that labor. When the Spanish West Florida planter John Mills, quoted in the epigraph that begins this chapter, pointed to the "Great numbers of Africans" and "great numbers brought down the River from Kentuckey, Cumberland Virginia, Maryland" as a threat to the stability of the region, he did not seem to view the distinctions between these overlapping trades as particularly important. Each brought "Negroes" who were dangerous (and available for purchase, an opportunity of which he admitted he had recently availed himself despite his concerns) and whom Mills worried would someday rebel.[12] Mills was an Anglo-American, meaning that he at least shared a language and some culture with enslaved Americans. For his francophone neighbors, the distinction between the trades was likely even less important. For them, both trades brought in culturally alien strangers.

Perhaps unsurprisingly, considering this overlap and blurring between the two trades, historians of the internal slave trade are often vague about how the early trade started and worked.[13] Partly this is because the early trade, far less structured than that of the antebellum period, left relatively little evidence. However, sourcing is not the only issue. The vagueness on when and how the trade began and how the early trade operated is also because there is no clear moment of origin of the trade as a distinct phenomenon. Enslaved Americans were moved west as soon as Anglo-Americans moved west. As more Anglo-Americans moved west, enslaved Americans moved with them. As the volume of the movement increased, it inevitably became more structured with the development of slave trade specialists and infrastructure devoted to the slave trade. It also changed with broader changes in American society, such as with the closing of the international slave trade in 1808 and the maturation of a national capitalist economy during the mid-1800s. This chapter details one period of profound change for the trade in the lower Mississippi valley: when it overlapped with and then replaced a recently resurgent international slave trade and became truly "internal" to a single national market, thus beginning the process of becoming the sophisticated antebellum trade process that is commonly invoked by the moniker.[14]

Of course, both slave trades were processes for forcibly relocating newly or long-enslaved peoples from Africa or of African-descent to the lower Mississippi valley to fulfill the insatiable hunger of the region's enslavers for labor to extract wealth from the soil via cotton and sugar. The human implications of these systems should be obvious: enslavement for Africans and social and familial rupture and alienation in a diverse, exploitative, and brutal slave society for all those forcibly moved to the region. This process would have been experienced as trauma, a trauma the enslaved dealt with in a variety of ways, including in 1811 through violent rebellion. The slave trades were also a central way Africans and African-descended people experienced the modernizing world of the early 1800s. They were put into motion by the desires of Atlantic World capitalists and forced to construct new lives, families, communities, cultures, and identities.[15] Much as with the adoption of cotton and sugar, lower Mississippi valley elites and their Atlantic partners were impressively innovative in how they acquired labor, but that innovation was yet another means to transmute human suffering and exploitation into profits via cotton and sugar.[16]

Much more so than with the cotton and sugar technological systems, the slave trades were directly influenced and structured by governmental action, with governments closing and reopening the slave trades and at times regulating them. Most often, they did so because of fears that imported enslaved people threatened stability, as was the case when the Spanish government closed the international slave trade in 1796 in response to the Haitian Revolution and the Pointe Coupee Conspiracy. However, more idealistic concerns about the slave trade also influenced governmental action, particularly the closing of the international trade by the United State in 1808. Enslavers often, although not always as is shown by their support of the 1796 ban, pushed back against these government actions, arguing that their desire for labor trumped other concerns. They usually won the argument and managed to reopen or keep open the flow of enslaved people. When they lost the argument, they ignored new restrictions and imported them anyway.

The period around the Louisiana Purchase, when Louisianans attempted to both accommodate themselves to their new rulers and influence those rulers' policies, reveals what was likely the most important example of a successful effort to reverse restrictions on slave importations. When setting up the territory of Orleans (as what became the modern state of Louisiana was called), Congress banned the international and internal slave trades.[17] An 1804 memorial to Congress from residents of the territory, which contained a number of complaints about the new government, argued for reopening the slave trades, particularly the international trade. The memorial argued that fairness dictated that Louisianans should have the right to determine the future of the trade. It pointed out that the African trade was "free to all the Atlantic states, who chuse to engage in it" and dismissed any need to engage arguments over the trade's justness. The memorial explained why the slave trade was necessary, relying on the old argument that "the necessity of employing African labourers . . . arises from climate, and the species of cultivation, pursued in warm latitudes" and the need to use enslaved labor to maintain the levees. They claimed the results of a failure to reopen the trade would be grim: "Cultivation must cease, the improvements of a century be destroyed, and the great river resume its empire over our ruined fields and demolished habitations."[18]

This memorial was not the only avenue through which the federal government was learning about regional dissatisfaction with slave trade restrictions. Soon after his arrival in New Orleans, Governor Claiborne received a report on conditions in rural Louisiana that claimed that "no Subject . . . [is] so interesting to the minds of the inhabitants of all that part of the Country which I have visited as that of the importation of brute Negroes from Africa." The informant claimed that reopening the slave trade "would go farther with them, and better reconcile them to the Government of the United States, than any other privilege that could be extended."[19]

Claiborne took this advice seriously and throughout the next year reported to his superiors in Washington that the true cause of dissatisfaction within the territory was the ban on the slave trade. In a letter to Secretary of State James Madison he reported that "on [the subject of the slave trade], the people generally appear to feel a lively interest, and the prevailing opinion expressed here is, that a prohibition would tend generally to the injury of the Province."[20] Once the memorial had been promulgated, Claiborne remained convinced that the slave trade was the most important grievance, writing in one report that "my opinion is that had the African trade been continued for a few years, no murmers against the Law of Congress would have been heard."[21]

Soon after the memorial was presented in Washington, Congress, as part of a broader reorganization of the territory, also partially acceded to the demand to reopen the slave trade, legalizing it between the territory of Orleans and the rest of the United States while keeping the direct international trade illegal.[22] Coupled with the reopening of the international slave trade in South Carolina, this act also de facto reopened the international trade to the lower Mississippi valley.[23]

Lobbying in favor of the slave trade was not limited to the American period, and elites lobbied both the Spanish and French about it. For example, in 1800, the New Orleans Cabildo held a debate over whether to insist that the Spanish government reopen the international slave trade. The Cabildo split evenly on whether to support lifting the ban, with six supporting doing so and six opposing it. Despite this fundamental disagreement, most speakers agreed that planters and farmers "required" more enslaved people. One opponent forthrightly recognized that "Agriculture requires that the quantity of negroes in this Colony be increased." Unsurprisingly, supporters saw cultivators' labor needs as fundamental to their arguments. One supporter argued that importing enslaved people was "the only way to develop this colony due to the new cultivation of the sugar-cane, the agriculture being unable to progress without labor." While most of the argument revolved around disagreements about the continued dangers of rebellion and the causes of the Haitian Revolution, the members of the Cabildo agreed that, on purely economic grounds, the reopening of the slave trade was justified.[24] In the end, the Spanish government sided with the supporters of the slave trade and reopened the international slave trade shortly after the debate.[25]

After the cotton and sugar revolutions, local support, especially among elites, for reopening or keeping open the slave trades was strong if not unanimous. When faced with restrictions, elites lobbied their governments to reopen or keep open the trades. Both the Spanish and American governments, despite reservations, agreed to reopen the trades when pressed to do so in the early 1800s, and, with the crucial and consequential exception of the closing of the international slave trade by the United States in 1808, locals were largely successful in keeping the slave trades open and largely unregulated.[26] Locals wanted enslaved labor for their cotton and sugar plantations and farms. With government support or at least acquiescence, they continued to look to the Atlantic World and their fellow Americans to fulfill that desire.

The shapes of the slave trades in the lower Mississippi valley during the late 1700s and early 1800s were complex. Prior to the closing of the international slave trade in 1808, Africa was by far the most important source of enslaved labor in the lower Mississippi valley. However, the region was never populous or economically important enough during the era of the international slave trade to demand much attention from those trading directly with Africa, and, after the Louisiana Purchase, the direct trade became illegal. Therefore, the African trade into the region was often complex, indirect, and even illicit. The second most important source of enslaved labor before 1808 was the rest of the United States, meaning both the "internal slave trade" (a misnomer in much of the region until unified under American control in 1810) and the migration of enslavers with the people they enslaved. This source would become the most important after 1808. The internal slave trade had not yet developed into a well-organized trade, operating in different ways as different actors scrambled to derive labor or profits from it. Besides these two main sources of enslaved people, a small but not inconsequential number were brought into the region from the Caribbean. As with the other two trades, the path of these people into the region were complicated, with some being added to shipments of Africans and others coming with enslavers relocating to the region. Together, these three sources provided labor for the region's sugar and cotton cultivators. They also brought new people into the region, who formed the basis of new communities of people of African descent or transformed existing ones.

The international slave trade was not newly important as of the late eighteenth century. It had been the source of the region's enslaved population from the early eighteenth century before stagnating during the late French colonial period. Under the Spanish, locals began importing more enslaved people, particularly after the American Revolution. One historian estimates that between twelve and fifteen thousand enslaved people, almost all of whom were Africans, were imported during the Spanish period, mostly after the American Revolution.[27] By the standards of many other colonies, these numbers were quite small. For example, the Trans-Atlantic Slave Trade Database documents 266,225 enslaved Africans disembarking in Jamaica between 1783 and 1803.[28] However, enslaved Africans being imported into the lower Mississippi valley were joining a relatively small population of enslaved people. A Spanish census found that the region had just over fifteen thousand enslaved people in 1785.[29]

The Louisiana Purchase led to a formal ban on the slave trade but only after a nine-month period when the slave trade remained open and at least a thousand enslaved people were imported.[30] After a ban that lasted a little more than a year, Congress legalized the importation of enslaved people from other parts of the United States, but not from abroad. Combined with South Carolina's legalization of the African slave trade, this action de facto reopened the international trade. During 1806 and 1807, dozens of ships arrived from Charleston carrying roughly nine thousand Africans.[31] As with the figures for the Spanish period, while this number seems small by the standards of other plantation colonies, relative to the population, just under forty-nine thousand enslaved people in 1810, it was significant.[32] Of course, we should also recognize that, outside of demographic abstractions, for those nine thousand individuals their arrival in the lower Mississippi valley was part of a larger forced journey that was life shattering, life altering, and life defining.

The legal African slave trade was typically characterized by transshipments via other ports.[33] Before the Louisiana Purchase, it largely consisted of Africans reexported from the Caribbean. Until the 1796 ban, Jamaica was the most common source for transshipped Africans, although they were also commonly brought from Dominica, St. Domingue, and Martinique. After the trade was reopened in 1800, Havana was the most common source. After the trade reopened again in 1805, transshipments came via Charleston.[34] Considering that planters and merchants generally referred to Africans brought via these trips as "brute" or "new" slaves, Africans were probably transshipped to the region rather quickly and did not spend much if any time in the Caribbean or South Carolina.[35] While transshipments were most important, some Africans were imported directly from Africa.[36] For example, in September 1803, an advertisement appeared in *Moniteur de la Louisiane* offering for sale "140 heads of blacks of the nations Congo and Manaings" who had "arrived directly from the coast of Africa."[37]

The importation of enslaved Africans, whether directly or indirectly, was organized by local merchants or as speculative ventures by outsiders who likely consigned many of the Africans to local merchants on arrival, illustrating the role of local merchants in operating the trade and attracting it to the region. The historian Douglas Chambers has analyzed local slave trade mercantile networks between 1783 and 1796, the peak of the slave trade during the Spanish period. He has identified twenty-five individual merchants or merchant houses that were likely slave traders. Chambers argues that most of those he has identified were small-scale traders who may have acted as wholesalers or retailers of enslaved people imported by other New Orleans or extraregional merchants. He has also identified several major slave traders who likely either organized slave trade trips, typically via the Caribbean, or acted as consignees for merchants from outside the region. Some of the more important of these merchants included the Irishman Daniel Clark Jr., the American Oliver Pollock (previously a Philadelphia resident who acted as Congress's representative in New Orleans during the American Revolution), and the French-born Jean Dupuy and Jean Baptiste Labatut.[38] Unfortunately, we do not know the details of this trade, but these merchants were likely taking advantage of contacts they had with Caribbean merchants.

This pattern of local merchants organizing ventures or acting as consignees continued in the American period. For example, in 1807 the New Orleans merchants Richard Reynal Keene and (once again) Daniel Clark contracted with Forbes, Munro, and Forbes of Nassau in the Bahamas to deliver "not less than seventy nor more than two hundred" enslaved people on a ship chartered by Keene and Clark. However, the plan went awry in some unspecified way, leading to the nondelivery of the enslaved people and a suit for $25,000 in damages.[39] Still, Keene and Clark's venture shows how New Orleans merchants worked with other Atlantic merchants to import enslaved Africans and other such ventures that did not end up in the courts were likely common.

More rarely, wealthy planters bypassed local merchants and organized their own shipments of enslaved Africans. In February of 1807, William Dunbar of Natchez wrote to two Charleston merchants asking for their assistance "to procure a Certain number of African slaves." He had been introduced to the merchants by the New Orleans merchant house of Chew and Relf, with whom he did substantial business. He informed them that he had £3,000 set aside to purchase enslaved Africans and for expenses and specified that he preferred the enslaved people to be from twelve to twenty-one years old and "well formed & robust."[40]

Local merchants and planters sought out the trade, hoping to both involve themselves in a lucrative commerce and provide (for themselves or others) labor to produce the goods their wealth depended on. In fact, marking clear boundaries between merchants and planters is somewhat deceptive. Often merchants were procuring labor for the plantations they owned and operated. Many international slave traders were major sugar and cotton planters, showing the strong connection between slave trade profits and rural development. Daniel Clark was a sugar planter, land speculator, and local booster who had his finger in every aspect of the region's development.[41] His uncle, also Daniel Clark, who imported or acted as the factor for the importation of Africans into Natchez in the late 1780s, was a cotton planter and land speculator.[42] In 1810 the Frenchman Pierre Sauve, identified by Chambers as a likely slave trader, owned a sugar plantation in Orleans Parish with an enslaved labor force of eighty people.[43] For many, planting and slave trading (and other mercantile activities) went hand in hand, a pattern we will see again with the internal slave trade.

Planters and merchants (who were often one and the same) used connections with merchant houses elsewhere in the Atlantic World to procure enslaved Africans for the lower Mississippi valley. In some cases, outsiders shipped Africans to the region as speculative ventures, often assigning them to local consignees for sale. Regardless of the exact method used, in the twenty-five-year period between 1783 and 1808 merchants and planters forcibly imported more than twenty thousand Africans through the legal international slave trade.[44] While they had little control of how this technological system operated outside of the region, they acted to gain access to it and direct a small part of it to enrich themselves and their fellow enslavers.

On January 1, 1808, the United States outlawed the international slave trade. Residents of the lower Mississippi valley seem to have, by and large, acquiesced to the ban, at least formally. Very little local discussion of the ban has survived.[45] While overt resistance to the slave trade ban might not have occurred, covert resistance (or covert indifference) was common. As we have seen, smuggling had a long tradition in the region, and the smuggling of enslaved Africans appears to have become commonplace after 1808, although it is unlikely that the number of Africans being smuggled was more than a fraction of the numbers being imported legally before 1808.

Slave smuggling was facilitated by international instability and the privateers common to warfare during the period.[46] Four cases against slave smugglers brought before the Superior Court of the Territory of Orleans between July 24 and September 1, 1810, reveal how smuggling operated. In two of the cases, the enslaved Africans were introduced via Bayou Lafourche, a waterway that connects with both the Mississippi and Gulf of Mexico, showing how smugglers used the complex waterways of the area to avoid customs officials. The number of enslaved people in the cases varied, with the smallest involving 5 individuals and the largest 153. In three of the four cases, the smugglers were privateers, in two cases bringing in Iberian slave ships captured in the Caribbean. However, not only disreputable outsiders were involved in such smuggling. The fourth case, with 105 enslaved people, involved Honore Fortier, a prominent local planter and merchant who seems to have orchestrated the smuggling trip. Finally, despite the cases, most of the enslaved people seem to have never been seized, nor the smugglers punished. These trips probably benefited both the smugglers who profited and the planters and farmers who got new labor.[47]

Another case illustrates how prominent merchants bent the law to smuggle enslaved people and the complexity of that smuggling. This trip involved three merchant houses from three different cities (Pensacola, Charleston, and New Orleans) and a Brazilian slave trader. In 1811, Benjamin Chew and Richard Relf, close business associates of Daniel Clark, sued a Brazilian slave trader and a Charleston merchant house "for their services in & about the business of the Ship *Bellona*," a Portuguese vessel, whose "business" was to transport three hundred enslaved people from the coast of Africa to Spanish West Florida.[48] Relf and Chew's role was to use their contacts in West Florida to gain entry for the slave ship. Documents suggest that they bribed a Spanish official (likely the governor or intendant) to produce documents giving the cover story that they intended to smuggle the enslaved people into American territory. In reality, they planned to sell them into the area around Baton Rouge in nominally Spanish territory (the area had revolted the previous summer against Spanish rule but had not yet been incorporated into the United States). Still, considering the subterfuge involved, it is far from clear what the actual goal of the trip was and telling that smuggling into American territory was being used as a cover story for smuggling enslaved people into Spanish territory.[49]

Merchants with resources and connections were more than willing to break and bend the rules to supply planters and farmers with enslaved labor and expected that enslavers would be more than happy to play along. Just how extensive this smuggling was is impossible to know although federal court cases brought against smugglers indicate that thousands of enslaved Africans were smuggled into Louisiana during the 1810s.[50] In addition, the African share of the population of Louisiana parishes that recorded origins of enslaved people in official documents did decline in the 1810s but still remained remarkably persistent, suggesting significant smuggling (see fig. 1).[51] In the 1810s, at least two-fifths of adult enslaved people appearing in estate inventories on the German Coast, which was just up the Mississippi River from New Orleans, were listed as Africans. Individual planters benefited from the smuggling. For example, when Michel Fortier, slave smuggler Honore Fortier's father, died, his 1819 estate inventory (taken eleven years after the international slave trade ban) revealed the he owned a very Africanized sugar plantation with 67 (48 percent) of the 140 adult enslaved people in the inventory listed as Africans.[52]

Sources are almost universally silent on the dynamics of the trade once newly enslaved Africans arrived in the region and how they were treated when they first arrived on the region's plantations and farms. In fact, outside of legal documents and advertisements, Africans were rarely mentioned or discussed in writing. C. C. Robin, a Frenchman who had resided in the colony for several years around the time of the Louisiana Purchase and a critic of slavery, published a book on his experiences and, uniquely, recorded his impression of the treatment of recently imported Africans. According to Robin, enslaved Africans were sold as soon as they arrived. He claimed that sick ones were often sold at reduced prices to surgeons who would "speculate on curing them." The rest of the Africans "purchased by the planters, are minutely examined." According to Robin, "The Creole purchaser will examine a negro in every part." The "every" is important to him as he emphasizes that planters searched for "some sign of his virility" in the hopes of guaranteeing "reproductive capacity." Robin concluded that these "examinations become so familiar to these unfortunate creatures, that modesty is soon a stranger to them."[53]

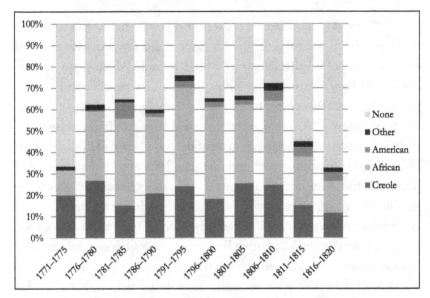

Fig. 1. Origins of enslaved people aged fifteen or older in Louisiana estates, 1771–1820

Sources: Figures calculated using data from the Louisiana Slave Database. The data for this chart were drawn only from estate inventories in the database. Categories used by the database were more specific than the ones used here. I have organized the database's specific categories into general ones. The sample size of each five-year period in chronological order is 683; 1,302; 1,173; 2,301; 1,986; 1,600; 1,512; 2,677; 3,787; and 7,696.

Robin also related what he saw as the typical experience of the newly enslaved Africans once they were transported to their enslaver's plantation or farm. According to Robin, the large planters generally followed a process in integrating Africans into their workforces. While he did not ever use the term, in many other parts of the Americas, this process would have been called "seasoning" or "acclimatization."[54] According to Robin, the Africans were "gradually introduced to work." They were made to "wash often, to take strolls from time to time, and . . . they are made to dance." They were also mixed into groups with older enslaved people to learn plantation work habits. Robin, as a critic of slavery, was careful to note that these "attentions" were not "dictated by any consideration of humanity" but rather "economic necessity." He continued that many enslavers, because of poverty or greed, did not follow this process.

In these cases, the Africans had to do "hard and constant work" immediately upon their arrival. As a result, they "die of disease, or even more often of depression."[55]

Even with Robin's description many questions about the experience of newly enslaved Africans are left unanswered. Most importantly, we have little way of knowing, beyond reasonable inferences, how the Africans themselves experienced these harsh changes in their lives. However, we do know that Africans commonly reacted by attempting to escape. Africans recently brought to the region were more likely to appear in runaway slave advertisements. In a collection of 854 runaway slave advertisements placed in Louisiana newspapers between 1801 and 1820, Africans appeared often in runaway slave advertisements during the peak period of the international trade, whereas, once the trade became illegal, Africans became a rarity in the advertisements (see fig. 2). For example, between 1806 and 1810, 26 percent of all enslaved people in runaway slave advertisements were described as Africans and surely some of the 43 percent given no origin were Africans, considering the very brief nature of many of those advertisements. Over the same period about 39 percent of adult enslaved people in Louisiana estate inventories were listed as Africans (see fig. 1). However, over the next fifteen years, Africans appearing in the advertisements declined far more rapidly than did their apparent share of the population, down to 7 percent between 1816 and 1820. Over the same period, Africans made up at least 15 percent of adult enslaved people in surviving Louisiana estates. This suggests that recently arrived Africans were more likely to show up in the advertisements, either because they were more likely to attempt to escape or, alternatively, enslavers were more worried their absence was not temporary.[56]

Robin's account paints a grim, if unsurprising, picture of newly enslaved Africans being humiliated at purchase and then through pure luck either subjected to a seasoning process designed to ease them into their new lives or immediate and brutal demands that might lead to their quick death. The runaway slave advertisements suggest that many Africans reacted by escaping. Africans were being broken into a new life of servitude growing cotton or sugar for the region's planters and farmers. One suspects that Robin, despite his criticisms of the system, was too sanguine about the seasoning process. Surely all newly arrived Africans suffered

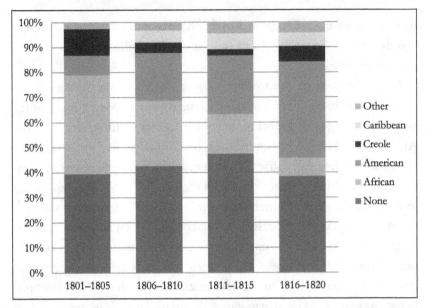

Fig. 2. Origins of escapees in runaway slave advertisements in Louisiana news-papers, 1801–1820

Sources: Figures calculated using advertisements from the following news-papers: *Ami de Lois, Baton Rouge Gazette, Louisiana Courier, Louisiana Gazette, Louisiana Herald, Louisiana Rambler, Moniteur de la Louisiane, New Orleans Daily Chronicle, Orleans Gazette, St. Francisville Timepiece, Telegraph, Union.* The sample size of each five-year period in chronological order is 38, 223, 333, and 260.

greatly, physically and psychologically, in their new home. Planters and merchants, spurred by the profits of cotton and sugar, used their Atlantic mercantile connections to import thousands of Africans into the region in the years following the reopening of the trade by the Spanish in 1800. These importations forever changed the fate of the individual Africans imported and the region itself.

While enslaved Africans were easily the largest group involuntarily re-located to the region until at least the closing of the international slave trade in 1808, enslaved people from other groups were also being moved to the region. Enslaved Caribbean Creoles were a constant, if somewhat minor, presence in the region (see fig. 1; Caribbean Creoles make up the bulk of the "other" category). Most enslaved Caribbean Creoles appear to have come from Jamaica prior to 1809 and then St. Domingue after 1809. Between 1771 and 1808, 50 percent of enslaved Caribbean Creoles appearing in Louisiana documents were Jamaicans; 20 percent were from St. Domingue. Between 1809 and 1820, 81 percent of enslaved Caribbean Creoles appearing in Louisiana documents were from St. Domingue; 10 percent were from Jamaica. The influx of enslaved Caribbean Creoles was never as numerically important as that of the other major groups (Caribbean Creoles had their highest presence in estates between 1806 and 1810 with 2.1 percent of all enslaved people), and probably mostly consisted of enslaved people who were added to cargoes of Africans in the Caribbean or came with enslavers traveling to the region.[57]

The shift to enslaved St. Dominguans coincided with just such a relocation of enslavers. In 1809, thousands of St. Domingue refugees fled from St. Yago de Cuba, where they had settled after fleeing St. Domingue in the wake of the Haitian Revolution. These refugees had been expelled from Cuba in 1809 because of popular and official anti-French sentiments during the Napoleonic wars.[58] The entry of these refugees' slaves was in direct contravention to the 1808 ban on the international slave trade. After some initial hesitation and in the face of some local opposition spurred by fears of introducing enslaved people and free people of color who had experienced (and perhaps taken part in) the Haitian Revolution, Governor Claiborne allowed enslavers to introduce the enslaved people into the territory.[59] Ultimately, the US Congress allowed the permanent settlement of the refugees by creating a one-time exception to the slave trade ban.[60] One historian estimates that twelve thousand Saint-Domingue refugees entered Louisiana after the Haitian Revolution began.[61] It's unclear how many of these refugees were enslaved, but one estimate claimed that about one-third of those who entered in 1809 were.[62]

Enslaved Caribbean Creoles, especially Haitians, tended to clump in New Orleans and in urban occupations because their enslavers tended to remain in the city.[63] One does find the occasional enslaved Caribbean Creole on rural plantations. For example, of the 140 enslaved adults on Michel Fortier's plantation in Orleans Parish in 1819, four were from St. Domingue, and five were from Jamaica. However, as the Fortier example shows, one rarely finds more than a handful on any plantation. Estate inventories from two regions with significant origin data for enslaved people through 1820 (the German Coast and Orleans Parish) show the rarity of enslaved Caribbean Creoles in rural Louisiana. Of the 887 enslaved people appearing with an origin in German Coast estate inventories in the 1810s, only nineteen (2 percent) were from the Caribbean. In sharp contrast, of 1,311 enslaved people appearing in estate inventories with an origin in the 1810s in Orleans Parish (which included New Orleans), 143 (11 percent) were from the Caribbean.[64]

Enslaved Caribbean Creoles were culturally important in New Orleans but a minor addition to the population in the rural lower Mississippi valley.[65] While they were not unimportant in the countryside, they were a vector for "dangerous" ideas circulating around the Caribbean, their arrival was usually not directly caused by the economic changes unleashed by the sugar and cotton revolutions. While some enslaved Caribbean Creoles did work in the cotton and sugar fields, their arrival was not directly related to cultivators' desire for labor. Enslaved Caribbean Creoles were mostly an incidental, if important, addition to the local population, in sharp contrast to enslaved Africans and Americans.[66] While local elites played a role in the international and internal slave trades, they had only a very limited role in the arrival of enslaved Caribbean Creoles and often resisted it as dangerous.

The other major influx of enslaved people during the period was that of enslaved Americans (often referred to as "American slaves" in the region) via the internal slave trade and enslaver migration. Enslaved Americans were far from an incidental addition to the local population. Enslaved Americans were being brought to the region in response to economic conditions. Whether being brought with an enslaver intending to settle or a merchant or planter hoping to make money from a slave trading trip or gain labor for themselves, the trade was driven by the desire for labor by locals growing cotton and sugar and, after 1808, the ban on the international slave trade. In concert with extraregional actors, residents of the lower Mississippi valley were developing a technological system that fulfilled their labor wants and increased the profits they could make from the cotton and sugar systems. This was the period when the relatively minor flow of enslaved Americans to the region began to surge and become predominant.

The size and forms of this forced migration are difficult to trace. Partly this is because many of the enslaved Americans brought to the region were not traded at all but instead brought by Anglo-American colonizers, leaving little direct evidence besides the presence of the enslavers and enslaved in the region.[67] For example, in 1783, Benjamin Farar, a recent immigrant from South Carolina and resident of Pointe Coupee, enslaved 153 people, of whom 43 were recorded as Creoles of South Carolina, 29 as Creoles of Virginia, and one as a Creole of Pennsylvania.[68] While Farar was somewhat atypical in the very large number of enslaved people he brought with him, he was certainly not unique in bringing enslaved people with him when he migrated to the region.

Another reason the trade is difficult to trace is that many of the enslaved Americans who were traded were brought via a haphazard and unstructured trade that left little direct evidence. Still, pieces of evidence do give us glimpses of the various routes by which enslaved Americans were traded to the region during this early period of the internal slave trade. These glimpses paint the picture of a somewhat chaotic but also increasingly organized and predictable trade.[69]

One of the more important early internal slave trade routes came down the Mississippi River from Kentucky and Tennessee. Small-scale traders brought enslaved people to be lodged in New Orleans for sale or sold along the way. For example, on May 21, 1804, John Hardeman "of Tennessee" sold five enslaved people to residents of Iberville Parish, located along the Mississippi River.[70] An 1811 guidebook includes a document that records all the goods, including 286 enslaved people, descending the Ohio River from near Louisville, Kentucky, between November 24, 1810, and January 24, 1811.[71] Many of these enslaved people likely ended up in the lower Mississippi valley. During the first decade of the 1800s, the slave trader Isaac Franklin (who would later play an important role in developing the more organized and sophisticated antebellum internal slave trade as a part of the slave-trading firm Franklin, Armfield, and Ballard) and his brothers made several slave-trading trips from Tennessee to the lower Mississippi valley. In this period early in the development of the American banking system and credit networks, the Franklin brothers often found it difficult to collect the money they were owed for the people they sold, a feature of the trade that was likely common and retarded the growth of large slave-trading firms.[72] Still, at a minimum hundreds of enslaved people were being moved down the western rivers annually as early as 1810. By the late 1810s, this trade accelerated dramatically with the post–War of 1812 cotton boom.[73]

Another common way enslaved Americans were traded to the region was by planters who made slave-purchasing trips to the East Coast, particularly to the Chesapeake, where local enslavers had enslaved labor forces beyond their needs. Many of these planters discovered that, once in the East, they were connecting into already well-developed slave-trading networks. As early as 1801, a correspondent reported to Winthrop Sargent, the former Mississippi Territory governor turned cotton planter, from the Eastern Shore of Maryland that two of their acquaintances were leaving soon to return to Natchez with eighty to ninety people they had purchased there. The correspondent shared that he had purchased fifteen people and planned to purchase several more.[74]

Such trips continued to be common nearly two decades later. Remember that Charles Morgan had claimed that his original plan had been to purchase people in Virginia before discovering an alternative "supply" in New Jersey. Joseph Erwin, a sugar and cotton planter in Iberville Parish, made at least two trips in the late 1810s to the Chesapeake Bay and bought at least sixty-two people.[75] Erwin was not only buying the people for his own use. When he returned from his first trip, he stopped in Natchez and sold some of the people he had purchased.[76] Still, Erwin must have kept some of the people, as his enslaved labor force grew from 68 people in 1810 to 194 people in 1820.[77] Much as it had with the international slave trade, for many slave trading and planting were closely connected.

Local merchants also took part in the internal slave trade as speculative ventures. For example, on June 28, 1809, the merchant firm Hillen and Wedenstrandt advertised "27 valuable Negroes" "purchased on the Rappahannock River" for sale "on board the Schooner Sally Ann" along with "5,000 Front Bricks."[78] As in this instance, enslaved Americans often came with other cargoes, indicating that the traders were not specialized in the slave trade but merely taking on enslaved people as one of several goods. In fact, those selling large groups of enslaved people in New Orleans were rarely dedicated slave traders. For example, in January 1809 John Clay, probable brother of Henry Clay and a local merchant, offered thirty enslaved Virginians brought to the region on the brig the *Louisiana Packet* along with baker's flour, lard, butter, soap, tobacco and bricks.[79] I have found no other examples of Clay or Hillen and Wedenstrandt advertising people for sale. Merchants and merchant firms rarely placed more than a single advertisement in the paper for large shipments of enslaved Americans during the period.

As with the African slave trade, merchants and planters were more than willing to bend and even flout the law to increase the flow of enslaved Americans to the region. The anecdote that began this chapter shows how Charles Morgan and his coconspirators in New Jersey bent and broke the law to send enslaved New Jerseyans to the sugar and cotton plantations of the lower Mississippi valley. They were far from alone in engaging in illicit activities to send people to the region for enslavement there.[80] For example, the *Baltimore Patriot* published a letter from New Orleans that was written to a Baltimore resident to inform him that a girl working in the letter writer's boarding house had been stolen from the Baltimore resident and smuggled to New Orleans. The newspaper's introduction to the letter claimed that the kidnapping of enslaved and free African Americans in Baltimore for sale to the lower Mississippi valley was common.[81] In the mid-1820s, Philip Hickey, a planter near Baton Rouge who had lived in the area for several decades, brutally abused a boy for (truthfully) telling a stranger he had been abducted from Philadelphia. He then released the boy to Philadelphia's high constable, who had been sent to the region by the city's mayor to rescue abductees. The boy died just eight days after his return to Philadelphia. Hickey was comfortable purchasing an abducted free African American and surely would have been willing to do so early in the 1800s, when abductees were already being carried to the Deep South.[82] Kidnappings of free people of color, slave stealing, and other illicit practices were ongoing if small parts of the internal slave trade.[83]

In the aftermath of the sugar and cotton revolutions, enslavers and merchants were bringing enslaved people from other parts of the United States into the lower Mississippi valley by a variety of means and in increasing numbers. What is most striking about the trade during this period is its lack of formal structure. Enslaved Americans were not usually brought to the region by dedicated "slave traders" but rather by a diverse group of actors who typically engaged in slave trading as a side venture or to fulfill their own labor wants. Most of these opportunistic slave traders would have considered themselves planters or merchants, not slave traders. Structures to service the trade were certainly being created. Planters who traveled east discovered that dedicated slave traders existed on the East Coast to service those who appeared there with money to purchase enslaved people.[84] Trading small numbers of people down the western river system had become an annual activity for men on the make, and some, like the Franklin brothers, made the trade a regular business, although, tellingly, they often had a hard time getting paid for the people they sold. Charles Morgan and his confederates had created a structured, if illicit and transitory, business for trading enslaved New Jerseyans to the region. Still, in these years, the internal slave trade was more of an unorganized, desperate scramble for enslaved labor or the profits from their sale than an organized business.[85] Still, by taking part in that desperate scramble, local elites and planters were actors in the development of the internal slave trade and its replacement of the international trade.

By the 1810s, enslaved Americans were the most important stream of enslaved people being brought into the region. Unfortunately, their experiences are difficult to excavate. No contemporary writer recorded his impression of how they were treated on arrival or how they dealt with the trauma of being separated from their family and community. Solomon Northup, an African American from New York who was kidnapped and sold into slavery on Louisiana sugar and cotton plantations in the 1840s, gives insight into the dynamics that must have been at play. In his narrative, Northup related the experiences of the enslaved people he met. Most memorable was the affecting story of Eliza, who experienced the terrible trauma of her children being sold away from her in New Orleans. According to Northup, she continued to mourn for her children until she was "a thin shadow of her former self" and died miserably, implicitly as a result of beatings from her final enslaver. As for Northup himself, while he formed positive relationships with other enslaved people and even some whites, unsurprisingly he continued to grieve for the loss of his family and continued to search for ways to get back to them.[86] At the same time, the fact that so many enslaved Americans migrated with their enslavers, especially in this early period of the internal slave trade, might have complicated enslaved people's experiences, as many moved with family and friends, creating a situation that would likely have been less alienating than that experienced by those sold to new enslavers.[87] Still, while experiences of forced migration would not have been uniform, they would rarely have been positive.

Evidence from the East Coast illustrates the malevolent effects this forced migration had on enslaved Americans. During the Early Republic, enslaved Americans were aware that the lower Mississippi valley, with its cotton and sugar plantations, was a place to be dreaded. Adam Hodgson, an Englishman who traveled in North America between 1819 and 1821, made a habit of conversing with the enslaved people he met. According to him, "The very name [of New-Orleans] seems to strike terror in the slaves and free Negroes of the middle States," driving some to suicide to avoid being sent there. He also related the rumor among some enslaved and free African Americans in Virginia that the American Colonization Society (which was dedicated to ending slavery through colonizing all African Americans out of the United States) was a cover for sending enslaved people to New Orleans.[88] Charles Ball, who grew up in Maryland and was sold to a South Carolina cotton planter in 1805, recalled that he had considered suicide while being moved south due to his dread of cotton plantations. He also wrote "that the slaves who are driven to the south often destroy themselves."[89] Soon after the sugar and cotton revolutions, enslaved Americans had learned to dread the Second Middle Passage and the cotton and sugar plantations of the Deep South.[90]

As had enslaved Africans, enslaved Americans appear to have reacted to their forced movement to the lower Mississippi valley by attempting to escape from their new enslavers. Between 1806 and 1810, 19 percent of enslaved people in Louisiana runaway slave advertisements were Americans (see fig. 2), while over the same period only 5 percent of adult enslaved people in estate inventories were. The proportion of enslaved American escapees increased rapidly over the next fifteen years to 39 percent between 1816 and 1820. The proportion of enslaved Americans in estate inventories, after peaking at 5 percent between 1806 and 1810, stagnated at around 4 percent during the 1810s (see fig. 1).[91] Enslaved Americans' presence in these advertisements suggests a grim situation for enslaved American (and a worrisome one for enslavers). Either enslaved Americans were attempting to escape at a very high rate or their absences presented unique concerns. Some of the advertisements suggest that enslavers were anxious that enslaved Americans might permanently escape from enslavement, a worry rarely expressed in advertisements for other enslaved people. The enslaver of Bob (escaped from Pointe Coupee) suspected that he had escaped onto a "Kentucky boat" bound for New Orleans.[92] The enslaver of Jack (originally from Baltimore) believed he was attempting to return there.[93] Enslavers often suspected that enslaved Americans from the Atlantic Coast, Kentucky, and Tennessee would attempt to return to those places, either by boat or foot, presumably to reunite with family and friends.

For the enslaved the Second Middle Passage was an immense tragedy, disrupting and destroying familial and social connections and forcing them to spend their lives laboring in the harsh world of sugar and cotton. However, for the region's elites it was a triumphant achievement. Planters and merchants had once again shown their ability to innovate by developing (in concert with enslavers and merchants on the East Coast) a slave trade system that could replace the international slave trade, providing them with the labor they demanded to produce profits via sugar and cotton.

Besides the traumas and dislocation enslavers and merchants imposed on enslaved Africans, Americans, and Caribbean Creoles by moving them to the region, forcibly moved people would also have had to make new lives in an increasingly diverse and potentially alien free and enslaved population. The influx of enslaved peoples into the region during the late eighteenth and early nineteenth centuries dramatically changed the composition of the region's African and African-descended populations. By the 1770s, the region's African-descended population had, after decades of low importations of enslaved people, become largely creolized (i.e., born in the region and having an Afro-Louisianan culture). This changed beginning in the 1780s as large imports re-Africanized parts of the region.[94] While more difficult to date, following the sugar and cotton revolutions other parts of the region became "Americanized" because of enslaver migration and the growth of the internal slave trade. In addition, throughout the region, the enslaved population became more diverse with people from Africa, the Caribbean, and the United States mixing with creolized populations already present.

As a result of this diversity, the enslaved had to learn to live in a world of strangers, many of whom were culturally alien. They developed new and unique cultures that were different than the region's prior African American cultures and distinct from the African American cultures of the rest of the United States. Diversity was also important to enslavers (and other whites) whose enslaved labor forces consisted, at least in part, of strangers who were also often culturally alien. For francophones enslaved Americans, and not just Africans, would have fallen into the latter category. This alien population presented enslavers with challenges of communication and control and produced a great deal of worry and even fear in the free population.

Re-Africanization began during the indigo and tobacco booms of the late 1780s and was reinforced and continued after the sugar and cotton revolutions. Prior to the surge in the slave trade in the 1780s, the lower Mississippi valley's enslaved population contained very few Africans after decades of low importations (see fig. 1). This reversed in the 1780s as Africans became, at the very least, a large minority of the enslaved population in areas where origins were recorded. An appreciable African component of the enslaved population persisted into the 1810s in parts of the region when 17 percent of adult enslaved people appearing in estate inventories were still listed as Africans. During the late 1700s and early 1800s, the lower Mississippi valley's African-descended population was easily the most Africanized of any in North America.[95] While Africans were brought to all parts of the region (recall the sale of African enslaved people in Natchez in the late 1780s), they were likely most important in the sugar areas around New Orleans, the main port of entry for Africans.[96]

Americanization happened in some parts of the region following the sugar and cotton revolutions. In the areas where officials regularly recorded origins in estate inventories (New Orleans, the German Coast, and Pointe Coupee), enslaved Americans were an increasing but always small presence in the early 1800s (see fig. 1). Enslaved Americans were far more common in frontier areas settled by Anglo-Americans in both Louisiana and Mississippi, areas dominated by cotton cultivation. These areas saw dramatic free and enslaved population increases throughout the period, well beyond natural increase. Considering that the enslaved populations created had nearly equal numbers of men and women (meaning that the African slave trade, which delivered to the region more than two men for each woman, was not a significant contributor), the enslaved people rapidly populating these regions were coming from the rest of the United States.[97] For example, in 1820 Rapides Parish, located on the Red River and with a rapidly growing enslaved population, had a ratio of 1.15 adult enslaved men for each adult enslaved woman. The annual increase of the enslaved population of Rapides Parish between 1810 and 1820 had been 12.4 percent, well above any reasonable level of natural increase.[98] During the early 1800s, the cotton plantations and farms of Mississippi and Louisiana depended more heavily on enslaved Americans than did the sugar plantations in the countryside around New Orleans, which still depended heavily on enslaved Africans into the 1810s. Americanization and re-Africanization occurred in parallel in different parts of the region. At the same time, enslaved people from all backgrounds ended up throughout the region. Enslaved Americans ended up working on sugar plantations, Africans ended up working on cotton plantations, and Caribbean Creoles ended up working on both.

Still, discussing enslaved Africans, Americans, and Caribbean Creoles as groups is problematic and gives a misleading sense of the dynamics at play in the region. These groups were not uniform but rather diverse. Enslaved Caribbean Creoles included Jamaicans, Haitians, Cubans, and individuals from other Caribbean islands. Even enslaved regional Creoles were not uniform with enslaved people referred to as Creole who had been born in the francophone areas of the southern parts of the lower Mississippi valley, the anglophone areas around Natchez, and even the Illinois country. These people would not have shared the same formative experiences and, in some cases, would not even have spoken the same languages. Still, in most cases, local references to Creoles meant francophones born in the southern parts of the lower Mississippi valley.

Unsurprisingly, captives brought from Africa came from a wide variety of ethnic origins. Louisianans typically recorded not just that enslaved people were Africans but also which ethnic group they were thought to belong to. Of course, one should be skeptical about the designations given by Euro-Americans and Europeans, who would have been deeply ignorant of Africa itself, to Africans. These origins did not necessarily have a direct relationship to the self-identities of enslaved Africans, which were themselves moving targets in a world in constant flux. Still, many of these designations likely reflected communities with shared cultural features that would have meaningfully structured the lives of enslaved Africans.[99] The large number of designations that appear in the documents suggests a great deal of diversity. From 1781 to 1820 dozens of different ethnicities or places of origin were given for Africans in estate inventories.[100]

However, enslaved Africans were not a mass of relatively small ethnic groups of equal importance.[101] For example, Africans labeled "Manding" (who would have come from Senegambia) were relatively important throughout the period, with 10–15 percent of Africans with origins in this group. However, one group stands out from the others: the Congolese. From around 20 percent of enslaved Africans in the 1780s, the proportion of enslaved Congolese peaked at over 40 percent at the end of the period.[102] The slave trade must have been preferentially bringing captives from West Central Africa in its final years. While outside of official documents and runaway slave advertisements the region's residents almost never commented on the ethnicities of the people they enslaved, they must have recognized the changing makeup of their labor forces and the increasing importance of Congolese. A rare exception to this silence suggests that they did. In 1803 a Frenchman wrote a description of Louisiana that included a vocabulary of Congolese words intended to be used by French immigrant planters to communicate with enslaved Congolese.[103]

The other major group being brought into the region in response to the commodity booms was enslaved Americans. Enslaved Americans entering the region were also not uniform in their origins. Between 1781 and 1820, of enslaved Americans given a specific origin in Louisiana documents, 13 percent came from Kentucky or Tennessee, 26 percent from the Carolinas or Georgia, and 6 percent from the Mid-Atlantic or New England. However, over this period, the largest contingent, at 55 percent, came from Virginia or Maryland. In fact, one trend that stands out over the period is the increasing importance of enslaved Virginians and Marylanders over the first two decades of the nineteenth century (from 35 percent of enslaved Americans given a specific origin in the 1780s to 67 percent in the 1810s).[104] The importance of the relatively recently colonized Kentucky and Tennessee also became greater with their share approaching nearly 20 percent by the 1810s.[105] The internal slave trade was increasingly focused on the Upper South, the region that would be the dominant source of the trade throughout the antebellum period. The diversity among enslaved Americans might not have been as important culturally as that among enslaved Africans and Caribbean Creoles, considering that so many came from areas (the Chesapeake, Kentucky, and Tennessee) that shared similar cultures. Still, enslaved people in the Atlantic states were not uniform in their regional cultures. Those from the Carolinas and Georgia would have had a distinct culture from those elsewhere, thus adding further to the lower Mississippi valley's complex cultural gumbo.[106]

A large amount of ethnic and regional diversity was introduced into the African and African-descended population before and during the sugar and cotton revolutions. As a result, enslaved people forcibly brought into the region were thrown into living situations surrounded by foreign and very different people, both enslaved and free. Even those from similar backgrounds were often strangers to one another. One can surmise that this would have often created alienation of individuals and even conflict. Still, enslaved people brought into the region found ways to deal with their new living situation by accommodating themselves to the dominant cultures, learning to interact effectively with their peers from different origins and seeking out individuals who shared their ethnic and cultural background.[107]

Runaway slave advertisements placed in the region's newspapers provide a window into these dynamics. For example, in 1802, four enslaved people escaped from Alexandre Harang's sugar plantation near New Orleans. Harang suspected that they were trying to escape to the other side of "the lake," most likely Lake Pontchartrain, as they had taken a boat. In the advertisement he took out to find them, Harang gave their names and descriptions. Pierre-Marc was thirty years old, five feet six inches tall, "well-built," and worked as a sawyer and carpenter. Janvier was twenty-eight to thirty years old, five feet four to five inches tall, "overweight," and had "red" skin. Thomas was thirty to thirty-two years old, five feet two inches tall, "big," and "very black." Jeannette was aged twenty-five to twenty-six years old, "slender and thin" with a "long figure," "black," and with "cuts in her skin like the negroes of her country."[108]

As this last descriptor reveals, Jeannette was an African. So were the other three. Harang claimed that Pierre-Marc and Thomas were Senegalese, Janvier was a Nar, and Jeannette was a Nago. They had come from diverse African backgrounds, but in Louisiana had attempted to escape together. Harang's description of Pierre-Marc, along with their taking of a boat, might give a clue as to their goal. According to the advertisement, Pierre-Marc spoke Spanish, English, and French, an impressive linguistic achievement. Even more strikingly, he spoke Mobilian, a trade pidgin spoken along the Gulf Coast among Native Americans and European traders.[109] Pierre-Marc must have already been in the region for some time and taken part in the trade with Native Americans. As such, he probably had an abnormally large amount of knowledge of the region's geography. Perhaps he planned to take his fellow escapees into Native American country and attempt to use his linguistic and cultural skills to find some sort of freedom there.[110]

This group illustrates how enslaved people, once in the lower Mississippi valley, adapted to their new lives and communities. To be so linguistically astute, Pierre-Marc would have had to learn a great deal about the world to which he had been forcibly brought. Even his fellow escapees, almost certainly not as cosmopolitan as he, had put aside their ethnic differences to attempt to escape together as part of a new community of people of African descent. While the region's new African and African-descended residents were adapting to their new world, they did not accept without challenge its power structures. Like enslaved people throughout the Americas, they adapted and resisted at the same time, a fact that caused concern for whites who exploited and lived among this alien population. Alexandre Harang must have wondered in what other ways the strangers he enslaved might be conspiring against him. Certainly, such thoughts must have occurred to him nine years later when a man he enslaved named Atys attempted to strike him with a stick and then stabbed another white man.[111] While the story of Pierre-Marc and his confederates is particularly striking, similar stories of enslaved people from throughout the Atlantic World learning new languages and escaping alone or with others appeared regularly in the region's newspapers.

Still, the possibilities of linguistic accommodation and cross-ethnic solidarity likely had their limits, suggesting the very real possibility for alienation among the enslaved. For example, while Pierre-Marc and many other enslaved people became skilled in English, French, and Spanish (32 percent of Africans appearing in runaway slave advertisements in Louisiana were said to speak at least a little of one of the languages), many other enslaved people appear to have, at least at the moment they escaped, not learned the languages spoken by their enslavers. Some enslavers, perhaps pointedly, mentioned in runaway slave advertisements that the people they enslaved had not learned the region's languages. For example, in the sample of runaway slave advertisements from Louisiana, thirteen escapees were said to speak English poorly and another twenty-two were said to speak French poorly. In addition, sixty-two enslaved Americans were listed as speaking only English, a likely alienating fact since many of the escapees lived in the largely francophone region around New Orleans.[112]

Of course, enslaved African and African-descended people had or were developing ways of communicating in their communities other than the dominant European languages. At times, albeit rarely, these other means of communication were referenced in runaway slave advertisements. Rarely, whites recognized that enslaved people were communicating in French Creole, a language mixing elements of French, African languages, and elements of other languages as well. In 1811, a Congolese woman named Rozette was said to speak Creole French.[113] That same year Pauline, from the Windward Islands, was also said to speak Creole French.[114] At other times, the advertisements make clear that durable networks of communication in African languages existed and were even utilized by whites. For example, in 1807, the city jail of New Orleans advertised that two Congolese men had been placed in the city jail. They "speak only the language of their country." However, the advertisement also included that they "say they came here in the same vessel; that they belong to different masters, and reside on Sugar plantations, situate below the city on the right bank of the river."[115] These two Congolese men had said a great deal for only being able to speak an African language. Most likely those running the city jail had enlisted an enslaved person who spoke both French and Congolese as a translator. These advertisements, while unusual, show that the region's diverse slave communities were both continuing to use their native languages and developing or adopting the means to communicate across cultural and ethnic lines within the slave community.

However, this example of enslaved Congolese continuing to communicate predominantly in their native language suggests that we should not exaggerate the potential for cross-ethnic solidarity. Intraethnic solidarity likely came far more easily to enslaved people living in the region's diverse populations. For example, instances of cross-ethnic escapes were rare. Escaping alone or with people from a similar background was far more common. In 1816 "six American negroes, not speaking a word of French" escaped from a plantation in Acadia.[116] In 1804, two unnamed Congolese escaped together from Harang's plantation.[117] And, of course, those two Congolese men who could not speak any European language ended up in jail together in 1807. In fact, an analysis of groups appearing in Louisiana runaway slave advertisements shows that mixed group were a minority (six or eight of thirty-five groups depending on how one defines ethnicity).[118]

Runaway advertisements suggest that the diverse members of the region's enslaved population reacted to their situation in a variety of ways including partial accommodation to the dominant culture or continued aloofness. Some enslaved people also found ways to create cross-cultural communication and accommodation. However, enslaved people usually preferred individuals from a similar background when attempting to escape, which suggests that cross-cultural accommodations had their limits. Enslaved people usually preferred to deal with diversity in the slave community by searching out individuals who shared their own background. Scholars have shown that, in New Orleans, when possible, members of the same African ethnicity tended to seek each other out and form social and fictive kinship bonds.[119]

Driven by surging importations of enslaved people from throughout the Atlantic World, increasing diversity was a central fact of life for the region's enslaved people in the late 1700s and early 1800s. Members of these diverse communities developed ways to deal with their new and potentially alienating lives. Enslaved people new to the region were not typically completely isolated among an alien population. Many enslaved people shared ethnicities and languages and sought one another out. Many enslaved people were also learning the dominant languages of the region and using them to communicate with one another (as well as the free population). Finally, enslaved people were forming and learning Creole languages that allowed them to communicate and create new African American communities or interact with the ones that already existed in the region. However, diversity was a complicated factor in the lives of the enslaved. Many enslaved people, likely used to culturally homogenous communities or at least ones with limited and predictable diversity, probably experienced it as a negative fact of their lives. While little evidence of this has survived, enslaved people from different backgrounds probably came into conflict with one another, perhaps sometimes violently.[120] However, enslaved people did, by necessity, find ways to mitigate the potentially negative effects of diversity within the enslaved population and began the process of forming new African American communities out of that diversity.[121]

In the years after the sugar and cotton revolutions, planters and merchants in the lower Mississippi valley scrambled to bring enslaved people to the region to man the region's plantations and farms. They, typically successfully, fought attempts by the region's governments to prevent or regulate the influx. They covertly ignored what bans were instituted when it served their purposes. They brought enslaved people from all three of the sources available to them: Africa, the Caribbean, and the United States. Africa dominated prior to 1808 but was increasingly eclipsed in the 1810s by the United States. In fact, the rise of the internal slave trade and Anglo-American enslaver migration was the most important divergence during this period from trends that had long predated the sugar and cotton revolutions. Enslaved Americans went from being a minor addition to the population to the main source of new labor. Elites had used their extraregional connections to successfully direct a small proportion of the international slave trade to the region and participate in the development of a system, the internal slave trade, that first complemented and then replaced the international slave trade.

These trades and enslaver migration transformed a creolized enslaved population into one that was Africanized, Americanized, and diverse. Enslaved people from the region and those being brought to the region experienced massive and traumatic disruptions to their lives. They dealt with these disruptions by embracing old and new communities. Many of the most recently arrived reacted by trying to escape. Overall, this entire experience would have been immensely disruptive and traumatic. Yet, by necessity Africans and African Americans persevered.

In the next chapter, we will turn to one of the most direct results of the creation of this large, diverse, and restive enslaved population: the 1811 German Coast Insurrection. Enslavers and other elites had worried for years that enslaved people, encouraged by their numbers and driven by resentment at their treatment, would rise in rebellion. Hundreds of them did exactly that in 1811 in the largest slave rebellion ever to happen in North America and in what would be the greatest challenge to the region's slave system until the Civil War. Ironically, this challenge would be interpreted by the region's elites as proving that their worries had been overblown, and they would, in fact, be able to hold on and keep control of and profit from their lucrative system indefinitely.

5

ENSLAVERS TRIUMPHANT

The Blacks have been taught an important lesson—their weakness.

—Territory of Orleans House of Representatives, 1811

On the night of January 8, 1811, hundreds of enslaved people enacted the worst nightmare of their enslavers: they rose in rebellion. The rebellion began on Manuel Andry's sugar plantation, located in St. John the Baptist Parish, just upriver from St. Charles Parish on the German Coast. According to Andry, a group of enslaved people had attempted "to assassinate [Andry] by the stroke of an axe" and "ferociously murdered" his son.[1] By the end of the next day, the rebels had marched over twenty-one miles downriver, as far as the Fortier plantation in Orleans Parish, just upriver from New Orleans. During this march, they had collected a force estimated at between two hundred and five hundred people and at least some weapons while burning plantation houses and scattering free and enslaved refugees into the swamps and city. On January 9, enslavers knew what it was to fear the people they enslaved.[2]

Transformations in the region's slave society over the previous two decades (a surging, alienated enslaved population; the escalating labor demands on plantations and farms; and a particularly brutal slave regime built on violently intimidating a restive enslaved population) driven by the cotton and sugar revolutions came to a head in the German Coast Insurrection of 1811, the largest slave revolt ever to occur in North America.[3] While the precise goals and motives of the revolt will probably always remain shrouded in mystery, it was the clearest expression of enslaved people's dissidence from enslavers' worldview and their most direct attempt to overthrow or undermine it. They failed to do either. The rebellion was easily defeated by an ad hoc force of eighty men, and the region's elite followed that defeat with an orgy of judicial and extrajudicial violence aimed at the enslaved people who had dared to rise against them. In the end, the revolt's results showed that, by 1811, the social and economic organization of the region as an export-oriented slave society was not fragile but rather resilient, with the ability to protect itself from challenges.

The lower Mississippi valley's elites recognized this resilience. Ironically, they interpreted the revolt as a ratification of their region's social order. Rather than reacting to the revolt with fear that the system was in danger of complete collapse (as they had after the uncovering of the 1795 Pointe Coupee Conspiracy), elites in the region reacted with triumphalism and exemplary violence. They made an example of the rebels with summary executions, torture, judicial executions, and the grisly display of bodies and body parts. They rewarded enslaved people who had remained loyal and hence shown, at least in the minds of enslavers, that not all the enslaved opposed the region's social organization or, at the very least, were too intimidated to resist it. They crowed about their triumph and how it showed their society could keep their restive enslaved population under control. Finally, they took no actions like those of the Spanish government after the Pointe Coupee Conspiracy. They did nothing to cut off or even regulate the importation of people via the internal slave trade, and they made no changes to the region's slave laws. The lesson of the German Coast Insurrection was that force would be enough to keep the region's enslaved population under control. No one would be allowed to challenge the profits that sugar and cotton had produced for the region's elite.

Before turning to the German Coast Insurrection and its aftermath, it is worth taking stock of the changes the lower Mississippi valley had undergone in the sixteen years leading up to the rebellion. The central argument of this book is that the adoption of sugar and cotton rehabilitated the region's slave system and propelled it toward the boisterous second slavery of the Antebellum South ruled over by a class of self-confident planters and merchants. After 1795, cotton and sugar proved to be prosperous (excepting a few years when international events intervened), leading to boom times in the lower Mississippi valley.

Cotton was, for the most part, a very profitable crop, with the typical estimate of the annual returns per enslaved person working it being around $200.[4] Excepting slumps during the Embargo of 1807 and the War of 1812, cotton prices remained relatively high throughout the first twenty-five years following its adoption.[5] Around the time of the Louisiana Purchase, the New Orleans merchant James Pitot wrote that cotton meant that "ease then finally took the place of want among a great many planters, and wealth soon banished financial embarrassment and privations among several others."[6] Quality issues also receded in importance and, if anything, the region's cotton came to be seen as a superior type of short-staple cotton. For example, in 1807, the Natchez cotton planter Winthrop Sargent, the former governor of the Mississippi Territory, received a letter from a Liverpool merchant claiming that manufacturers were surprised that it was "Bourbon Seed" cotton (the fuzzy seed type of cotton that was lower quality than smooth-seed sea island cotton) considering its high quality. He claimed that "there is no description of Cotton which comes to this market more saleable than New Orleans."[7] This was not true, as sea island cotton continued to demand higher prices. However, it still must have been music to Sargent's ears, as he had been intimately involved in early efforts to improve the quality of Mississippi's cotton.

Sugar planters were also earning large revenues from their plantations. In fact, their revenues outstripped those of cotton planters and proved more resilient. One booster claimed in a newspaper article widely reprinted throughout the country that sugar production returned an annual revenue of $350 per enslaved person. This booster even listed the number of enslaved people and revenues for eleven sugar planters, figures that bolstered his claims about the lucrative nature of sugar. The author claimed that these figures showed "the superior advantages enjoyed by the planters established on the Mississippi, over those of any other part of the union, or perhaps of any other country."[8] They also showed "the superior advantages" of sugar plantations over other plantations on the Mississippi itself.

The commodity boom did not only lead to economic prosperity for many free residents; it also had striking emotional effects as well. The attitude of many planters and merchants transformed from anxiety and despair in the mid-1790s to jubilation and excitement just a few years later. Much of the evidence for this is retrospective, as individuals looked back at their earlier problems from the perch of returned prosperity. However, this transition can be seen as it happened in Pointe Coupee planter and merchant Julien Poydras's business letters. Between 1798, during the depths of his economic troubles, and 1800, once he had fully committed to cotton cultivation, the tone of these letters dramatically changed. In the earlier letters, Poydras was often preoccupied by the (dismal) prospects of his indigo crops and his other business problems. In a few of the letters, the tone was very emotional, with Poydras musing on the base nature of man or his disillusionment with life. For example, in a letter to his brother, he wrote an almost poetic rumination on life:

> The aged soul is tired and withered by the reverses, troubles and cruel experiences of men: it becomes hardened and never smiles on idle dreams of fancy, which always disappear at the moment you believe you can catch them. It is no longer the time of happy ignorance nor the time when desires and seducing illusions surmount all the obstacles which might be in the road of a blissful imagination; like the believe [sic] that all is well in the perfumed air of flowers, which really is only a trap to hide the thorns.[9]

Poydras did not have a very positive outlook on life during the economic crisis of the 1790s.

However, after he switched to cotton cultivation, Poydras's letters became optimistic, even exuberant, focused on the profits to be made. In a spring 1800 letter, he wrote that, once his cotton gins were built, "we shall speak no more of credit, only of good opportunities."[10] In another letter he tried to convince his correspondent to switch his plantation's crop to cotton by detailing its economic benefits. A Madame Bourgeai "used twenty pickers and made 5,000 piastres." However, even more could be made. "The Englishmen [i.e., Anglo-Americans] on the other side [of the Mississippi] made even more, however their negroes are better pickers than ours." He exhorted his correspondent to "wake up to this work, think it over and you shall find profit."[11] With cotton, the tone of Poydras's letters had gone from despondent to electric with excitement. Although retrospective and self-serving, Étienne Boré's 1803 narrative about his adoption of sugar has a similar narrative arc.[12] Sugar and cotton rehabilitated both the pocketbooks and spirits of enslavers.

The opportunity to profit directly or indirectly from cotton and sugar sparked rapid growth in the region's populations, transforming it from an imperial backwater to the rapidly expanding western anchor of the American Republic's Deep South.[13] The region saw a large increase in both voluntary and forced immigration in the late 1700s and early 1800s that transformed the region from one that, in 1785, had a relatively small non–Native American population of under thirty thousand people centered on New Orleans to one that had, in 1810, a sizable non–Native American population of over one hundred thousand people that had spread throughout the region.[14] The two main forms this immigration took, voluntary immigration of free people and the forced immigration of enslaved people, were fundamentally different yet intimately connected phenomena. The voluntary immigration of free people was driven by the reasonable hope that moving to the region would increase one's economic prospects. The forced immigration of enslaved people, discussed in the previous chapter, was largely driven by the hope that moving enslaved people to the region would increase the economic prospect of whoever was forcing the movement, be it someone who planned to sell the enslaved person or to exploit their labor. These experiences were fundamentally different but connected through the cotton and sugar revolutions.

Two obvious questions to ask would be who the people were who were moving to the region, and, in the case of free migrants, why they had done so. As we saw in the previous chapter, we can say a surprising amount about who the enslaved people in the region were, or at least where they had been brought from. A similarly detailed examination of the white population is not possible. Still, using the evidence available to us, we can give a general outline of the origins of free immigrants. They were a diverse group. Julien Poydras, and Jean Baptiste Riviere were both French. Daniel Clark Jr. was Irish. John McDonogh, a merchant and planter in New Orleans, was from Baltimore. John Mills, a planter near Baton Rouge, was from New York. Charles Morgan, a planter in Pointe Coupee

Parish and slave smuggler, was from New Jersey. Joseph Erwin, a sugar and cotton planter and slave trader, was from Tennessee. Thousands of migrants from St. Domingue entered the region in the two decades after the Haitian Revolution. Such examples could be continued ad nauseum. The region attracted immigrants from most of western Europe, probably all the American states, and throughout the Caribbean. Still, one area served as the main "hearth" for migrants to the region during this period. Americans from the older slave states on the Atlantic seaboard and the newer slave states of Tennessee and Kentucky were moving into the region in large numbers.[15] The group was particularly important, as they brought at least some of the people they enslaved with them, providing labor and influencing the dynamics of the slave community.

Thousands of free whites poured into the region. In 1785, the free white population was just over twelve thousand. By 1810, it was nearly fifty thousand in the areas tallied in that year's federal census.[16] These white migrants were mostly men, reflecting the boom-time atmosphere. In 1810, according to the federal census, the region had 1.5 adult white men for every adult white woman, a striking imbalance in a region colonized by Europeans nearly a century before. Some areas were even more imbalanced, such as Concordia Parish, just across the river from Natchez, which had a ratio of 2 to 1.[17] By 1820, the imbalances had become even more pronounced, with the areas included in the 1810 census having 1.7 adult white men for every adult white woman.[18] While these imbalances paled in comparison to those in later western mining towns or early Jamestown, reflecting the preexisting settlements and the fact that families were migrating to the region, these numbers do suggest something of a "boom" atmosphere of men on the make pouring into the region to profit directly or indirectly from sugar and cotton.

Unsurprisingly, considering the sugar and cotton revolutions, most of these men came to the region to make money. Booster literature emanating from the region focused almost exclusively on the economic advantages of the area when enticing migrants, reflecting the opportunities created by the sugar and cotton revolutions.[19] Letters sent by those migrants, often trying to convince others to join them, also took economics as the main, and perhaps only, lure for potential migrants. For example, over the course of several years, the Kentucky transplant Nathaniel Cox urged his acquaintance, Gabriel Lewis, to relocate to the region. To convince Lewis, Cox made a nakedly economic argument. Cox argued that Lewis's capital would be put to better use in the lower Mississippi valley than in Kentucky, where it was in danger of decline.[20] He urged him to bring his main form of capital, the people he enslaved, to the region. Once there, "they would certainly make you a hansome [sic] fortune in ten years by the cultivation of cotton."[21] Cox's arguments were typical of those made (both publicly and privately) to attract free migrants to the region.[22] White men came to make money, ideally via enslaved people's labor and typically via cotton and sugar.

Of course, that population of enslaved people was also expanding rapidly in this period resulting from the final years of the international slave trade, enslaver migration, and the expansion of the internal slave trade. The number of enslaved people in the region grew from just over fifteen thousand enslaved people in 1785 to nearly fifty thousand in 1810 in the areas of the region tallied in that year's federal census.[23] In the rural areas, the enslaved population grew, both in absolute terms and relative to the free population. For example, between 1805 (the first year with census data) and 1810, the enslaved population of Mississippi's Jefferson County (located in cotton country) grew from 972 people to 1,694 people and from 38 percent of the population to 43 percent of it. By 1820, the enslaved population had grown to 3,635 people and 53 percent of the population.[24] Between 1804 and 1810, the enslaved population of St. Charles Parish (located in sugar country) grew from 1,582 people to 2,321 people and from 66 percent of the population to 71 percent of it. By 1820, the enslaved population had grown to 2,989 people, or 77 percent of the population.[25]

Throughout the region, enslaved people were being concentrated in larger slaveholdings. In St. Charles Parish the proportion of households that enslaved more than twenty people increased from 18 percent in 1804 to 26 percent in 1810 and 38 percent in 1820 (see fig. 3). The average number of people enslaved per household increased from 12.7 in 1804 to 17.4 in 1810 and 26.5 in 1820. Increasingly, enslaved people could expect to live on larger slaveholdings (see fig. 4). In 1804, 30 percent of enslaved people lived on plantations with more than fifty enslaved people, in 1810, 51 percent did, and in 1820 66 percent did. Not a single enslaved person had lived on a plantation with one hundred or more enslaved people in 1804; in 1810, 9 percent did, and in 1820 23 percent did.[26]

In cotton-growing Jefferson County, concentration was much less severe but still occurring. The proportion of households that enslaved more than twenty people increased from 4 percent in 1805 to 7.5 percent in 1810 and 9 percent in 1820 (see fig. 3). The average number of enslaved people per household also increased, from 3.4 in 1805 to 4.0 in 1810 and 6.9 in 1820. The county also saw an increase in the proportion of

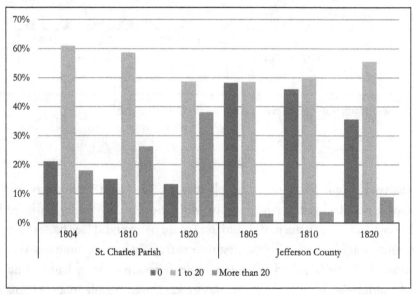

Fig. 3. Proportion of households by slaveholding size

Sources: Figures calculated using the 1804 St. Charles Parish territorial census schedules, the 1805 and 1810 Jefferson County territorial census schedules, and the 1810 and 1820 federal census schedules. For St. Charles Parish's 1804 census schedules see "General Census of St. Charles Parish, 1804," Conrad, *St. Charles,* 389–407. For St. Charles Parish's 1810 census schedules, see *Population Schedules of the Third Census of the United States, 1810, Louisiana,* reel 10, 423–30. For Jefferson County's 1805 and 1810 census schedules, see the Mississippi, US, State and Territorial Census Collection, 1792–1866. For St. Charles Parish's 1820 census schedules see *Population Schedules of the Fourth Census of the United States, 1820, Louisiana,* reel 30, 67–72. For Jefferson County's 1820 census schedules see *Population Schedules of the Fourth Census of the United States, 1820, Mississippi,* reel 58, 49–60.

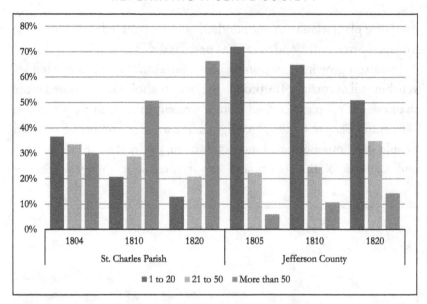

Fig. 4. Proportion of enslaved people by slaveholding size

Sources: See sources for figure 3.

enslaved people living on larger plantations. In 1805, 28 percent of enslaved people lived on plantations with more than twenty enslaved
people, in 1810 35 percent did, and in 1820 49 percent did (see fig. 4). The
county was also seeing for the first time extremely large plantations with
more than one hundred enslaved people. Jefferson County had had no
plantations with more than one hundred enslaved people in any census
before 1820. In 1820, it had two with 158 and 101 enslaved people, accounting for 7 percent of all enslaved people in the county.[27]

Overall, the most striking commonality between St. Charles Parish
and Jefferson County was rapid growth of the number of enslaved people
in absolute terms and per household. Still, the details of this growth were
quite different. In St. Charles Parish, slave ownership was rapidly concen-
trating (with nearly two-thirds of all St. Charles Parish's enslaved people
living on plantations with more than fifty enslaved people by 1820),
whereas in Jefferson County more gradual concentration was occurring,
with those enslaving fewer than twenty-one people continuing to enslave most enslaved people (if only barely) through 1820. This difference
is unsurprising considering the different economics of cotton and sugar.

Cotton could be grown productively by anyone, whereas sugar could not be. At the same time sugar was far more profitable than cotton. While concentration of slaveholdings happened throughout the regions, these two features caused more rapid concentration of wealth in sugar regions than cotton regions.

As the profits from sugar and cotton, the robust migration of free whites, and the growth (and concentration) of the enslaved population illustrate, by the early 1800s, the region's elites had put behind them the economic crisis of the mid-1790s. However, that did not mean that they were wholly at ease. Many of them worried about the stability of the society they had created, a society that depended on the rapid importation of enslaved people, people whom they knew were not the content dependents of antebellum slaveholder mythmaking. In 1806, territory of Orleans governor William C. C. Claiborne wrote Thomas Jefferson that the continued advance of sugar production raised the possibility of an "insurrection on the part of that unfortunate race of men in which we are likely to abound."[28] The next year, the Baton Rouge area cotton planter John Mills wrote that "the day is fast approaching when the whites will fall a sacrifice to the Blacks."[29] Elites knew that enslaved people were a threat to their control and profits. In 1811, these worries would be proven at least partially justified by the German Coast Insurrection.

The German Coast Insurrection was rooted in the conditions of the rapidly growing population of enslaved people in the lower Mississippi valley. As should already be clear, those conditions were harsh and grim. We have already discussed two factors determining these conditions: a surging, alienated enslaved population and the grueling labor demands on the region's sugar and cotton plantations and farms. Connected to these factors but also inherent to any slave system was the resistance of enslaved people to enslavers' demands and the use of physical coercion (i.e., violence) by enslavers to overcome that resistance. Violence and conflict were central to slave systems in the Americas (and elsewhere). The former slave and abolitionist Olaudah Equiano defined slavery as a "state of war."[30] The notion that slavery was characterized by constant conflict and violence (i.e., was a "state of war") was accepted by residents of the lower Mississippi valley. For example, the cotton planter John

Mills described his relationship with the people he enslaved as a constant and calculated violent struggle for control and dominance that he expected enslaved people might well win in the long run via sheer numbers and resentment.[31] He and many other enslavers (as shown by their reaction to the German Coast Insurrection) certainly would have answered affirmatively Equiano's question, "Are you not hourly in dread of an insurrection?"[32]

Enslavers' dread arose from the fact that enslaved people did not passively accept their demands and resisted or at least evaded them through various actions including work slowdowns, sabotage, escaping, and even violence.[33] For example, enslaved people regularly attempted to escape from enslavers. The motivations to escape varied and could include avoidance of punishment, unwillingness to work, escape to freedom, and escape back to wherever the enslaved person had friends and family.[34] Regardless of the motivation, by escaping, enslaved people denied their enslavers' their labor. The perusal of any regional newspaper from the period shows that escape attempts were quite common. In 1802, Louisiana's only newspaper, *Moniteur de la Louisiane,* notified the public that Pierre-Marc, Janvier, Thomas, and Jeannette had escaped from the plantation of Alexandre Harang on the night of August 29.[35] In 1811, a notice in the *Louisiana Courier* informed the public that Tom, an enslaved man from Baltimore and "well known in town as a Baker or vendor of bread" had escaped on the night of March 11.[36]

Enslaved people in the lower Mississippi valley, just as enslaved people did everywhere, also resisted enslavers in more subtle ways. For example, the enslaved defied enslavers' attempts to control their movement, creating spaces outside of enslaver control. The 1800 Spanish investigation of the murder of Cola, enslaved by Étienne Boré, revealed that enslaved people ignored the orders of their enslavers not to visit certain plantations and even ran a rice-selling ring right under their noses. The evidence given in the case indicates that whites living on plantations were painfully unaware of even the most basic activities of enslaved people during their non-work time. It also revealed that enslaved people readily moved between plantations.[37] Many observers commented on (and often bemoaned) this relative freedom of movement.[38] Local governments passed laws to regulate enslaved people's movements and periodically republished them to

remind enslavers of legal requirements, suggesting they were not rigorously enforced.[39]

Other subtle acts of resistance like work slowdowns, sabotage, and
theft are difficult to document, but the descriptions given by observers
of the region's enslaved people would suggest that they were commonplace. Pierre-Louis Berquin-Duvallon wrote that enslaved Louisianans
were "lazy, libertine, and given to lying." In contradiction to this claim of
laziness, he also wrote that "the good negro, during the hours of respite
allowed him, is not idle." Instead, "he is busy cultivating the little lot of
ground granted him, while his wife . . . is preparing food."[40] This contradiction suggests that Berquin-Duvallon recognized that at least some of
the enslaved were not inherently lazy, only lazy when working for their
enslaver. French colonial commissioner Pierre Clément Laussat largely
agreed with this portrayal of enslaved Louisianans. According to him,
"one cannot expect fidelity, punctuality, or attachment" from an enslaved
person who "aims only to cheat his master, steal from him, and work as
little as possible." Enslaved people were "sluggish deceitful, and on the
lookout for a chance to neglect their obligations with impunity."[41] Observers generally agreed that the region's enslaved people were shiftless
and deceitful, suggesting subtle resistance to slavery.

Another subtle form of resistance was enslaved people's acquisition of
knowledge their enslavers would have preferred they not have. In and
of itself, the spread of information did not directly undermine slavery.
Yet during these revolutionary times, many enslavers worried about
it and tried to prevent it, seeing it as a potential long-term threat. For
example, Mills wrote that enslaved people were "kept in Ignorance as
much as possible."[42] However, enslavers were unsuccessful in doing so.
Enslaved people were at least somewhat aware of the Haitian and French
Revolutions. Certainly, they would have been aware of the former once
enslaved St. Dominguans began to trickle into the colony. In the case of
the latter, evidence gathered after the Pointe Coupee Conspiracy of 1795
suggests enslaved people knew at least something about the French Revolution and its ideas.[43] A year later, the elite Creole Joseph de Pontalba
complained about sailors from a French corsair spreading radical ideas to
the enslaved.[44] News of revolutionary events and ideas could not be kept
away from enslaved people.[45]

The most extreme and dangerous possible form of slave resistance was interpersonal violence. This could take the form of an enslaved person resisting punishment, getting into a fistfight with their enslaver or an overseer, murdering the enslaver or overseer, or, in the most extreme example, rising in rebellion. Criminal court cases from Orleans Parish suggest violent acts against enslavers and overseers regularly occurred. For example, in 1810 and 1811, besides those tried for involvement in the German Coast Insurrection, two enslaved men named Azri and Atys were hanged for assaulting their enslavers, an enslaved woman named Rose Marie was indicted for the attempted poisoning of her enslaver, and an enslaved man named Andre was convicted of "having revolted against the overseer" and was sentenced to twenty-five lashes and working for two years with a chain around his leg.[46]

While the resistance of enslaved people in the lower Mississippi valley might appear unexceptional for a slave society, many observers concluded that, in aggregate, it represented a real threat to whites' stable pursuit of profits and even, perhaps fancifully, the region's continued control by whites. For example, in a letter written to Thomas Jefferson shortly after the handover of Louisiana, Isaac Briggs, appointed surveyor of the Mississippi Territory the year before, identified slavery as the greatest threat to stable American governance in the region. He wrote to Jefferson that "the number of slaves in this country is already great, and the infatuated inhabitants are in the habit of increasing it by large importations." He claimed that the enslaved were "acquainted, far better than their oppressors, with almost every path and every retreat" and were "capable of secresy [sic], and many of them of considerable system." Enslaved people were "already discontented and disposed to throw off their yoke, on the least prospect of success." As a result, enslavers were "alarmed and think to find their safety in rigorous discipline," but "this will but hasten the crisis, and [make] the catastrophe more dreadful." With his mind turning to the "sanguinary scenes of St Domingo," Briggs chose to quote Jefferson's famous statement that "'I tremble for my Country, when I reflect that God is just—that his Justice cannot sleep forever—and that there is no attribute of the Deity which can take part with us in such a contest.'" Briggs concluded that "the Divine Author of Nature has indeed made this

Country a *Paradise*—but man has converted it into a *Pandemonium*."[47] Briggs was far from the only observer to reach the conclusion that slave resistance (resulting from surging importations of enslaved people and enslaver violence) had produced an inherently unstable social order.

Enslaved people in the lower Mississippi valley pushed back against or subtly undermined enslavers' demands and control. As Briggs reported, enslavers, with the backing of the Spanish and American states, attempted to control the people they enslaved, and in the end, they, by and large, succeeded in doing so to a degree that allowed them to continue to profit from their labor even if many feared, as did Briggs, that this control was fragile. We have already seen how some planters used managerial hierarchies, particularly enslaved drivers, to control enslaved people. We have also seen that enslavers paid enslaved people to incentivize Sunday work and overwork. In fact, enslavers commonly used positive inducements, from payment for work and goods produced by enslaved people on provision grounds to freedom for favored enslaved people, to control the enslaved.

Despite the use of positive inducements, most central to enslavers' tactics of control were violence and the enlistment of state power. At the most basic level, enslaved people worked every day under the threat of the whip. Laussat noted that "there exists an organized hierarchy of drivers, chiefs, and overseers, always whip in hand."[48] Benjamin Henry Latrobe recorded that he "saw an overseer direct[ing] the repair of the levee with a long whip in his hand."[49] Mills claimed that "for small faults," enslaved people were "punished with 10 or 12 strokes over the naked Back, with a Cow Hide."[50]

More formal punishments were forthcoming for enslaved people who committed some misdemeanor, failed to meet production goals (as detailed by Charles Ball and Solomon Northup), or angered their enslaver or overseer. Latrobe described several such scenes. In one, Mrs. Tremoulet, his landlady, punished a house servant whom Latrobe thought "modest, obliging, & incredibly active" for not making a bed "at the hour prescribed." Tremoulet "had her stripped quite naked, tied to a bed post, & she herself... whipped her with a Cowskin till she bled."[51] Natchez cotton planter and scientist William Dunbar declared that he would make an enslaved man "declare under the lash" whether he had stolen some horses.[52] John Mills detailed what he believed to be the typical formal punishment for enslaved people:

> Generally, . . . they are staked down, that is, three stakes is drove into the ground in a triangular manner about six feet apart. The culprit is told to lie down, (which they will do without a murmer), flat on the belly, the Arms is then extended out, side ways, and each hand tied to a stake hard and fast. The feet is both tied to the third stake, all stretched tight, the overseer, or driver then steps back 7, 8 or ten feet and with a raw hide whip about 7 feet long well plaited, fixed to a handle about 18 inches long, lays with great force and address cross the Buttocks, and if they please to assert themselves, they cut 7 or 8 inches long at every stroke.[53]

In the end, enslavers' threat and use of violence lay at the base of slavery in the lower Mississippi valley, just as it did everywhere else the institution existed.

Slave control was not left solely to individual enslavers. Enslavers had the backing and support of the state. Slave patrols were required by both the Americans and Spanish. Considering the large numbers of escapees and the relative freedom of enslaved people's movements, many enslaved people either successfully evaded the patrols or the patrols were not very effective. Still, the patrols were at least at times active tools of control. After the Pointe Coupee Conspiracy the Spanish governor ordered slave patrols to launch concerted dawn raids on slave quarters in search of arms and refugees.[54] In 1808, a slave patrol captured two escapees in St. Charles Parish.[55] During the War of 1812, the head of the slave patrol in St. Martin Parish reported "that in going his Rounds last night . . . he found and seized in the cabin of François the Slave of Marcel Patin . . . two guns and in the cabins of Jean Louis and Temon . . . each one gun which he likewise seized," indicating that the parish's slave patrol was searching slave cabins for weapons.[56]

The state bolstered the slave regime in other ways, especially after the tools of the state fell unambiguously into local elites' hands with the extension of American sovereignty. Once that happened, they set about stripping slave codes of most features that might soften the institution.[57] Under the Spanish, the situation had been more ambiguous, as Spanish officials often served imperial concerns that trumped those of local enslavers and, for strategic reasons, valued stability over profits from the exploitation of enslaved labor.[58] Still, the state, under both the Spanish and the Americans, propped up slavery. It created the legal structure, through slave codes and other ordinances that gave legal validation to enslavers' power over the people they enslaved and validated the degraded status of the enslaved themselves as well as their very status as property. Enslavers in or near New Orleans could even turn enslaved people over to the city government for "correction" as part of the city's chain gang.[59] In the cases of extreme crimes or resistance, the state imposed its authority directly over enslaved people through the judicial system.

As in all slave societies, enslaved people in the lower Mississippi valley resisted their enslavement, and enslavers used various tools and tactics to minimize the effects of that resistance. Still, observations from the period suggest that the region's slave system was harsh even by the standards of slave societies (although likely not as harsh as the brutal slave regimes of the Caribbean).[60] The best evidence for this is the horror with which many observers reacted to what they witnessed in the region. This was true even for those who had prior experiences with slavery. Adam Hodgson, a merchant from Liverpool and opponent of slavery, traveled throughout the United States and Canada between 1819 and 1821. Despite his opposition to slavery, he was surprised by how mild slavery appeared to be in the Chesapeake and the Carolinas. He found enslaved people, against his expectations, to be "intelligent" and well-mannered and the abuses less severe than he expected.[61] His experience in the lower Mississippi valley differed dramatically. In Natchez, he found planters who, despite seeming "respectable, liberal and humane," casually shot and killed enslave people who had attempted to escape, forced enslaved people to work under the threat of the lash and the gun, asked guests to administer severe corporal punishments to enslaved people, and tolerated the mistreatment of the enslaved by their overseers. According to Hodgson, "The poor slaves are toiling with little rest or respite from morn to night—for here I observe they seem to work many hours longer than in Carolina." Hodgson judged the lower Mississippi valley's slavery to be the worst in the United States.[62] This sort of response was common among travelers and new-comers to the region.[63]

While most observers merely noted what they observed without looking for causes (beyond slavery itself) or pointed to a vague notion of regional culture (often rooted in prejudices against "Creoles"), others pointed to the effects of the sugar and cotton revolutions, particularly the importation of thousands of alien and alienated enslaved people.[64] John Mills described the lower Mississippi valley's elites as driven by greed to buy more and more people who were then severely disciplined and abused. Mills argued that the blame for this abuse lay squarely on the need to control those large numbers of alien enslaved people. While arguing that he did not approve of "that Inhumane commerce, of tear-ing them from their native country and friends by force of arms, or by treachery or finesse," he also asserted that the harsh treatment of the en-slaved in a place with so many was a necessary evil. His correspondent, his New York cousin Gilbert Jackson, living "in a country, where slavery was scarcely known, as your Negroes was in general, always treated more like servants than Slaves," could not understand the threat they lived under in the lower Mississippi valley.[65]

According to Mills and other observers, the great cruelty and danger endemic to the area's slave society was a result of the infusion of alien en-slaved people driven by the prosperity brought by cotton and sugar. Mills also would have likely pointed to the crops themselves, both due to their profitability and production demands, as causes of the mistreatment. In fact, he directly connected abuse and neglect with an insatiable hunger for profits from the crops in lieu of all else, going so far as to argue that planters even neglected their own needs in their quest for profits.[66] In the end, many observers agreed that slavery in the lower Mississippi valley was characterized by extreme brutality, even in comparison with other slave societies, and a particularly restive and resistant enslaved population that posed a constant threat to elite profits and control.[67]

These tensions in the years following the sugar and cotton revolutions came to a head in the 1811 German Coast Insurrection. As we have seen, the revolt began during the night of January 8 on Manuel Andry's sugar plantation in St. John the Baptist Parish and expanded over the course of the next day while the rebels marched south along the Mississippi River toward New Orleans.[68] The makeup of the revolt was diverse, much like the enslaved population itself. The man usually identified as the main leader, Charles Deslondes, was a driver on Andry's plantation and either a Creole or from St. Domingue. Two other possible leaders, Kook and Quamana, enslaved by the Virginian transplant James Brown, were Africans, probably Akan. A rebel named Simon was originally from Baltimore and had tried to escape the previous July. A perusal of the remaining names shows a mix of French, English, and African names indicating a rebellion made up of members of all the major groups composing the enslaved population of the region. Even maroons emerged from the swamps behind the plantations to join the revolt while, ironically, many enslavers went in the opposite direction.[69]

Little direct evidence has survived about the rebels' motives, goals, and plans. Jupiter, a suspected rebel captured over a month after the revolt, claimed he had rebelled to go to New Orleans to kill whites.[70] Jupiter's is the only clear statement of motivation that has survived, and perhaps his was the goal for many: revenge for abuse, extreme labor demands, and being brought to the region. One anonymous observer suggested that the revolt was a paroxysm of rage aimed not at any goal but rather the harsh situation in the region: "It appears to have been a desperate sally of a few wretches, determined no longer to submit to the hardship of their situation."[71] In this view, enslaved people had been pushed too far by the planters and were striking back in frustration and anger.

Still, stopping at simple revenge as a possible motivation is unsatisfactory, especially when explaining a rebellion involving hundreds of people in a place that was a crossroads of various revolutionary traditions. Perhaps some enslaved people had visions of a true revolution, of overturning the slave system and creating something new in its place. They would have had the example of Haiti to guide them. Information on the revolution was available to enslaved people, and at least a few enslaved Haitians lived on the German Coast, and many more lived in New Orleans.[72] Enslaved people had also been exposed to the radical ideals put forward by the French Revolution and to the American rhetoric of equality and republicanism by enslaved Americans and Anglo-American immigrants.

Tellingly, early reports of the revolt focused on the claim that the leader was either an enslaved or free man of color from St. Domingue.[73] At least some of the rebels were likely inspired by these revolutionary examples and ideas.

Africans who took part in the rebellion likely had their own motivations and goals. Historians who have studied African-led slave revolts in the Americas have found that these rebels' motivations and goals were often based in their preenslavement experiences in Africa refracted through their experience of enslavement. Such goals often focused on creating autonomous and even sovereign African spaces in the Americas. Except in extraordinarily rare circumstances, such ambitions were tempered by the fact that Africans did not find themselves living among individuals from the same backgrounds as themselves.[74] In the case of the German Coast Insurrection, a diverse mix of people from Africa, other slave societies in the United States, and the region were involved in the rebellion, suggesting that any "African" component would have been highly attenuated if still likely present.

Finally, the revolt might even have been motivated, at least initially, by far more immediate factors. For example, it might have begun as an attack fueled by grievances against Manuel Andry and his son that then spiraled out of control as they failed to successfully kill Andry. It might have been their plan to kill him and his son in the dead of night and, with no witnesses, return to their quarters, hoping to get away with it. Killings of abusive overseers and enslavers did happen at times in slave societies in the Americas.[75] However, once Andry escaped, his attackers might have felt they had little choice but to rise in revolt. Their numbers could have swelled as individuals with their own motives and goals joined them on the spur of the moment.[76]

When it comes to the motivations and goals of the revolt, we are left with a wide range of possibilities. Most likely, the motivations and goals would have been diverse and complex, and the rebels themselves probably disagreed about why they were rebelling and to what end. Still, considering the history of the previous two decades with the revolutionary currents entering the region and the intensification of work associated with the sugar and cotton revolutions, the rebels would likely have had on their minds Haiti, various revolutionary ideals, and the harsh world within which they found themselves. Most likely would have agreed with a leader of an 1806 conspiracy in Cuba (which was itself undergoing transformations similar to those in the lower Mississippi valley) who declared to his followers, "We can't bear the whites any longer, it is time to kill them."[77]

At the very least, the revolt shows that several hundred enslaved people on the German Coast and in Orleans Parish were ready and willing to take up arms again their enslavers. This did not surprise those enslavers. Upon hearing about the revolt, most planters seem to have immediately jumped to action, either to flee or take up arms. They did not hesitate with disbelief that the people they enslaved would rebel. Planters were more than ready to believe that the people they enslaved wanted them dead. With the planters and other whites gone to the swamps, New Orleans, or across the river, the rebels took control of the countryside on the German Coast. The enslaved people of the German Coast had challenged and called into question the very foundation of the economic and social organization of the lower Mississippi valley.

However, we should not too quickly romanticize or overemphasize that challenge.[78] Elites had tools to meet such a challenge, tools that proved all too effective in defeating it. Immediately after receiving news of the revolt, territory of Orleans governor William Claiborne began to put into motion the coercive tools available to him. On learning of the revolt on the morning of January 9, Claiborne went to General Wade Hampton, commander of American forces in the region, and informed him of the uprising. Hampton immediately proceeded upriver with what troops he could gather: two companies of volunteer militia and thirty regular soldiers. On the way, they overtook a company of US Navy seamen who joined his force.[79] Claiborne gathered the militia of the city augmented by the "brave Tars" of the merchant vessels in the port and a company of free men of color.[80] Claiborne also sent a circular to the "Militia Colonels and Parish Judges" enclosing "the best account of an Insurrection, I can give, which has broken out on the Coast" and commanding them to "order strong Militia patroles [sic] by day and night; and cause a strict police among the Slaves to be maintained."[81] In the face of the threat of a slave insurrection, all elements of free society came together to oppose it. The rebels were unlikely to find any solidarity outside their own ranks.

Hampton's small force arrived at the rebels' position on the morning of January 10, but when they attacked, the rebels had already withdrawn.[82] Ultimately, local whites put down the revolt. According to Manuel Andry, on whose plantation the revolt started, he had, by the morning of January 10, "collect[ed] a detachment of about eighty men" who were "so happy to meet the brigands . . . colors displayed and full of arrogance." Upon meeting them, they charged and "made considerable slaughter." Many rebels escaped, but Andry "immediately ordered several strong detachments to pursue them through the woods, and at every moment our men bring them in or kill them." By the end of the next day, he informed Claiborne that "the first chief of the bandittis named Charles Deslondes has fallen into our hands, and several others appear to have commanded in second are now in my power." He and his men had also found "many runaways dead in the woods." While these dead might have been the result of the battle, Andry and his men were also almost certainly meting out their own justice.[83]

Realistically, barring great luck, the rebels probably never had a chance of success. At best they had some weapons and a few individuals with military experience before their enslavement in Africa or perhaps during the Haitian Revolution.[84] The region's free residents, on the other hand, were well armed and often had at least some military experience through service in the militia or the Spanish army. They also vastly outnumbered the rebels, with thousands of whites and free people of color living in New Orleans and the countryside around New Orleans and on the German Coast (over four thousand adult white men lived in the area according to the 1810 census). This was not the Caribbean, with its immense enslaved majorities.[85] They could also depend on the US Army and Navy and not just Hampton's small force. A much larger force was upriver at Baton Rouge supporting the incorporation of formerly Spanish West Florida into the United States. Had the rebels managed to stave off Hampton and the local militia, that force surely would have come downriver to confront the rebels, as would militia forces from other parishes. Finally, the rebels had nowhere to go. Unlike in St. Domingue, there were no mountains to which the rebels could flee. Louisiana did have its swamps, but living in these was difficult and certainly impossible for a large group. As one observer stated, "The nature of the country . . . does [not] . . . afford a safe retreat to considerable bodies of brigands."[86] As a coherent force, they were bound to a narrow band of land between the river and the swamps. While the rebels might have symbolically challenged the planters' rule, a successful revolt, at least one of this scale, was not a realistic possibility. Tellingly, they were defeated by an ad hoc force of eighty men, apparently with no fatalities among the attackers.[87]

While the coercive power of the planters and the state was apparent in the response to the revolt, that power and the willingness of elites to put it to bloody use became most apparent as they put down the revolt and in its immediate aftermath. By and large, most elites probably agreed with Andry when he wrote Claiborne that "a GREAT EXAMPLE" needed to be made of the rebels.[88] That "example" proved to be an orgy of vengeful bloodletting. One observer reported that a rebel captured early in the revolt "was killed after he became a prisoner, for what reason I know not, unless to gratify the revengeful feelings of the planters—they turned him loose in a lane and shot him as he ran."[89] Samuel Hambleton, a US Navy official, wrote to David Porter, the post's former commander about the "characteristic barbarity" of the planters during the revolt. According to Hambleton, after the revolt had been put down, "Several [of the captured rebels] were wrested from the Guards & butchered on the spot." The cruelest treatment was reserved for Deslondes, the identified leader of the rebellion: "Charles had his Hands chopped off then shot in one thigh & then the other, until they were both broken—then shot in the Body and before he had expired was put into a bundle of straw & roasted!"[90]

Once direct coercion and revenge had destroyed the organized revolt, captured or scattered its survivors, and meted out immediate "punishments," the coercive power of the planters and the state was far from finished making "a GREAT EXAMPLE" of the rebels. Trials of suspected rebels were held between January 13 and 15 in St. Charles Parish on the plantation of Jean-Noël Destréhan, a sugar planter noteworthy for his modesty and humanity according to Pierre Clément Laussat and the next year to become one of the first Louisianans elected to the US Senate. The tribunal consisted of Destréhan, Alexandre Labranche, Cabaret (probably Pierre-Marie Cabaret de Trepy), Adelard Fortier, and Edmond Fortier. They were all sugar planters of St. Charles Parish, enslaving 100, 83, 64, 76, and 56 people, respectively, in 1810.[91]

Interrogations, as recorded, were simple matters, very different from the long depositions taken when the Spanish had been in power.[92] Suspects were recorded as having merely named confederates in the revolt and specified their crimes. More must have been said: the planters did not convict all the accused of involvement, so exculpatory evidence was likely given but not recorded. The tribunal condemned eighteen people to death and exonerated six. Those condemned were to be executed "with the least delay, by means of a militia detachment . . . , to be shot, each one in front of the residence to which he belonged." To further the exemplary nature of the punishment, the court ordered that "the heads of those executed would be cut off and put up on the ends of a pike, at the place where each one of the guilty had suffered the just punishment for his crimes." The court explained that this was done to make "a terrible example for all the criminals who might in the future violate the public tranquility."[93]

The "example" set by the St. Charles tribunal was not the only one. At least eleven more suspected rebels were tried in the City Court of New Orleans between January 16 and February 16. Ten were found guilty. Most were hung at various plantations or in the city. The bodies of the executed were left exposed as an example. One, Jean, was given thirty lashes and was forced to watch the execution of one of the condemned "on account of his youth." A final enslaved man was condemned to be shot in private and his body returned to his family because his uncle had turned him over to authorities. One suspect was found not guilty because three planters, including St. Charles tribunal members Alexandre Labranche and Jean-Noël Destréhan, had encountered him fleeing from the rebels and teased him that he was probably the real leader of the rebels.[94]

The suspects tried in New Orleans had been tried before tribunals composed of elite whites, including the planter and merchant Daniel Clark Jr., the planter and future governor of Louisiana Jacques Villeré and sugar pioneer Étienne Boré. Tellingly, four of the jurors were delegates to the constitutional convention that would begin meeting later that year.[95] These juries, much like the one convened in St. Charles Parish, were made up of the elite of the community. These trials were nakedly the acts of that elite against those who had attempted to subvert their rule and profits.[96]

At least twenty-six enslaved people were executed by the judiciary, and many more had been killed in battle or murdered after being captured.

The most common estimate is that roughly one hundred enslaved people died during and after the revolt. François Xavier Martin, who lived in New Orleans at the time of the revolt, claimed in *The History of Louisiana* that "sixty-six of them were either killed during the action [i.e., battle] or hung on the spot, immediately after," and "the corpses of others were afterwards discovered" in the swamps. Martin continued that "sixteen were sent to the city for trial," where they were "convicted and executed" and "their heads were placed on high poles, above and below the city, and along the river as far as the plantation on which the revolt began."[97]

The killings and executions were of course meant to cow the enslaved population and show them what would happen to those who resisted slavery. The bodies and body parts put on display must have been seen by virtually all the enslaved people who lived on the German Coast and in Orleans Parish. Many enslaved people would have known someone killed in the revolt or have been forced to witness an execution. Many even further away would have heard about the violence and mass death. That was the intent of those who ordered the public executions and displays of bodies and body parts. Unsurprisingly, little evidence has survived of how the enslaved interpreted the results of the revolt. Some must have been intimidated and frightened by the scale and ferocity of whites' response. Some must have seen this as another expected feature of the unjust and harsh system the rebels had acted against. Few could have viewed the events with indifference. Regardless, the revolt and its aftermath would have been traumatic for enslaved people on the German Coast and in Orleans Parish and a warning to any enslaved person who heard about it as to what would happen if they rebelled. The effects of this trauma are impossible to know with certainty. However, the lack of future revolts is telling.

A few enslaved people benefited from the rebellion. Enslavers and the state moved to reward those who had shown exemplary loyalty. As was usually the case during a slave revolt, most enslaved people had not joined the rebels, instead retreating to the woods, staying on the plantations, or fleeing to New Orleans. A few enslaved people had aided whites, and a resolution by the legislature called for judges on the German Coast to form juries to identify those who had done so.[98] A judge in St. Charles Parish convened such a jury on February 20, taking the depositions of five enslavers about the actions of four enslaved people. Dominique had warned at least two enslavers directly and one indirectly of the conspiracy. Pierre, a driver, had learned of the revolt and warned his enslaver.[99] At least one man was manumitted after the revolt. Bazile, who belonged to the estate of a deceased sugar planter in St. Charles Parish, had extinguished the fires in the plantation house set by the "brigands" and resisted them, saving the plantation house from destruction. A notice placed in the *Louisiana Courier* announced to the public that, barring any protests, Bazile would be free thirty days after its publication.[100]

The region's elites had used all the tools available to them to put down the revolt and turn it into a vivid example of what would happen to those who resisted slavery. They defeated the rebels in battle. Then, in the immediate aftermath, they tortured and murdered at least one suspected leader and murdered several other unnamed rebels. Afterward, they held trials for the captives, found most guilty, and executed almost all of those convicted. At the same time, they displayed the heads and bodies of enslaved people killed during and after the revolt to intimidate the enslaved population. Finally, they promised to free those enslaved people who had aided enslavers in escaping or resisting the revolt. Planters had shown the enslaved and themselves the effectiveness of the tools they possessed to keep the region under their control and operating to their benefit.

Despite the effectiveness of the elite's coercive tools, one might still expect elite confidence to have been shaken by such a large slave revolt. Certainly, the paroxysm of violence seems to have gone beyond what was strictly necessary to bring the region back under control and perhaps reflected the violent expurgation of fears that both predated and resulted from the revolt. If only because of the size of the revolt, we might expect enslavers to show at least a little self-doubt and fear. However, excepting immediate panic, especially in New Orleans, reaction appears to have been effective. Claiborne and Hampton quickly put the wheels of state coercion into motion. Many planters and other whites fled the rebels, but many also joined with armed bands and militia companies, often on plantations across the river, which were unthreatened by the rebels. The group that put down the revolt had done just this, organizing itself across the river from the rebellion and then crossing the river to fight the rebels.

For enslavers (and many other free people), the eighty men in that group were surely the heroes of the moment.

Rather than shaken confidence, the apparently dominant response to the rebellion among enslavers was triumphalism. The answer of the territorial House of Representatives to the governor's annual speech, given shortly after the rebellion, encapsulated this response. The members of the house began by offering "public condolence for the loss of our Citizens who fell a sacrifice to the fury of the Blacks" (two whites had been killed during the revolt) and sympathies for "the private afflictions, and individual misfortunes." However, they immediately switched gears to "felicitate ourselves and our fellow citizens that the disaffection was partial, the effort feeble and it suppression immediate." The example given by the suppression "has been terrible." By and large, the enslaved had evinced "great fidelity." And the "Citizens, and Strangers" had manifested a "Zeal and spirit worthy the occasion." The whites had "learned that our Security depends on the order and discipline of the Militia." However, "the Blacks" had also "been taught an important lesson—their weakness."[101] These were not the words of a society shaken to its core. Rather, they were the words of a self-confident society that had met the worst the people they enslaved had to offer and triumphed. They had feared the surging and alien enslaved population for years. The day of reckoning had finally come, and they had come out on top.

Official actions taken in the aftermath of the revolt also indicate a general lack of deep anxiety once the fighting and trials had ended. In contrast to the Spanish government in 1795, the American territorial government did relatively little. Claiborne urged the legislature to place new restrictions on slave imports from the rest of the United States and to reorganize the militia to more effectively counter slave unrest.[102] The legislature took no action on the former suggestion (planters wanted enslaved labor) but did pass a new militia law aimed at increasing the discipline of the militia and its responsiveness to crisis.[103] In addition, the legislature petitioned the federal government to station additional troops in the region.[104] Finally, rather than moving to either restrict enslaved people or ameliorate their condition, the legislature made no changes to the slave code until late December 1814, nearly four years after the revolt.[105] The legislature did not see the revolt as reason to make major changes to the organization of the region's slave society. They believed that an increase in coercive power would be sufficient.

In addition, in the immediate aftermath of the revolt, planters signaled their continued commitment to slavery through the purchase of enslaved people and plantations. For example, on October 22, 1810, the estate of the sugar planter Louis-Augustin Meullion had been inventoried. At his death he had enslaved seventy people and owned a large plantation. His property was valued at $91,258. On January 28, 1811, the property was auctioned off, a mere eighteen days after the revolt had been put down, on the same plantation that had been defended by Bazile. Two of the estates' enslaved people had even been killed in the insurrection. Despite these seemingly unpromising conditions, the sale went off without a hitch. Fifty-one people were sold that day, with three more sold on March 9. Bazile and several others were set free. Overall, the estate brought in over $130,000, almost $40,000 more than it had been appraised at.[106]

This is far from the sole example of the continued commitment to slavery and plantation agriculture. Hampton believed that the crushing of the revolt had increased the region's stability and thus prospects. Soon after the end of the revolt, he informed the secretary of war that "the insurrections are crushed for some years at least."[107] He concretely signaled his belief in the stability and prosperity of the region by investing in local property. Hampton purchased a sugar plantation from New Orleans merchant and planter Daniel Clark within two months of the revolt.[108] In March 1811, he offered another planter $70,000 for a large piece of land near Baton Rouge.[109] By 1829, Hampton was the largest sugar planter in the lower Mississippi valley, producing immense amounts of sugar via the labor of over four hundred enslaved people on the plantation purchased from Clark.[110]

While the predominant response to the revolt was a combination of lustful vengeance, triumphal crowing, and confidence that the slave regime was on a solid footing, some local elites must have been more hesitant or at least have been more deeply affected by the violent events. A rare glimpse at greater unease in the wake of the revolt is a passing comment made by a traveler, Bernhard, Duke of Saxe-Weimer Eisenach, over a decade after the events of 1811. The duke visited the sugar plantation of

Michael Andry, a surviving son of Manuel Andry, who had "the reputation of being very severe to his negroes." The duke offered as a possible explanation that "twelve years ago an insurrection of the slaves broke out at his habitation, in which one of his brothers was murdered, and his father received three severe wounds with [an] axe."[111] The revolt had, unsurprisingly, not slipped from local memory. At the very least, the region's free residents carried on the memory of when the people they enslaved had risen against them, a warning of what was possible in the brutal world they had created.

While more lasting unease must have been present among the lower Mississippi valley's free residents after the insurrection, little evidence of it has survived. Whatever there was remained locked away in their minds, out of sight to future historians. In the end, it is difficult not to conclude that elites, by and large, reacted to the largest slave revolt in North American history, a revolt that was a result of the new order elites had imposed in the lower Mississippi valley to profit from sugar and cotton, with a mixture of relief and triumphalism. They concluded that the course of the revolt had ratified the stability of their society. They could continue the basic course they had laid out over the previous two decades with little fear that the enslaved population would successfully waylay them.

CONCLUSION

The Divine Author of Nature has indeed made this Country
a *Paradise*—but man has converted it into a *Pandemonium.*

—Isaac Briggs to Thomas Jefferson, January 2, 1804

The German Coast Insurrection of 1811 and the reaction of the region's
elites to it showed that much had changed since 1795 when the Pointe
Coupee Conspiracy had thrown elites into a panic. In 1795, the region's
elites feared that the revolutionary ideas of France and Haiti would
spread to their province, spurring an unstoppable challenge to their slave
regime. At the same time, they suffered a severe economic crisis as their
main cash crops, tobacco and indigo, collapsed. Together, these factors so
destabilized slavery that elites panicked when enslaved people conspired
against them and supported drastic action to bring slavery back under
control, including the closing of the slave trade. In fact, the situation was
perceived as so dire that at least some elites believed slavery was possibly
headed for extinction.

In 1811, all of that seemed behind them. The French Revolution was
dead (or, depending on one's point of view, dormant). Haiti was independent, but its revolution had never successfully spread beyond its
island even if its example still lurked in the background of every slave
society. The lower Mississippi valley was now firmly part of the United
States, and local elites largely controlled the region's governments. Most
importantly, cotton and sugar had exploded across the region, bringing
unparalleled profits. The lower Mississippi valley's elites had successfully transformed the region into a profitable and expansive slave society with mighty planters and merchants ruling over a restive enslaved
population that was, nonetheless, under enough control to create huge
profits.

The events of 1811 also reveal more profound realities about the lower Mississippi valley's slave regime. In 1800, a member of the New Orleans Cabildo had warned his peers not to "expose ourselves to losses because of our greediness" by ignoring "the terrible experience in the French Santo Domingo."[1] Despite this warning, "greediness" defeated caution. Spain reopened the slave trade, and enslavers resisted all attempts to restrict it and them. In addition, they drove enslaved people mercilessly on their plantations and farms to increase profits. Despite the enslavers' actions, subsequent events show the warning was off the mark. In 1811, planters crushed the largest slave revolt in North American history and proved to themselves that they could both indulge their "greediness" and avoid "the terrible experience in the French Santo Domingo." Of course this was not the last perceived challenge to their rule, as slave conspiracies would continue to be uncovered, and enslaved people continued to resist enslavers' demands.[2] In particular, the War of 1812 elevated fears about slave resistance, fears justified when hundreds of enslaved people fled to British invaders in 1815.[3] Yet it is difficult not to conclude that elites learned the lesson well that a large, alien, and resistant enslaved population could be effectively controlled by the threat and use of coercive violence. In the face of crisis, their system had proved resilient, adaptable, and sturdy.

By 1811, elites had largely shaped the region to match their desires. The elite vision for the region was one in which those with capital and access to credit could use that capital and credit to purchase land, enslaved people, and capital goods to benefit from the new export crops of cotton and sugar. Harvests of the crops would then be shipped out of the region by merchants who would also benefit from the reorientation of the local economy. To make this vision a reality, locals mastered the growing and processing of the new crops. They also convinced consumers outside the region that the goods they produced were of a satisfactory quality to purchase. Finally, they continued to work to improve the operation of their enterprises by experimenting with new crop strains, new equipment, and even wholly new enterprises. They nimbly adopted, adapted, and improved the cotton and sugar technological systems.

One of the most important ways enslavers shaped their region was through the molding of enslaved labor forces. They imported large numbers of enslaved people from any available source to man their cotton and sugar plantations and farms, tapping into the extant international slave trade and taking part in the development of the internal slave trade. Enslavers controlled those enslaved people through harsh discipline and coercive tools such as slave patrols and military force. They broke the enslaved population to new labor regimes and developed or adopted new labor practices in the process (e.g., the "pushing" system). Finally, when enslaved people attempted to directly challenge the new regime in the German Coast Insurrection, they crushed them, teaching them a "lesson" that they hoped would serve to keep the region under control for years to come. Elites successfully remade their region in the late eighteenth and early nineteenth centuries into one of the most lucrative but harshest slave regions of North America. The lower Mississippi valley in the years around 1800 is a classic example of the creation of a second slavery, in its case a second slavery consisting of an intertwined economic system built on sugar and cotton.[4]

As this narrative should suggest, the region's elites had an overwhelming preponderancy of *agency* in creating this second slavery.[5] They decided what crops were to be grown. They decided how labor would be organized. They made immense fortunes from the new economy. Certainly, enslaved people used their own agency to resist enslavers' demands, but while these efforts were not complete failures, they only had limited successes. Enslaved people managed to win some concessions in that enslavers typically continued to recognize customary labor-free times, pay for extra work, allow enslaved people to market their own goods, and even move about with a great deal of freedom. Enslaved people also developed their own languages and cultures that were somewhat aloof from those of their enslavers. However, when enslavers' needs and desires conflicted with enslaved people's needs and desires, those of enslavers almost always won, the clearest example being the transformation of Sunday work during the harvest from voluntary to involuntary on sugar plantations.

While local elites did have a great deal of agency in remolding the region, we should not overestimate that agency. The sugar and cotton revolutions were not only the result of actions by a particularly nimble local elite bending the landscape and enslaved people to their will. Besides the local actors who asserted their own, often countervailing, agency, those elites were always interacting with outside forces largely beyond their control. The political crisis of the 1790s and its retreat in the early 1800s occurred mostly (although not entirely) because of events taking place in Europe and the Caribbean. Similarly, while locals worked hard to make the cotton and sugar revolutions happen, these events were in great part a response to outside economic and political forces. Cotton swept over not only the lower Mississippi valley but also much of Tennessee and the backcountries of Georgia and South Carolina.[6] All these regions were reacting to the surging demand for cotton in the Atlantic World. The cotton revolution was overdetermined. While the sugar revolution was more contingent, considering that the crop was not an obvious fit for the region's environment, it too was also in large part a reaction to outside events, in this case the collapse of the St. Domingue sugar industry, which drove up sugar prices and provided crucial skilled labor in the form of refugee sugar makers.[7] Local elites did make the crop revolutions but not in a framework of complete local control. They were always reacting to and taking advantage of their situation within a larger world.[8]

However, even these reactions show how flexible and active these elites were. They knew about the opportunities their world offered. They learned about commodity prices abroad, products that could be grown and sold, and how to market these products once adopted. They also searched for and found sources of enslaved people so that they would have the labor they desired to produce more of the new crops. While it is difficult to imagine a path by which the region would not have adopted cotton and possibly sugar as well, their adoptions were not only the result of economic determinism. Rather, these changes were the result, in the moment, of a very nimble and aware group of Atlantic World capitalists who recognized they faced challenges, searched for solutions to those challenges, found them in different technological systems, and worked to implement and improve those systems. Local elites, through their choices and actions, determined the speed and shape of these crop revolutions even if the revolutions themselves might have been inevitable. They, not impersonal extraregional forces, made the lower Mississippi valley what it was.

Regional elites would have agreed with this conclusion and were proud of what they had achieved. The residents of Natchez and its Spanish government recognized the revolutionary nature of the cotton gin introduced by John Barclay and promised to richly reward him for it.

Étienne Boré fought to be recognized as the founder of sugar production and to this day holds a prominent place in the history of Louisiana. Charles Morgan was lauded for creatively finding a way to smuggle enslaved New Jerseyans to New Orleans. Boosters sent letters to newspapers and correspondents extolling the region's economy and the opportunities it provided for white men, particularly enslavers in the Atlantic states. For regional elites, and many nonelite free people as well, the adoptions of sugar and cotton and all the actions taken to support the production of the new crops were indeed a "triumph," as one observer claimed.[9]

We, looking back over two hundred years later, find the implications far more disturbing. Certainly, elites used cotton and sugar to transform a marginal colonial region on the edge of empires into a vibrant slave society that was soon to be a center of a dynamic and expansionist "Deep South." However, this was only made possible through the brutalization and exploitation of enslaved laborers from Africa or of African descent. The switch to cotton and sugar degraded the lives of enslaved people living in the region and spurred the introduction of many thousands more over the decades to come, destroying the lives those people had had in their places of origin. One can only imagine the emotions of the enslaved New Jerseyans who were suddenly uprooted from their lives in a society where slavery was dying and flung onto the harsh plantations of the lower Mississippi valley. In fact, the life of a typical rural enslaved person in the lower Mississippi valley was surely harsher in 1810 than it had been in 1780. That life was also surely more degraded than that of a typical enslaved person in the Chesapeake and perhaps any other slave society in North America. Enslaved people on the East Coast of the United States believed this to be the case and dreaded the possibility of being shipped to New Orleans. For those individuals, the sugar and cotton revolutions meant the possible alienation from family and community and a harsh and, in the case of sugar, shortened life. The immense wealth of the region's elite was built upon cruelty toward and the suffering of tens of thousands of peoples of African descent. As Isaac Briggs so pithily noted, local elites had converted "a *Paradise* ... into a *Pandemonium*."[10]

Elites in the region understood what they were doing and embraced the cruelty and oppression their society was built on. They grabbed onto cotton and sugar as means to quickly produce great wealth from their capital. To do so, they desired large numbers of enslaved people. They viewed these enslaved people as merely a means to the end of producing that immense wealth. They spoke of them as economic units and treated them as such. They pushed them hard and mistreated them when it was to their advantage. They gave them favors and privileges when that was to their advantage. Certainly, a great deal of day-to-day variety existed among enslavers. Surely some viewed themselves as paternalists caring for their extended multiracial families, while others avoided cruelty for religious and humane reasons. However, little evidence for such enslavers has survived. A large amount of evidence of cruel and harsh enslavers has survived. The region's slavery was a callous and cruel institution that was the key and indispensable cog in the capitalist machine that elites had built to produce so much wealth from cotton and sugar for their own enrichment.

The region's merchants, planters, and government officials worked together to make the sugar and cotton revolutions successful, and they took great pride in their success. They would rule over what would become one of the wealthiest plantation societies in North America, a plantation society that continued in the coming decades to follow the economic and social paths created at the time of the sugar and cotton revolutions. The fears and anxieties of the 1790s had been exiled. No longer would the region's planters fear that slavery was a fragile institution. Over the next five decades, the region would pull more and more enslaved people into the cotton and sugar systems and successfully extract more and more profits from them and the soil via those systems. For the region's enslaved people, this was the beginning of a long nightmare that would see them living and working in some of the harshest conditions North American slavery had to offer without even the dimmest hope that it would soon come to an end. Elites had created a paradise for capital but a pandemonium for social relations in the countryside. The economy and the social structure it spawned was, in large part, what local elites had long dreamed of and hoped to finally create when they switched to cotton and sugar in 1795. By 1811, they had succeeded. Their slave society had been replanted and was now flourishing, fertilized by the immense suffering of the enslaved.

Appendix

USING GWENDOLYN MIDLO HALL'S
LOUISIANA SLAVE DATABASE

Historians know a great deal about the demographic profile of enslaved people in parts of the lower Mississippi valley. Government officials in Louisiana often recorded detailed information about the region's enslaved people in legal documents such as slave sales and estate inventories. These records often included such useful information as age, sex, and place of origin. While the ages and sexes of enslaved people were commonly recorded in official documents throughout the Americas, the recording of origins was less common. While the origin of this practice is difficult to pinpoint with precision, it seems to have been a result of Spanish control. Prior to the 1770s and full implementation of Spanish sovereignty, origins were rarely recorded. After that year, origin recording became common although not universal. The practice then persisted in some parts of Louisiana well into the American period.[1]

In addition, due to the region's tradition of meticulous record keeping, thousands of documents have survived that contain detailed data on Louisiana's enslaved people.[2] Much of these data have been organized into a database by the historian Gwendolyn Midlo Hall, the Louisiana Slave Database. This database contains thousands of entries for the late 1700s and early 1800s.[3] While Hall's database is a critical resource for identifying trends in the demographic profile of the region's enslaved population, like any resource it has limitations and gaps and must be handled carefully. In this appendix, I explain how I have used the database in this book.

While I use the database to look at some other aspects of the enslaved population (e.g., gender balances), the predominant way I use it is to discuss the origins of enslaved people. In most instances, I use data from estate inventories as they are more likely than sales to reflect the actual makeup of the region's enslaved population considering they are snapshots of slaveholdings at a moment (the death of the enslaver or the enslaver's spouse). Between 1771 and 1820, 24,717 enslaved people appeared in Louisiana estate inventories that have been included in the database. Of those, 10,883 (44 percent) enslaved people were listed with an origin.[4] The other major document type, slave sales, is likely subject to some obvious and not so obvious biases. Most obviously, not all enslaved people were equally likely to appear in a slave sale at any given time. However, I have used slave sales and other document types when the number of estate inventories are too limited to give a significant amount of data. When I have done so, I have indicated that.

When working with enslaved people's origins, I present data for enslaved people aged fifteen or older (referred to as "adult" in the text). My assumption, supported by the data, is that most enslaved people brought to the region were adults, and most children were Creoles (i.e., born in the region). In addition, when most observers were considering the nature of the local population, they were typically commenting on the adult population rather than the entire population. Adult enslaved people were the most valued workers and the greatest potential threats to the stability and profitability of the region's slave society. Therefore, to get a sense of what the enslaved population looked like to local and outside observers, I have focused most of my analysis on the adult population. Between 1771 and 1820, 16,213 enslaved people fifteen years of age or older appeared in estate inventories in Louisiana. Of those, 8,626 (53 percent) enslaved people were listed with an origin.[5]

While a great deal of data on enslaved people's origins have survived, two cautions are necessary for interpreting that data. First, the data recorded is dependent on the ability of European and European-American officials to correctly ascertain enslaved people's origins. For such general origins as "Creole," "African," or "American," they most likely could in most cases (although instances of misidentification between these crude categories almost certainly occurred). For more specific origins, particularly precise African origins, the accuracy of such claims are more open to question. Precise African origins, while likely having some actual relationship to enslaved people's geographic origins in Africa, were often a creation of Europeans trying to categorize the people they were enslaving rather than a reflection of the actual identities of Africans prior to their enslavement. Of course, Africans' identities also transformed after enslavement and their experiences both on the Middle Passage and in America.[6] As such, I use these origins impressionistically rather than as a precise reflection of the actual origins or self-conception of Africans.

Second, the data are uneven over time and place. Officials commonly recorded origins in the Spanish period and, after the Louisiana Purchase, in regions where government documents were recorded in French. Data on origins are most extensive on the German Coast (St. Charles and St. John the Baptist Parishes), in Pointe Coupee Parish, and in Orleans Parish as officials in those areas continued to regularly record origins through 1820 and beyond. In other parts of the region, particularly those dominated by Anglo-Americans, the recording of origins was virtually nonexistent, especially after the Louisiana Purchase. For example, 86 percent of estate inventories recorded in English did not give origins for any enslaved people inventoried; only 25 percent of French-language inventories did not give origins for any enslaved people inventoried.[7] As such, conclusions drawn about enslaved people's origins from the database are only useful for certain parts of the region over the whole period under study here.

In the end, Hall's database tells us a great deal about the origins of enslaved populations in certain parts of the region (those dominated by francophones) and very little about other parts (those dominated by anglophones). We must treat it with great care when drawing conclusions about the entire region. Still, when used carefully and in combination with other sources (especially census data), it can be an invaluable resource for insights into the demographic characteristics of the enslaved population of the region.

NOTES

Introduction

1. Joseph de Pontalba to Jeanne des Chappelles, September 20 and October 24, 1796, *The Letters of Joseph X. Pontalba to His Wife*, 302–5, 374. I use the term "Creole" as it was used at the time: to denote an individual born in the region who usually spoke French as his first language. It was applied equally to whites, enslaved people, and free people of color. That said, the term can be "slippery" at times, as it might also be used to refer to individuals not actually born in the region but who had assimilated into local society.

2. Din, *Spaniards, Planters, and Slaves*, 185–86.

3. John Watkins to William Claiborne, February 2, 1804, *Official Letter Books of W. C. C. Claiborne, 1801–1816*, 2:10.

4. Claiborne to Thomas Jefferson, April 15, 1804, *The Territorial Papers of the United States*, vol. 9, *The Territory of Orleans*, 222.

5. Clark, *New Orleans*, 1–201; Ingersoll, *Mammon and Manon in Early New Orleans*, 3–180; Powell, *The Accidental City*, 1–196; Usner, *Indians, Settlers, and Slaves in a Frontier Exchange Economy*.

6. Clark, *New Orleans*, 187–92, 206–14.

7. Clark, *New Orleans*, 187–88, 191–92.

8. Din, *Spaniards, Planters, and Slaves*, 152.

9. Narrett, *Adventurism and Empire*, 195–203; Wood, *Empire of Liberty*, 185–89.

10. Hall, *Africans in Colonial Louisiana*, 343–74; Din, *Spaniards, Planters, and Slaves*, 154–93.

11. For example, see Martin, *The History of Louisiana*, 263–67. The switch in crops has been mentioned in most histories of the region during the period around the Louisiana Purchase. See, for example, Ingersoll, *Mammon and Manon in Early New Orleans*, 181–209; Powell, *The Accidental City*, 258–61.

12. For example, see Russell, "Cultural Conflicts and Common Interests." While the sugar revolution is fundamental in her study, Russell's focus is not the process of the sugar revolution but rather how it abetted the creation of a new elite class of

Creoles and Anglo-Americans. The sugar revolution also figures prominently in Ingersoll's and Powell's studies but is not the focus.

13. Recent books published about the lower Mississippi valley around the time of the Louisiana Purchase have focused on New Orleans: Faber, *Building the Land of Dreams;* Johnson, *Slavery's Metropolis;* Powell, *The Accidental City.* This tendency holds true in almost all periods of the region's history.

14. The classic statement of the concept of the second slavery comes from Tomich, *Through the Prism of Slavery,* 56–71. In addition, see Tomich and Zeuske, eds., "The Second Slavery"; Tomich, "The Second Slavery and World Capitalism"; Kaye, "The Second Slavery." See Tomich et al., *Reconstructing the Landscapes of Slavery* for a recent comparative study of the second slaveries of Brazil, Cuba, and the American South using visual evidence. Tellingly, the American South section focuses on cotton cultivation in the lower Mississippi valley.

15. Baptist, *The Half Has Never Been Told,* 47–49, quotes on 47 and 49.

16. For some of the more important examples of the history of second slavery and cotton in the United States (although not all of these authors use the term second slavery), see Baptist, *The Half Has Never Been Told;* Beckert, *Empire of Cotton;* Beckert and Rockman, eds., *Slavery's Capitalism;* Johnson, *River of Dark Dreams;* Rothman, *Flush Times and Fever Dreams;* Rothman, *Slave Country.*

17. An American, "To the Editor of the Louisiana Gazette," *Louisiana Gazette,* August 8, 1806.

18. See Tomich et al., *Reconstructing the Landscapes of Slavery,* 39–50, 87–122, for an overview of Cuba's second slavery.

19. For the history of sugar in the lower Mississippi valley during the antebellum period, see Follett, *The Sugar Masters;* Sitterson, *Sugar Country.*

20. See Rood, *The Reinvention of Atlantic Slavery,* for a second slavery aloof from cotton that involved the deep entanglement of modernizing slave systems in Brazil, Cuba, and the Upper South.

21. Arthur, *The Nature of Technology,* 28, 54; quote on 28.

22. Tomlins, *Freedom Bound,* 5.

23. Arthur, *The Nature of Technology,* 28.

24. McClellan and Dorn, *Science and Technology in World History,* 345–46, 365–71.

25. Ferrer, *Freedom's Mirror,* 327.

26. For the broader history of local political control as a part of "English liberty" and how it was used to draw exclusionary boundaries see, for example, Greene, *Exclusionary Empire.*

27. Faber, *Building the Land of Dreams.* Faber makes the crucial point that some of these changes began during the very brief period of formal French control and were then consolidated under American sovereignty. In taking these actions, elites were curbing the more flexible (but still strongly hierarchical) slave and racial laws imposed on the region by the Spanish. See Din, *Spaniards, Planters, and Slaves,*

especially the preface and conclusion, and Landers, *Black Society in Spanish Florida,* 183. Also see Johnson, *Wicked Flesh,* 187–218.

28. Adelman and Aron, "From Borderlands to Borders," 822.

29. Hammond, *Slavery, Freedom, and Expansion in the Early American West;* Hammond, "Slavery, Settlement, and Empire"; Rothman, *Slave Country.* For examples of works more focused on the founders and the federal government see Fehrenbacher, *The Slaveholding Republic,* 28–47, 253–63; Finkelman, *Slavery and the Founders;* Freehling, *The Reintegration of American History,* 12–33; Freehling, *The Road to Disunion,* 1:121–43.

30. Hammond, *Slavery, Freedom, and Expansion in the Early American West,* 169.

31. For other works that have studied the expansion of slavery on a local- or regional-level see Dupre, *Transforming the Cotton Frontier;* David Libby, *Slavery and Frontier Mississippi,* 37–59; Klein *Unification of a Slave State;* Russell, "Cultural Conflicts and Common Interests"; Baptist, *Creating an Old South.*

32. One does find statements by enslavers expressing discomfort with slavery's expansion or slavery itself. However, these statements are rare and appear to have had little broader impact.

33. "To the Members Composing the Convention," *Louisiana Gazette,* November 16, 1811.

34. The literature on capitalism and the modernity of the Antebellum South is immense. For recent examples on capitalism and the Antebellum South see Baptist, *The Half Has Never Been Told;* Beckert, *Empire of Cotton;* Beckert and Rockman, *Slavery's Capitalism;* Clegg, "Capitalism and Slavery"; Follett et al., *Plantation Kingdom;* Johnson, *River of Dark Dreams;* Kaye, "The Second Slavery." For a collection of essays on the Antebellum South's modernity see Barnes et al., *The Old South's Modern Worlds.* The introduction is particularly useful for thinking through the South's relationship to modernity.

35. The harshness and degradation of slave conditions in this period and later on sugar and cotton plantations and farms has been identified by many historians. See, for example, Baptist, *The Half Has Never Been Told,* 111–44; Berlin, *Many Thousands Gone,* 325–57; Follett, *The Sugar Masters,* 46–89; Ingersoll, *Mammon and Manon,* 193–95; Johnson, *River of Dark Dreams,* 151–75, 209–43; Tadman, "The Demographic Costs of Sugar."

36. Hall, *Africans in Colonial Louisiana,* 358.

37. Usner, *American Indians in the Lower Mississippi Valley,* 73–127.

38. For the most recent comprehensive overview of the ethnic cleansing of Native Americans, see Saunt, *Unworthy Republic.*

1. The Crisis of the 1790s

1. Stanley Clisby Arthur, foreword to *The Letters of Joseph X. Pontalba to His Wife,* i–viii.

2. Pontalba to Chappelles, February 25, 1796, *The Letters of Joseph X. Pontalba to His Wife*, 5–6, quotes throughout.

3. Pontalba to Chappelles, May 3, 1796, *The Letters of Joseph X. Pontalba to His Wife*, 101–2, quotes throughout.

4. Pontalba to Chappelles, March 17, 1796, *The Letters of Joseph X. Pontalba to His Wife*, 46–47.

5. Julien Poydras to Felix De Materre, August 22, 1795, "Letterbook of private and commercial correspondence of an indigo and cotton planter," 10.

6. For an overview see Powell, *The Accidental City*, 249–56. Various historians have touched on the region's enslaved people's interactions with the French and Haitian Revolutions. For interactions during the late Spanish colonial period with the revolutions, see Hall, *Africans in Colonial Louisiana*, 316–74; Roberts, "Slaves and Slavery in Louisiana," 35–100; Din, *Spaniards, Planters, and Slaves*, 133–93. For later interactions, particularly as related to the 1811 German Coast Insurrection, see Buman, "To Kill Whites," 25–65; Paquette, "'A Horde of Brigands?'" For Jacobinism in Louisiana see Liljegren, "Jacobinism in Spanish Louisiana." For free people of color in Louisiana and the French Revolution see Hanger, "Conflicting Loyalties."

7. While many historians have noted the crisis of the 1790s, not all have, and those who have usually dismiss it as transitory and not particularly severe. This is odd, as the records of the region are replete with locals complaining (and even panicking) over events. For example, neither Ingersoll, *Mammon and Manon in Early New Orleans*, nor Rothman, *Slave Country*, extensively acknowledge it. Din, *Spaniards, Planters, and Slaves* does discuss the events of the crisis in greater depth but largely dismisses them as overblown and not taken particularly seriously by locals. Hall, *Africans in Colonial Louisiana*, argues for the depth of the challenge to the slave system posed by the Pointe Coupee Conspiracy but has little to say about elite panic in response to it or the economic problems that afflicted the region at the same time and fed that panic. Powell, *The Accidental City*, 249–56, agrees that the period of the mid-1790s saw a crisis in the region's slavery due to economic stagnation and revolutionary currents. However, as Powell's project is a sweeping synthetic account of the period, he deals with this crisis only briefly. Perhaps the best discussion of the panic engendered by the Pointe Coupee Conspiracy is in chapter 2 of Roberts's "Slaves and Slavery in Louisiana." Roberts illustrates the deep challenge to the system posed by the enslaved in the early years of the Haitian Revolution. However, he does not connect these problems to the economic collapse occurring at the same time, nor does he show how these crises were ultimately resolved, as those issues are outside of the scope of his study.

8. Clark, *New Orleans*, 3–157; Dawdy, *Building the Devil's Empire*; Hall, *Africans in Colonial Louisiana*, 1–155; Ingersoll, *Mammon and Manon*, 3–144; Powell, *The Accidental City*, 1–128; Usner, *Indians, Settlers, and Slaves in a Frontier Exchange Economy*; Vidal, *Caribbean New Orleans*.

9. Berlin, *Many Thousands Gone*, 195–215; Clark, *New Orleans*, 46–60, 128–34; Powell, *The Accidental City*, 92–105, 127–28; Usner, *Indians, Settlers, and Slaves in a Frontier Exchange Economy*, 33–43, 44–76.

10. Powell, *The Accidental City*, 96.

11. Clark, *New Orleans*, 158–80, 221–25; Din, "Empires Too Far"; Narrett, *Adventurism and Empire*, 141–63; Powell, *The Accidental City*, 164–96, 317; Woodward, "Spanish Commercial Policy in Louisiana."

12. Powell, *The Accidental City*, 165, 172–74, 181–85, 192–93; Woodward, "Spanish Commercial Policy in Louisiana."

13. For an overview of this dynamic up to 1803, see Narrett, *Adventurism and Empire*. For the War of 1812, see Rothman, *Slave Country*, 119–62. One can see the continued threats to the "bordered" world of the lower Mississippi valley even after the War of 1812 in Clavin, *The Battle of Negro Fort*.

14. Clark, *New Orleans*, 187–92, 206–14, 228, and 232–48; Woodward, "Spanish Commercial Policy in Louisiana," 151–64.

15. Slave sales, Daniel Clark to Various Buyers, October 2 to October 4, 1787, *Natchez Court Records*, 44–45.

16. "Extract of a letter from a gentleman in New-Orleans to his friend in this city, dated April 25, 1792," *Independent Gazetteer*, June 2, 1792.

17. See note 6 in this chapter for secondary sources on Louisiana and the French and Haitian Revolutions. See Clark, *New Orleans*, 238–45, for changes in trade relationships.

18. Narrett, *Adventurism and Empire*, 195–203, and Wood, *Empire of Liberty*, 185–89.

19. Carondelet, "Military Report on Louisiana and West Florida."

20. Carondelet, *Circulaire*, 1–2.

21. Din, *Spaniards, Planters, and Slaves*, 152.

22. Carondelet, *Circulaire*, 1–3, quotes throughout.

23. Calculated from census data in Usner, *Indians, Settlers, and Slaves in a Frontier Exchange Economy*, 114–15.

24. Carondelet, *Circulaire*, 1, 3–5, quotes on 1 and 4.

25. Pontalba to Chappelles, September 1, 1796, *The Letters of Joseph X. Pontalba to His Wife*, 267–68, quote on 268.

26. Pontalba to Chappelles, September 13, 1796, *The Letters of Joseph X. Pontalba to His Wife*, 287–89, quotes on 288.

27. Pontalba to Chappelles, September 18, 1796, *The Letters of Joseph X. Pontalba to His Wife*, 298–99, quotes throughout.

28. Pontalba to Chappelles, September 20, 1796, *The Letters of Joseph X. Pontalba to His Wife*, 302–4, quote on 302–3.

29. Pontalba to Chappelles, September 13, 1796, *The Letters of Joseph X. Pontalba to His Wife*, 287–89, quotes on 287–88.

30. Johnson, "Denmark Vesey and His Co-Conspirators." Johnson cautions us to read enslaved people's testimony taken in the investigation of a conspiracy carefully and not to take it at face value.

31. Usner, *Indians, Settlers, and Slaves in a Frontier Exchange Economy*, 114, 182.

32. Hall, *Africans in Colonial Louisiana*, 362–65.

33. The best evidence for this is Julien Poydras's discussions of his travails with indigo. Poydras to Marre, June 18, 1796; Poydras to Claude Poydras, August 25, 1796; Poydras to Marre, August 28, 1796; and Poydras to Marre, November 1798, "Letterbook of private and commercial correspondence of an indigo and cotton planter," 16, 21–22, 24, 52.

34. The conspiracy has been covered extensively by other scholars, so there is little need to go into the details here. For secondary sources on the Pointe Coupee Conspiracy see Hall, *Africans in Colonial Louisiana*, 343–74; Din, *Spaniards, Planters, and Slaves*, 154–93. The records of the investigation are available in "Criminal Proceedings Instituted against the Blacks of Pointe Coupee for the Crime of Revolution or Conspiracy against the Whites," in Spanish Judicial Records, no. 3434.

35. Hall, *Africans in Colonial Louisiana*, 349–51, quotes on 350.

36. Hall, *Africans in Colonial Louisiana*, 351.

37. Pontalba to Chappelles, March 6, 1796, *The Letters of Joseph X. Pontalba to His Wife*, 22–23, quotes throughout.

38. Meeting, April 25, 1795, *Records and Deliberations of the Cabildo*, vol. 4, book 1, 6, reel 91–16.

39. Fleurian to Miguel Fortier, April 22, 1795, *Records and Deliberations of the Cabildo*, vol. 4, book 1, 7, reel 91–16.

40. Bringier to Fortier, April 23, 1795, *Records and Deliberations of the Cabildo*, vol. 4, book 1, 18–20, quotes on 19, reel 91–16.

41. Din, *Spaniards, Planters, and Slaves*, 135, 177–80. Also see Din, "Carondelet, the Cabildo, and Slaves," in which he argues the regulations went unenforced due to lack of attention and funding in contrast to an older strand claiming that a wave of repression followed the Pointe Coupee Conspiracy. See Hall, *Africans in Colonial Louisiana*, 376–79, for this argument.

42. Din, *The New Orleans Cabildo*, 171–72.

43. Meeting, February 19, 1796, *Records and Deliberations of the Cabildo*, vol. 4, book 1, 91–92, reel 91–16.

44. Din, *Spaniards, Planters, and Slaves*, 185–86. The government had already banned all importation of enslaved people from the Caribbean. The 1796 decision extended the ban to Africans brought directly from Africa.

45. Quoted in Gayarré, *History of Louisiana*, vol. 3, *The Spanish Domination*, 433.

46. Pontalba to Chappelles, October 24, 1796, *The Letters of Joseph X. Pontalba to His Wife*, 374.

47. I have uncovered no such evidence, and no secondary source discusses evidence for this claim. What antislavery sentiment there was in Spain was to be found

among liberals and not imperial officials who were typically more interested in expanding slavery while at the same time ameliorating enslaved people's conditions. See Berquist, "Early Anti-Slavery Sentiment in the Spanish Atlantic World."

48. The classic discussion of Spanish decision making is Whitaker, *The Mississippi Question*, 176–86.

49. Pontalba to Chappelles, March 27 and 30, 1796, *The Letters of Joseph X. Pontalba to His Wife*, 66–67, 70–72.

50. Pontalba to Chappelles, April 30, 1796, *The Letters of Joseph X. Pontalba to His Wife*, 97–98, quote on 98.

51. Armand Duplantier to his brother, January 10, 1796, Armand Duplantier Letters.

52. Meeting, August 16, 1800, *Records and Deliberations of the Cabildo*, vol. 4, book 3, 203–16, quotes on 207 and 212, reel 91–16.

53. Clark, *New Orleans*, 191–92.

54. "Memorial al Rey de los Habs de Natchez" (Memorial to the King from the Inhabitants of Natchez), September 15, 1791, Legajo, 212, sheets 514–15, Santo Domingo Papers and Cuban Papers.

55. Governor Manuel Gayoso de Lemos, "Political Conditions of the Province of Louisiana," July 5, 1792, *Louisiana under the Rule of Spain, France, and the United States, 1785–1807*, 1:269–88, quotes on 286.

56. Clark, *New Orleans*, 187–88.

57. Pontalba to Chappelles, April 17, 1796, *The Letters of Joseph X. Pontalba to His Wife*, 74.

58. Poydras to Marre, August 6, 1795, "Letterbook of private and commercial correspondence of an indigo and cotton planter," 7.

59. Duplantier to his brother, January 10, 1796, Armand Duplantier Letters.

60. Gray, *History of Agriculture in the Southern United States to 1860*, 611; Holmes, "Indigo in Colonial Louisiana and the Florida," 347.

61. Étienne Boré, "Culture du sucre sa restauration en 1795 par Mr. Boré habitant" (Cultivation of sugar its restoration in 1795 by Mr. Boré inhabitant), June 27, 1803, Pierre Clément Laussat Papers.

62. Clark, *New Orleans*, 187–88.

63. "Memorial al Rey de los Habs de Natchez," September 15, 1791, Legajo, 212, sheets 514–15; untitled memorial of the inhabitants of Natchez, no date, Legajo, 213, sheets 479–80, Santo Domingo Papers and Cuban Papers.

64. "Memorial of the Inhabitants of Natchez," September 27, 1797, Legajo, 213, sheets 630–34, Santo Domingo Papers and Cuban Papers.

65. Pontalba to Chappelles, March 17, 1796, *The Letters of Joseph X. Pontalba to His Wife*, 46–47.

66. Poydras to Duplantier, June 14, 1795, "Letterbook of private and commercial correspondence of an indigo and cotton planter," 6.

67. Poydras to Brunaud Bros & Co., October 9, 1795, "Letterbook of private and commercial correspondence of an indigo and cotton planter," 11–12, quote on 12.

68. Poydras to Claude Poydras, August 25, 1796, "Letterbook of private and commercial correspondence of an indigo and cotton planter," 21–22.

69. Poydras to Claude Poydras, August 25, 1796, "Letterbook of private and commercial correspondence of an indigo and cotton planter," 22.

70. Poydras to Marre, June 18, 1796, "Letterbook of private and commercial correspondence of an indigo and cotton planter," 17.

71. Poydras to Marre, August 28, 1796, "Letterbook of private and commercial correspondence of an indigo and cotton planter," 24.

72. Poydras to Marre, November 1798, "Letterbook of private and commercial correspondence of an indigo and cotton planter," 52.

73. Poydras to Claude Poydras, August 25, 1796, "Letterbook of private and commercial correspondence of an indigo and cotton planter," 21.

74. Poydras to Petit, November 29, 1798, "Letterbook of private and commercial correspondence of an indigo and cotton planter," 52–53.

75. Calculated from *Population Schedules of the Third Census of the United States, 1810, Louisiana,* reel 10. Poydras's entry is on 377.

2. Making the Cotton Revolution

1. Affidavit, William Dunbar et al., September 10, 1795, Legajo, 32, Santo Domingo Papers and Cuban Papers.

2. The evidence for John Barclay's building of the first cotton gin comes from documents in the Santo Domingo Papers and Cuban Papers, specifically, letters from Carlos de Grand-Pré to Francisco Luis Héctor de Carondelet, September 23 and November 12, 1795, which contain several other relevant documents. The quote is from a September 23, 1795, letter. Both letters and documents they contained are in Legajo, 32, Santo Domingo Papers and Cuban Papers. Many of these documents are quoted in translation in Holmes, "Cotton Gins in the Spanish Natchez District."

3. Few previous works focus on this moment of transition to cotton. However, many works do touch on it, typically as part of a larger study, and some do explore the local dynamics of how the shift was made. See Chaplin, *An Anxious Pursuit,* 277–329; Klein, *Unification of a Slave State,* 238–68; Lakwete, *Inventing the Cotton Gin,* 47–71; Libby, *Slavery and Frontier Mississippi,* 37–59; Rothman, *Slave Country,* 45–54.

4. M'Gruder, "From a long letter written by Mr. M'Gruder, and published in the Orleans Gazette," *Frankfort Argus,* April 7, 1808.

5. See an American, "For the Louisiana Gazette," *Louisiana Gazette,* September 19, 1806, for a reference to how a farmer with no enslaved labor could produce cotton by utilizing "public gins."

6. "Succession of Leonard Marbury," *Archives of the Spanish Government of West Florida,* 6:59. The average sale price of 145 enslaved men between the ages of fifteen

and forty-nine sold in Louisiana in 1803 was $732. Calculated using data from the Louisiana Slave Database.

7. Gray, *History of Agriculture in the Southern United States to 1860*, 77.

8. Thomas, "Pre-Whitney Cotton Gins in French Louisiana."

9. Bouligny, *Louisiana in 1776*, 50

10. Thomas, "Pre-Whitney Cotton Gins in French Louisiana."

11. Lakwete *Inventing the Cotton Gin*, 72–96.

12. Din, *Spaniards, Planters, and Slaves*, 156–57.

13. Grand-Pré to Carondelet, September 23, 1795, Legajo, 32, Santo Domingo Papers and Cuban Papers.

14. Slave sales, Daniel Clark to Various Buyers, October 2 to 4, 1787, *Natchez Court Records*, 44–45.

15. 1792 Natchez Census, Mississippi, US, State and Territorial Census Collection.

16. Mortgage, Daniel Clark to John Barclay, February 10, 1795, *Natchez Court Records*, 109.

17. Mortgage, Daniel Clark to John Barclay, February 10, 1795, *Natchez Court Records*, 109.

18. 1792 Natchez Census, Mississippi, US, State and Territorial Census Collection, 1792–1866.

19. Quoted in Claiborne, *Mississippi as a Province, Territory and State*, 1:143.

20. Wailes, *Report on the Agriculture and Geography of Mississippi*, 167; Claiborne, *Mississippi as a Province, Territory and State*, 1:143; Moore, *Agriculture in Ante-Bellum Mississippi*, 21–22. This story was repeated recently in Tomich et al., *Reconstructing the Landscapes of Slavery*, 74.

21. Dart, "Bradford, David," and "O'Connor, John," "Succession of Philip Lewis Alston," *Archives of the Spanish Government of West Florida*, 7:228–33. "Succession of Leonard Marbury," *Archives of the Spanish Government of West Florida*, 3:267–72.

22. Affidavit of Clark et al., August 24, 1795, Legajo, 32, Santo Domingo Papers and Cuban Papers.

23. Affidavit, Dunbar et al., September 10, 1795, Legajo, 32, Santo Domingo Papers and Cuban Papers.

24. Barclay to Grand-Pré, September 21, 1795, Legajo, 32, Santo Domingo Papers and Cuban Papers.

25. Grand-Pré to Carondelet, September 23, 1795, Legajo, 32, Santo Domingo Papers and Cuban Papers.

26. Holmes, "Cotton Gins in the Spanish Natchez District," 165.

27. Grand-Pré to Carondelet, November 12, 1795, Legajo, 32, Santo Domingo Papers and Cuban Papers. Population calculated from "Resumen General del Padron del Dist de Natchez del Año de 1795" (General Summary of the Census of the Natchez District in the year of 1795), Legajo, 31, Santo Domingo Papers and Cuban Papers.

28. Holmes, "Cotton Gins in the Spanish Natchez District," 166.

29. Grand-Pré to Carondelet, November 12, 1795, Legajo, 32, Santo Domingo Papers and Cuban Papers.

30. Advertisement, John Barclay, March 19, 1796, Provincial and Territorial Records.

31. *George Cochran vs. James McIntyre,* November 13, 1795, *Natchez Court Records,* 286.

32. Hall, "A Brief History of the Mississippi Territory," 555.

33. Baron de Carondelet, "Continuation of the documents printed by order of the City Council, relative to the Canal Carondelet," *Louisiana Courier,* March 9, 1812, extracted from the *Moniteur de la Louisiane,* October 19, 1795.

34. Robin, *Voyage to Louisiana,* 201; Alexander Norie and Thomas Lily Partnership Agreement, Narcisse Broutin, notary, January–December 1802, 4:366, New Orleans Notarial Archives.

35. Poydras to Marre, November 1798, "Letterbook of private and commercial correspondence of an indigo and cotton planter," 52.

36. Poydras to Dunbar, March 24, 1797, undated, and June 25, 1798, "Letterbook of private and commercial correspondence of an indigo and cotton planter," 33, 38–41, 45–48; Holmes, "Cotton Gins in the Spanish Natchez District, 1795–1800," 169.

37. Poydras to Dunbar, no date (probably late 1797 or early 1798), "Letterbook of private and commercial correspondence of an indigo and cotton planter," 39–41, quotes on 40.

38. Poydras to Marre, October 1799, "Letterbook of private and commercial correspondence of an indigo and cotton planter," 65.

39. Poydras to Dulcide Barran, James Freret, and Cavalier and Petit, October 12, 1799; Poydras to De Mattre, December 20, 1799, "Letterbook of private and commercial correspondence of an indigo and cotton planter," 68–73, quote on 73.

40. Poydras to Cavalier and Petit, October 12, 1799, "Letterbook of private and commercial correspondence of an indigo and cotton planter," 71.

41. Poydras to De Mattre, December 20, 1799, "Letterbook of private and commercial correspondence of an indigo and cotton planter," 73.

42. Poydras to De Mattre, March 13, 1800, "Letterbook of private and commercial correspondence of an indigo and cotton planter," 74.

43. Poydras to Freret, August 28, 1800, "Letterbook of private and commercial correspondence of an indigo and cotton planter," 88.

44. Poydras to Dunbar, June 30, 1799, "Letterbook of private and commercial correspondence of an indigo and cotton planter," 59–60, quote on 59.

45. Hall, "A Brief History of the Mississippi Territory," 554.

46. All the witnesses appeared more than once after 1798 in the various volumes of the *Archives of the Spanish Government of West Florida* as participants in legal cases and property transfers.

47. John Sibley to Claiborne, October 10, 1803, *The Territorial Papers of the United States* vol. 9, *The Territory of Orleans,* 75.

48. "List of Louisiana's Imports and Exports in 1800 and 1801" and "List of Louisiana's Imports and Exports in 1802," Dispatches from US Consuls in New Orleans.

49. Evan Jones to John Marshall or the Secretary of State, May 15, 1801, Dispatches from US Consuls in New Orleans.

50. Calculated from "General Census of St. Charles Parish, 1804," in Conrad, *St. Charles,* 389–407.

51. Dunbar to Green and Wainewright, October 2, 1807, *Life, Letters and Papers of William Dunbar,* 357.

52. *Population Schedules of the Fourth Census of the United States, 1820, Mississippi,* reel 57, 10.

53. John McBride, "Columbian Spinster," *Mississippi Herald and Natchez City Gazette,* August 25, 1807.

54. John McBride, "Columbian Spinster," September 15, 1807, and "Notice," December 3, 1807, both in *Mississippi Herald and Natchez City Gazette.*

55. Untitled selection of documents related to John Rollins's attempt to build a Columbian Spinster, *Archives of the Spanish Government of West Florida,* 17:48–52.

56. "Deposition of William Duvall, taken December 6, 1811," Provincial and Territorial Records. The file containing the deposition contains other documents related to the case, including a detailed schematic of "McBrides Machine For Ginning, Carding, and Spinning Cotton at one operation."

57. See Chaplin, "Creating a Cotton South in Georgia and South Carolina, 1760–1815," for a somewhat similar argument about textile production in South Carolina and Georgia. Chaplin does find more evidence for the actual adoption of such production during the economic dislocations caused by international instability of the first and second decade of the 1800s. Machines similar to the Columbian Spinster, and even called by that name, became more common in the antebellum period, including in the lower Mississippi valley. See Fort, *Bale o'Cotton,* 38.

58. "Extract of a letter dated Liverpool, August 10, 1801, to a Merchant in Philadelphia," *Newburyport Herald,* October 2, 1801.

59. Pitot, *Observations on the Colony of Louisiana,* 76.

60. See "A Cotton Gin Burning," 1803, in *Archives of the Spanish Government of West Florida,* 7:200–210. This is only one of several gin burnings in the early period of cotton production.

61. See Green and Wainewright, "Extract of a letter from a respectable Commercial House in Liverpool to their correspondent in this City," *Louisiana Gazette,* September 13, 1805.

62. Investigation of Benito Truly's Gin, begun May 19, 1796, Provincial and Territorial Records.

63. Investigation of Benito Truly's Gin, begun May 19, 1796, Provincial and Territorial Records.

64. Investigation of Benito Truly's Gin, begun May 19, 1796, Provincial and Territorial Records.

65. Richard Harrison's Petition to the Spanish Governor of Natchez, May 28, 1796, Provincial and Territorial Records. De Lemos's decree is appended to the end of the petition.

66. Investigation of Benito Truly's Gin, begun May 19, 1796, Provincial and Territorial Records.

67. "Presentments of the Grand Jury of Adams County," June 6, 1799, *Territorial Papers of the United States,* vol. 5, *The Territory of Mississippi,* 64.

68. "A Law to provide for the Inspection of Gins, Cotton Press, and cotton intended for exportation from this Territory," October 5, 1799, *Sargent's Code,* 117–18, quotes on 117.

69. "An Act suplementary [*sic*] to an Act entitled, 'an Act providing for the Inspection of Cotton,' passed the 10th day of March, 1803," November 11, 1803, *Acts Passed by the Second General Assembly of the Mississippi Territory during Their Second Session,* 2–3. Two newspaper notices were placed in late 1803 announcing that a cotton warehouse had been built and inspectors had been appointed. See untitled notices in *Mississippi Herald and Natchez City Gazette,* January 21, 1804. A later law passed by the general assembly shows that this warehouse had fallen "into decay and ruin." "An Act Providing for the Sale of the public Warehouse erected for the inspection of Cotton in the County of Washington," December 18, 1809, *Acts Passed at the First Session of the Sixth General Assembly of the Mississippi Territory,* 48–50.

70. Toulmin, *The Statutes of the Mississippi Territory.*

71. "Extrait du Journal de la Chambre des Représentans du Territoire du Orléans" (Extract from the Journal of the House of Representatives of the Territory of Orleans), *Moniteur de la Louisiane,* March 29, 1806.

72. "Extract of a letter from a respectable mercantile house in Liverpool to their correspondents at this place, dated 25th October 1803," *Union,* January 23, 1804.

73. "Extract of a letter from a respectable mercantile house in Liverpool to their correspondents at this place, dated 25th October 1803," *Union,* January 23, 1804.

74. Arthur, *The Nature of Technology,* 28.

75. Untitled advertisement, *Moniteur de la Louisiane,* October 2, 1802.

76. Dunbar to Green and Wainewright, February 25, 1806, *Life, Letters and Papers of William Dunbar,* 328.

77. Dunbar to Green and Wainewright, July 17, 1809, *Life, Letters and Papers of William Dunbar,* 363–64, quotes throughout.

78. Hodgson, *Letters from North America,* 1:11. In the book, Hodgson hides the name by referring to him as "Mr. W. D—." However, from context, it is clear who he is referring to.

79. Krichtal, "Liverpool and the Raw Cotton Trade," 80–93. For the population in 1785 see the 1785 Spanish census data in Usner, *Indians, Settlers, and Slaves in a Frontier Exchange Economy,* 114–15. For the 1810 population see the 1810 federal census data in *Urban Statistical Surveys,* 82–83. For the 1820 population see the 1820 federal census data in *Census for 1820,* 122–24.

80. Dunbar to Green and Wainewright, July 17, 1809, *Life, Letters and Papers of William Dunbar,* 363–64, quote on 364.

81. Dunbar to Green and Wainewright, July 17, 1809, *Life, Letters and Papers of William Dunbar,* 363–64, quote on 364.

82. Krichtal, "Liverpool and the Raw Cotton Trade," 97–98, quote on 98.

83. *Louisiana Advertiser,* May 6 to December 12, 1820.

84. *New Orleans Price Current and Commercial Intelligencer,* April 7, 1827.

85. Moore, *The Emergence of the Cotton Kingdom in the Old Southwest,* 10–11.

86. Claiborne to unknown, October 1, 1804, *Official Letter Books of W. C. C. Claiborne,* 2:344.

87. Dunbar to Green and Wainewright, February 25, 1806, *Life, Letters and Papers of William Dunbar,* 328.

88. Dunbar to Green and Wainewright, July 17, 1809, *Life, Letters and Papers of William Dunbar,* 363.

89. Francis D'Acosta, "New Pressing Machine," *Louisiana Courier,* November 16, 1810.

90. Samuel Briggs, illegible title, *Union,* February 23, 1804.

91. Lakwete, *Inventing the Cotton Gin,* 72–96.

92. See Chaplin, *An Anxious Pursuit,* 220–24, for an overview of cotton variety experimentation in South Carolina and Georgia around 1800.

93. Dunbar to Green and Wainewright, October 2, 1807, *Life, Letters and Papers of William Dunbar,* 356–57, quotes on 356.

94. Moore, *Agriculture in Ante-Bellum Mississippi,* 32.

95. Samuel Postlethwait to Green and Wainewright, November 22, 1810, *Life, Letters and Papers of William Dunbar,* 390.

96. Moore, *Agriculture in Ante-Bellum Mississippi,* 33.

97. Johnson, *River of Dark Dreams,* 8.

98. Olmstead and Rhode, *Creating Abundance,* 98–133.

99. Poydras to Meullion, September 15, [1800], "Letterbook of private and commercial correspondence of an indigo and cotton planter," 92.

100. For the 500-pound figure see, John Barclay to Carlos de Grand-Pré, September 21, 1795, Legajo, 32, Santo Domingo Papers and Cuban Papers. For the 1,000-pound figure see An American, "For the *Louisiana Gazette,*" *Louisiana Gazette,* September 19, 1806.

101. "Plantation Journal, 1819–1825," and "Plantation Journal, 1826–1830," David Rees Family Papers.

102. "Cotton Account Book, 1825–1828," David Rees Family Papers.

103. Din, *Spaniards, Planters, and Slaves,* 177–78, and "Black Code, An Act Prescribing the rules and conduct to be observed with respect to Negroes and other Slaves of this Territory," June 7, 1806, *Acts Passed at the First Session of the First Legislature of the Territory of Orleans,* 150–51.

104. Northup, *Twelve Years a Slave,* 194–96.

105. Ball, *Slavery in the United States,* and Northup, *Twelve Years a Slave.* See Pargas, "In the Fields of a 'Strange Land'" for a broader perspective on this adjustment.

106. Baptist, "Towards a Political Economy of Slave Labor," 33.

107. Baptist, "Toward a Political Economy of Slave Labor," 57–61; Baptist, *The Half Has Never Been Told,* 111–44.

108. Northup, *Twelve Years a Slave,* 165–68.

109. Ball, *Slavery in the United States,* 211–18.

110. Northup, *Twelve Years a Slave,* 163–69, quote on 167.

111. Ball, *Slavery in the United States,* 56.

112. Ball, *Slavery in the United States,* 13–70, 107–15, 146–65, 210–18, 266–74, 319–27, quote on 210.

113. Pargas, "In the Fields of a 'Strange Land,'" 570–72.

114. "Cotton Book of Edward F. Barnes, 1824–1830," Barnes-Willis Family Papers. "Cotton Account Book, 1825–1828," David Rees Family Papers.

3. Making the Sugar Revolution

1. Chaillot, "Clark, Daniel." An anonymous letter to the *Louisiana Gazette* claimed Clark was that author, An Inhabitant, "To the Printer of the Louisiana Gazette," *Louisiana Gazette,* September 23, 1806.

2. An American, "To the Editor of the Louisiana Gazette," *Louisiana Gazette,* August 8 and September 6, 1806, and An American, "For the Louisiana Gazette," *Louisiana Gazette,* September 19, 1806. These articles were published widely in newspapers outside of Louisiana.

3. An American, "To the Editor of the Louisiana Gazette," *Louisiana Gazette,* September 6, 1806.

4. An American, "To the Editor of the Louisiana Gazette," *Louisiana Gazette,* August 8, 1806.

5. For a general overview of the history of the sugar-making process and its spread into and within the Americas, see Mintz, *Sweetness and Power,* 20–52.

6. I have found little evidence of attempts by Louisiana sugar planters to learn about, invent, or discover new approaches to sugar production, either in labor management or technology. Evidence suggests they largely imported Caribbean practices and adapted them to the local climate. This is in marked contrast to the actions of contemporary sugar planters in Cuba as well as later Louisiana planters. Still, the general thinness of evidence for sugar planter practices in this period means that the possibility that

planters were innovating in some ways should not be wholly dismissed. Portuondo, "Plantation Factories"; Follett, *The Sugar Masters*, 22–25, 33–38.

7. The most direct exploration of the sugar revolution in Louisiana is Russell, "Cultural Conflicts and Common Interests," although Russell's focus is not the process of the sugar revolution. While the sugar revolution is fundamental to the remaking of the lower Mississippi valley around the time of the Louisiana Purchase and thus the origins of that core part of the Deep South, most works on the region have either treated it as a part of a different contemporary story or as background to the history of the mature sugar industry of the antebellum period. For the former see important examples such as Ingersoll, *Mammon and Manon in Early New Orleans*, 181–209; Powell, *The Accidental City*, 258–61; Rothman, *Slave Country*, 73–117. For important examples of the latter see Follett, *The Sugar Masters*; Rehder, *Delta Sugar*; Sitterson, *Sugar Country*.

8. M'Gruder, "From a long letter written by Mr. M'Gruder, and published in the Orleans Gazette," *Frankfort Argus*, April 7, 1808.

9. Rehder, *Delta Sugar*, 49–50.

10. See an American, "For the Louisiana Gazette," *Louisiana Gazette*, September 19, 1806, for an estimate of the capital needed to set up a sugar plantation.

11. Robin, *Voyage to Louisiana*, 76–77.

12. Bouligny, *Louisiana in 1776*, 50–51.

13. Boré, "Culture du sucre sa restauration en 1795 par Mr. Boré habitant," Pierre Clément Laussat Papers.

14. "[Translation] of a letter from a gentleman in New-Orleans to his friend in this city, dated April 25th, 1792." *Independent Gazetteer*, June 2, 1792.

15. Boré, "Culture du sucre sa restauration en 1795 par Mr. Boré habitant," Pierre Clément Laussat Papers.

16. Boré, "Culture du sucre sa restauration en 1795 par Mr. Boré habitant," Pierre Clément Laussat Papers.

17. Boré, "Culture du sucre sa restauration en 1795 par Mr. Boré habitant," Pierre Clément Laussat Papers.

18. Boré, "Culture du sucre sa restauration en 1795 par Mr. Boré habitant," Pierre Clément Laussat Papers.

19. Boré, "Culture du sucre sa restauration en 1795 par Mr. Boré habitant," Pierre Clément Laussat Papers.

20. Collot, *Voyage dans l'Amérique Septentrionale*, 2:224–32.

21. Laussat, *Memoirs of My Life*, 51.

22. Whitaker, *The Mississippi Question*, 93.

23. Meeting, August 16, 1800, *Records and Deliberations of the Cabildo*, vol. 4, book 3, 203–16, reel 91–16.

24. Many observers pointed to the convenience for the United States of having an internal supply of sugar. See, for example, An American, "To the Editor of the

Louisiana Gazette," *Louisiana Gazette,* September 6, 1806; Memorial to Congress by the Territorial House of Representatives, November 14, 1805, *The Territorial Papers of the United States,* vol. 9, *The Territory of Orleans,* 531; untitled article on the advantages of acquiring Louisiana, *Newburyport Herald,* July 15, 1803. For the reopening of the slave trade see "An Act further providing for the government of the territory of Orleans," *The Public Statutes at Large of the United States of America from the Organization of the Government in 1789, to March 3, 1845,* 2:322–23.

25. "Ley iiii. Que no se pueda hacer execucion en ingenios de azúcar" (Law 4. That an execution cannot be carried out against sugar mills), *Recopilacion de Leyes de los Reynos de las Indias,* 173.

26. Claiborne to Jefferson, May 1, 1804, *Official Letter Books of W. C. C. Claiborne,* 2:119–21; *Maria Luisa Senechal D'Auberville, widow of Francisco de Bouligny vs. Francisco Mayronne and Juan Bautista Degruys,* begun June 14, 1803, manuscript page 110, no. 4355, Spanish Judicial Records.

27. "An Act for laying a Duty on Goods, Wares, and Merchandise imported into the United States," *The Public Statutes at Large of the United States of America from the Organization of the Government in 1789, to March 3, 1845,* 1:24–27; the sugar tariffs are on 25.

28. Pontalba to Chappelles, March 26, 1796, *The Letters of Joseph X. Pontalba to His Wife,* 64.

29. Pontalba to Chappelles, November 2, 1796, *The Letters of Joseph X. Pontalba to His Wife,* 391.

30. Collot, *Voyage dans l'Amérique Septentrionale,* 2:224.

31. Boré, "Culture du sucre sa restauration en 1795 par Mr. Boré habitant," Pierre Clément Laussat Papers.

32. Calculated from *Population Schedules of the Third Census of the United States, 1810, Louisiana,* reel 10.

33. All figures calculated from "General Census of St. Charles Parish, 1804," Conrad, *St. Charles,* 389–407.

34. "List of Louisiana's Imports and Exports in 1800 and 1801"; "List of Louisiana's Imports and Exports in 1802," Dispatches from US Consuls in New Orleans Louisiana.

35. Jones to Marshall or the Secretary of State, May 15, 1801, Dispatches from US Consuls in New Orleans Louisiana.

36. *Population Schedules of the Third Census of the United States, 1810, Louisiana,* reel 10, 94.

37. *Agriculture of the United States in 1860,* 69.

38. For 1820 value see *Population Schedules of the Fourth Census of the United States, 1820, Louisiana,* reel 31, 77. For 1860 values see *Agriculture of the United States in 1860,* 69.

39. Clark, *New Orleans,* 305.

40. See Sitterson, *Sugar Country,* 145, for a brief overview of sugar boilers' work during the early 1800s. For an example of a sugar maker being employed to run the whole plantation see *Charles Lalonde Dapremont vs. Isabelle Arnaud Trepagnier,* docket nos. 25 and 70, April 19 and May 28, 1804, Territory of Orleans Superior Court. In these early years sugar makers looking for work advertised their knowledge of both the cultivation of sugarcane and manufacture of sugar. See "To Emigrants," *Daily Advertiser,* February 14, 1804.

41. Collot, *Voyage dans l'Amérique Septentrionale,* 2:230.

42. Untitled advertisement, *Moniteur de la Louisiane,* September 10, 1803; "Notice," *Louisiana Courier,* July 12, 1809.

43. Robin, *Voyage to Louisiana,* 108.

44. Information submitted by Patricio Urriel to transport some enslaved people to New Orleans, April 9, 1802, no. 4082, Spanish Judicial Records.

45. *Gil Eugenio Mabire vs. Francisco Mayronne and Juan Bautista Degruis,* May 29, 1800, no. 3913, Spanish Judicial Records.

46. "For Sale, A Gang of Negroes," *The Telegraphe, General Advertiser,* December 12, 1807.

47. Calculated using data from the Louisiana Slave Database. The data for the calculation was drawn from all available record types.

48. Only a handful of advertisements for enslaved sugar makers appeared in newspapers and relatively few sugar makers appeared in other documents. In addition, no observer I have found mentions the use of enslaved people to run a sugar house, much less a plantation. In contrast, white sugar makers appeared often in the newspapers and other documents and observers, with rare exceptions, saw them as a necessary factor in Louisiana's sugar industry. Follett, in *The Sugar Masters,* argues that some antebellum sugar planters systematically replaced white laborers with skilled enslaved people in all aspects of the plantation, including in the sugar house. Follett, *The Sugar Masters,* 122–29. It is certainly possible that planters in the early period used more enslaved sugar makers than is suggested here. However, if so, the evidence has not survived.

49. Robin, *Voyage to Louisiana,* 109. The architect Barthélemy Lafon designed and built sugar houses soon after sugar was introduced. See *Barthélemy Lafon vs. Jean Baptiste Riviere,* September 30, 1801, no. 4111, Spanish Judicial Records. Lafon was from France and had apparently never spent any time in the Caribbean. Therefore, he must have learned the skill in Louisiana. Travis, "Lafon, Barthélemy."

50. Collot, *Voyage dans l'Amérique Septentrionale,* 2:226.

51. Poydras to Dunbar, October 22, 1796; Poydras to Young, October 22, 1796, "Letterbook of private and commercial correspondence of an indigo and cotton planter," 27.

52. Robin, *Voyage to Louisiana,* 109.

53. "Talcott & Bowers," *Louisiana Courier,* July 5, 1809.

54. "For Sale," *Louisiana Courier,* September 13, 1811.

55. "To the Sugar Planters in Louisiana," *Louisiana Courier,* August 7, 1809.

56. [Berquin-Duvallon], *Travels in Louisiana and the Floridas,* 109–10.

57. "Louisiana and Mississippi," *Genius of Liberty,* August 3, 1819.

58. Francois Bossier, "For Sale," *Louisiana Courier,* November 13, 1820. See *Agriculture of the United States in 1860,* 69 for Natchitoches's nonproduction of sugar in 1860.

59. Pontalba to Chappelles, November 2, 1796, *The Letters of Joseph X. Pontalba to His Wife,* 391.

60. Collot, *Voyage dans l'Amérique Septentrionale,* 2:232. For comparison to the Caribbean, see Burnard, *Planters, Merchants, and Slaves,* 175. Burnard shows that, by the middle years of the 1700s, over half of rural Jamaican enslaved people lived on plantations with more than 150 slaves. Over 80 percent of rural Jamaican enslaved people lived on plantations with more than thirty-five enslaved people. By contrast, only 1 planter in Louisiana had more than 150 enslaved people in 1810, and that planter (Joseph Descuir of Pointe Coupee, with 171 enslaved people) was likely a cotton planter. Calculated from *Population Schedules of the Third Census of the United States, 1810, Louisiana,* reel 10. In 1820 6 Louisiana planters had more than 150 enslaved people, but of these only 3 were likely sugar planters (Wade Hampton of Ascension Parish with 461 enslaved people, Joseph Erwin of Iberville Parish with 194 enslaved people, and Lucien La Branche of Orleans Parish with 155 enslaved people). Through 1820, the number of enslaved people on sugar plantations in Louisiana lagged far behind what was typical in mature Caribbean sugar colonies. Calculated from *Population Schedules of the Fourth Census of the United States, 1820, Louisiana,* reels 30–32.

61. An American, "To the Editor of the Louisiana Gazette," *Louisiana Gazette,* September 6, 1806. Follett has found that this problem continued into the antebellum period. Follett, *The Sugar Masters,* 88.

62. Collot, *Voyage dans l'Amérique Septentrionale,* 2:225–27.

63. Pitot, *Observations on the Colony of Louisiana,* 74–75

64. William Taylor to John McDonogh Jr., April 8, 1804, John Minor Wisdom Collection (John McDonogh series).

65. Pitot, *Observations on the Colony of Louisiana,* 75

66. *New Orleans Price Current and Commercial Intelligencer,* April 7, 1827.

67. "To the Grocers of the City of Baltimore," *Daily Advertiser,* June 17, 1805.

68. Boré, "Answer to the Grocers of Baltimore," *Orleans Gazette,* September 18, 1805.

69. "To the Grocers of the City of Baltimore," *Daily Advertiser,* June 17, 1805.

70. "For the Orleans Gazette," *Orleans Gazette and Commercial Advertiser,* August 3, 1805. An 1827 accounting of the destinations of Louisiana sugar showed that 88 percent of sugar went to those four ports, with 50 percent going to New York alone. *New Orleans Price Current and Commercial Intelligencer,* April 7, 1827.

71. Collot, *Voyage dans l'Amérique Septentrionale*, 2:227–30.

72. Laussat, *Memoirs of My Life*, 52, 59.

73. Follett, *The Sugar Masters*, 22–23.

74. An American, "To the Editor of the Louisiana Gazette," *Louisiana Gazette*, September 6, 1806.

75. All figures calculated from "General Census of St. Charles Parish, 1804," Conrad, *St. Charles*, 389–407.

76. *Population Schedules of the Fourth Census of the United States, 1820, Louisiana*, reel 31, 72.

77. An American, "For the Louisiana Gazette," *Louisiana Gazette*, September 19, 1806.

78. Clark, *New Orleans*, 305–6, 310.

79. William Kenner & Co. to Joseph Erwin, March 3, 1818, Edward J. Gay Family Papers.

80. Clark, *New Orleans*, 308–11.

81. See Martin, "Slavery's Invisible Engine" for a broad discussion of slave mortgages.

82. Slave sales, Daniel Clark to Various Buyers, October 2 to October 4, 1787, *Natchez Court Records*, 44–45.

83. F. Bazile, "State of Louisiana," *Louisiana Courier*, December 13, 1813.

84. Advertisements from the following newspapers were used: *Baton Rouge Gazette, Commercial Advertiser, Louisiana Courier, Louisiana Gazette, Moniteur de la Louisiane, Orleans Gazette, St. Francisville Timepiece, Telegraph*.

85. For the Louisiana Bank, see Claiborne to Albert Gallatin, May 23, 1804, *Official Letter Books of W. C. C. Claiborne, 1801–1816*, 2:161; Claiborne to James Madison, January 13, 1805, *The Territorial Papers of the United States*, vol. 9, *The Territory of Orleans*, 368; *Ordinance Establishing the Louisiana Bank*. For the Bank of the United States, see Jefferson to Claiborne, April 17, 1804, *The Territorial Papers of the United States*, vol. 9, *The Territory of Orleans*, 225–26.

86. The Bank of Orleans and the Planters' Bank were incorporated in 1811. "An Act Incorporating the Planters' Bank in the City of New Orleans," April 15, 1811; "An Act to Incorporate the Bank of Orleans," April 30, 1811, *Acts Passed at the Second Session of the Third Legislature of the Territory of Orleans*, 86–101, 164–79. The Louisiana State Bank was incorporated in 1818. "An Act to Establish a State Bank, to be known by the name of The Louisiana State Bank," March 14, 1818, *Acts Passed at the Second Session of the Third Legislature of the State of Louisiana*, 78–91.

87. Haynes, *The Mississippi Territory and the Southwest Frontier, 1795–1817*, 216.

88. See, for example, Baptist, "Toxic Debt, Liar Loans, Collateralized and Securitized Human Beings, and the Panic of 1837."

89. Evan Jones and Paul Lanusse, "Louisiana Bank," *Louisiana Gazette*, December 28, 1804. See James Lyon, "Enquiry Relative to Banks [Extracted from the

'Union']," *Ordinance Establishing the Louisiana Bank*, 26–42, for another contemporary explanation of banks' utility.

90. Petition of Armand Duplantier for Bankruptcy Protection, docket no. 2967, April 2, 1811, Territory of Orleans Superior Court.

91. Pontalba to Chappelles, March 19, June 17, and September 8, 1796, *The Letters of Joseph X. Pontalba to His Wife*, 50–51, 180–81, 276–78. Pontalba mentions Riviere and his wife as attendees at parties and dinners held by the region's elites.

92. *Estate of Magdeleine Brazilier vs. Jean Baptiste Riviere*, docket no. 587, October 31, 1805, Territory of Orleans Superior Court.

93. "A Vendre, en totalité ou par moitié" (For sale, in whole or in half), *Moniteur de la Louisiane*, January 22, 1803.

94. *Estate of Magdeleine Brazilier vs. Jean Baptiste Riviere*, docket no. 587, October 31, 1805, Territory of Orleans Superior Court.

95. *Creditors of Jean Baptiste Riviere vs. Jean Baptiste Riviere*, docket no. 1052, December 13, 1806, Territory of Orleans Superior Court.

96. *Jean Baptiste Riviere vs. His Creditors*, docket no. 1707, June 17, 1808, Territory of Orleans Superior Court.

97. Petition of Jean Frances Merieult, docket no. 906, June 6, 1806, Territory of Orleans Superior Court.

98. An American, "For the Louisiana Gazette," *Louisiana Gazette*, September 19, 1806.

99. "Plantation Journal, 1826–1830," "Plantation Journal, 1831–1835," and David Rees to Elizabeth Rees, February 21, 1830, David Rees Family Papers.

100. Alexander Norie and Thomas Lily Partnership Agreement, Narcisse Broutin, notary, January–December 1802, 4:366, New Orleans Notarial Archives.

101. Contract, Guillaume Desk and Pierre Berguine, November 22, 1799, *St. Charles Parish, La., Original Acts, misc. court records, 1741–1899*, part 10–11, *1792–1795, 1796–1798*.

102. Benjamin Morgan, Untitled advertisement, *Louisiana Courier*, June 12, 1812.

103. "Journal et Relevé de Comptes depuis L'année 1814, Commencé de ce jour 14 Avril 1830 L'an de Grace," (Journal and Statement of Accounts since the year 1814, Begun on this day April 14 the year of our Lord 1830) Boucry Family Papers.

104. "Plantation Journal, 1831–1835," David Rees Family Papers.

105. "General Census of St. Charles Parish, 1804," Conrad, *St. Charles*, 389–407.

106. An Emigrant from Maryland, "To the Planters of Maryland and Virginia," *Daily National Intelligencer*, September 5, 1817.

107. Roberts, *Slavery and Enlightenment in the British Atlantic*, 131–60, quote on 132.

108. Laussat, *Memoirs of My Life*, 54–55

109. "From the Milledgeville Reflector: Some notices of the City of New Orleans and of the State of Louisiana," *City of Washington Gazette*, December 8, 1817.

110. Montulé, *Travels in America,* 89.

111. Two works that compare sugar with tobacco are Dunn, *A Tale of Two Plantations,* and Roberts, *Slavery and Enlightenment in the British Atlantic.* They unsurprisingly find the lives of enslaved people on sugar plantations to be much harsher than those on tobacco plantations. Also see Follett, "'Lives of Living Death'"; Follett, *The Sugar Masters,* 46–89; Higman, *Slave Populations of the British Caribbean;* and Tadman, "The Demographic Costs of Sugar."

112. For harvesting during the antebellum period see Follett, *The Sugar Masters,* 10–13, 46–47, 101–2.

113. Laussat, *Memoirs of My Life,* 60.

114. Northup, *Twelve Years a Slave,* 194.

115. "Plantation Journal, 1826–1830"; "Plantation Journal, 1831–1835," David Rees Family Papers. In 1831, Rees kept his journal through October. In 1832, the second year he operated his sugar house, he kept it year-round.

116. "Plantation Journal, 1831–1835," David Rees Family Papers; Northup, *Twelve Years a Slave,* 194–96.

117. Laussat, *Memoirs of My Life,* 54.

118. Conrad, *The German Coast,* 59–60, 91–92, 96–97. Five large estates were inventoried between 1803 and 1811 in St. Charles Parish. Of these only two included the jobs of the enslaved: that of François Trepagnier and his late wife Marie-Louise Labranche, inventoried in June of 1810, and that of Louis-Augustin Meullion, inventoried in October of 1810. In each case, the slave driver was listed first and had a particularly high appraised value ($1,300 in one case and $1,000 in the other). Both slave drivers were also listed as forty years old and natives of Louisiana. Another, much smaller estate, that of Alexandre Baure and Elisabeth Anne Trepagnier, listed a driver who was appraised at $900 and was also forty years old. He was also listed first in the list of enslaved people.

119. John Mills to Gilbert Jackson, May 19, 1807, John Mills Letters.

120. Northup, *Twelve Years a Slave,* 194, 209–10.

121. Roberts, *Slavery and Enlightenment in the British Atlantic,* 133–47.

122. An American, "For the Louisiana Gazette," *Louisiana Gazette,* September 19, 1806.

123. Calculated from the Louisiana Slave Database. When working with gender data from the Louisiana Slave Database, "adult" is defined as over thirteen to match the 1820 federals census's demographic categories for enslaved people.

124. All figures calculated from data in *Census for 1820,* 123–24.

125. *Population of the United States in 1860,* 192–93. St. Charles Parish still had an adult male-to-female ratio of 1.52. Here adult is defined as over fourteen to match how census data was reported in 1860. Tadman, *Speculators and Slaves,* 64–70

126. In 1820, New Orleans had an enslaved adult man-to-woman ratio of 0.49 (or roughly one man for every two women). Calculated from data in *Census for 1820,* 123–24.

127. "From the Milledgeville Reflector: Some notices of the City of New Orleans and of the State of Louisiana," *City of Washington Gazette,* December 8, 1817.

128. All figures calculated from *Census for 1820,* 18, 122–24.

129. See note 111 in this chapter. Also see Malone, *Sweet Chariot.*

130. Follett, "'Lives of Living Death.'"

131. *Agriculture of the United States in 1860,* 69.

132. "By N. Lauve," *Louisiana Courier,* November 6, 1815. This advertisement is the announcement of an auction at Maspero's exchange of a plantation in St. Tammany that had sixteen arpents planted in sugarcane.

133. Figures calculated from *Population Schedules of the Fourth Census of the United States, 1820, Louisiana,* reel 31, 180–84.

134. Figures calculated from *Population Schedules of the Fifth Census of the United States, 1830, Louisiana,* reel, 43, 130–57.

135. Most 1820 figures calculated from *Census for 1820,* 123–24. 1820 values for St. Tammany by size of enslaved population calculated from *Population Schedules of the Fourth Census of the United States, 1820, Louisiana,* reel 31, 180–84. 1830 figures calculated from *Population Schedules of the Fifth Census of the United States, 1830, Louisiana,* reel, 43, 130–57, 480–81, 676–77.

4. Remaking the Slave Trades

1. "Black Villainy," *Bangor Weekly Register,* June 4, 1818. This article was originally from *Relf's Philadelphia Gazette.* This article as well as many of the subsequent articles on the smuggling was republished widely.

2. This case is discussed in Hartog, *The Trouble with Minna,* 74–78. Hartog uncovered that the Morgan ring forged over one hundred enslaved people's consents to be moved to New Orleans.

3. "From the New-Orleans Chronicle, July 14," *New-York Daily Advertiser,* August 6, 1818.

4. "From the New-Orleans Gazette of July 15," *New-York Spectator,* August 7, 1818.

5. Untitled, *New England Palladium & Commercial Advertiser,* August 18, 1818.

6. Hartog, *The Trouble with Minna,* 77–78.

7. For Morgan's plantation in 1810, see *Population Schedules of the Third Census of the United States, 1810, Louisiana,* reel 10, 271. For Morgan's plantation in 1820, see *Population Schedules of the Fourth Census of the United States, 1820, Louisiana,* reel 31, 120.

8. Sebastián Calvo de la Puerta y O'Farrill the Marquis de Casa Calvo to the Cabildo, September 24, 1800, presented at the October 24, 1800, meeting, *Records and Deliberations of the Cabildo,* vol. 4, book 4, 13–29, quotes on 15 and 18, reel 91–16.

9. Claiborne to Jefferson, April 15, 1804, *The Territorial Papers of the United States,* vol. 9, *The Territory of Orleans,* 221–23, quote on 222.

10. Harms, *The Diligent*, 81–83. Harms shows how French slave traders carried goods from India, Germany, Sweden, and elsewhere, acting as middlemen for vast exchange networks that delivered desirable goods to the coast of Africa in exchange for enslaved Africans.

11. "American slaves" and "enslaved Americans" are something of misnomers, as, with advancing American sovereignty, enslaved people already in the region also became resident in the United States. However, it does give the sense, common in the region, that this group of enslaved people was distinct from enslaved people already living in the region and were often called "American" or, less commonly "English."

12. Mills to Jackson, May 19, 1807, John Mills Letters.

13. See Deyle, *Carry Me Back;* Gudmestad, *A Troublesome Commerce;* Tadman, *Speculators and Slaves.*

14. One of the clearest accounts of the development of the trade into and during the antebellum period is Rothman, *The Ledger and the Chain.*

15. Studies on this process are extensive for the effects of the international slave trade. See, for example, Hall, *Africans in Colonial Louisiana;* Hall, *Slavery and African Ethnicities in the Americas;* Heywood and Thornton, *Central Africans, Atlantic Creoles, and the Foundation of the Americas;* Mintz, "Enduring, Trying Theories"; Mintz and Price, *The Birth of African-American Culture;* Sweet, *Recreating Africa;* and Wheat, *Atlantic Africa and the Spanish Caribbean.* For broader explorations of the African Diaspora see, among many others, Falola, *The African Diaspora;* Gomez, *Reversing Sail, A History of the African Diaspora.*

16. When looking at this transitory period of the slave trade (i.e., from the international trade to the internal trade) scholars have typically looked very narrowly at how the trades worked in the lower Mississippi valley or more holistically at the entire picture of the trade throughout the United States. For the former see Chambers, "Slave Trade Merchants of Spanish New Orleans, 1763–1803"; Ingersoll, "The Slave Trade and the Ethnic Diversity of Louisiana's Slave Community"; Leglaunec, "Slave Migrations in Spanish and Early American Louisiana"; Leglaunec, "Notes and Documents." For the latter, see Deyle, *Carry Me Back,* chapter 1; Gudmestad, *A Troublesome Commerce,* chapter 1; Gudmestad, "Slave Resistance, Coffles, and Debates over Slavery"; Mcmillin *The Final Victims;* Rothman, "The Domestication of the Slave Trade in the United States"; Tadman, "The Interregional Slave Trade in the History and Myth-Making of the U.S. South"; Tadman, *Speculators and Slaves,* chapter 2.

17. Enslaved people could only be introduced if they were Creole or foreign born but introduced to the United States prior to May 1, 1798, and brought by an individual who intended to settle in the territory. "An Act erecting Louisiana into two territories, and providing for the temporary government thereof," *Public Statutes at Large of the United States of America from the Organization of the Government in 1789, to March 3, 1845,* 2:286.

18. *Memorial presented by the inhabitants of Louisiana to the Congress of the United States,* 18.

19. Watkins to Claiborne, February 2, 1804, *Official Letter Books of W. C. C. Claiborne, 1801–1816,* 2:3–13, quotes on 10.

20. Claiborne to Madison, March 1, 1804, *Official Letter Books of W. C. C. Claiborne, 1801–1816,* 2:13–14, quote on 14.

21. Claiborne to Madison, July 5, 1804, *Official Letter Books of W. C. C. Claiborne, 1801–1816,* 2:236–38, quote on 238.

22. "An Act further providing for the government of the territory of Orleans," *Public Statutes at Large of the United States of America from the Organization of the Government in 1789, to March 3, 1845,* 2:322–23. Prior to the new law, the territory was governed by the governor and a legislative council appointed by the president.

23. Shugerman, "The Louisiana Purchase and South Carolina's Reopening of the Slave Trade in 1803." Shugerman argues that South Carolina reopened the trade, at least in part, to take advantage of the market for enslaved people in Louisiana.

24. Meeting, August 16, 1800, *Records and Deliberations of the Cabildo,* vol. 4, book 3, 203–16, quotes on 206 and 210, reel 91–16.

25. Din, *Spaniards, Planters, and Slaves,* 205–9.

26. The governments of Louisiana and Mississippi periodically regulated the internal slave trade. In 1808, Mississippi's legislature enacted "An Act regulating the importation of Slaves, and for other purposes," which required a certificate from an imported enslaved person's place of origin attesting that they had never been convicted of certain crimes. *Acts Passed by the Fourth General Assembly of the Mississippi Territory during Their Second Session,* 37–40. In 1810, the territory of Orleans legislature enacted "An Act Concerning the introduction of certain Slaves from any of the states or territories of the United States of America," which banned the importation of any enslaved person who had been convicted of a capital crime. *Acts Passed at the First Session of the Third Legislature of the Territory of Orleans,* 44–49.

27. Leglaunec, "Slave Migrations in Spanish and Early American Louisiana," 195–96, 199, 202. Chambers in "Slave Trade Merchants of Spanish New Orleans, 1763–1803" estimates around 12,500 enslaved people over roughly the same period.

28. Trans-Atlantic Slave Trade Database.

29. Usner, *Indians, Settlers, and Slaves in a Frontier Exchange Economy,* 114–15.

30. "An Act erecting Louisiana into two Territories and providing for the Temporary Government thereof," *Public Statutes at Large of the United States of America from the Organization of the Government in 1789, to March 3, 1845,* 2:283–89. This law banned the slave trade on October 1, 1804. Claiborne interpreted his instructions to mean that he was to implement Spanish law as it had been, including on the slave trade. See Claiborne to Madison, January 31, 1804, Claiborne, *Official Letter Books of W. C. C. Claiborne, 1801–1816,* 1:352–53. For the number of enslaved people imported see Leglaunec, "Notes and Documents," 226.

31. Leglaunec, "Slave Migrations in Spanish and Early American Louisiana," 209, for the totals and Leglaunec, "Notes and Documents," 226–30, for the list of individual ships and their origins.

32. The 1810 figures calculated from 1810 federal census data in *Urban Statistical Surveys*, 82–83. The 1810 figure includes both the Mississippi Territory and territory of Orleans but not the "Florida parishes," which were transitioning to American rule as this census was taken and were, thus, not included.

33. See O'Malley, *Final Passages* for an overview of the British American transshipment trade, including with Spanish colonies like Louisiana.

34. Leglaunec, "Slave Migrations in Spanish and Early American Louisiana," 195–96, 199, 207.

35. O'Malley, *Final Passages*, 21–24. O'Malley finds that most Africans traded between American colonies were "New Negroes" who had been in the Americas for only a few days or weeks.

36. The Trans-Atlantic Slave Trade Database contains eighteen ships that landed 3,428 enslaved Africans directly from Africa in the lower Mississippi valley between 1783 and 1808.

37. Merieult, Untitled advertisement, *Moniteur de la Louisiane*, September 3, 1803.

38. Chambers, "Slave Trade Merchants of Spanish New Orleans, 1763–1803," 338–39. Chambers gives some biographical details for Clark, Dupuy, and Pollock. Pierre Clément de Laussat mentioned in his memoir that Labatut was from Bayonne. Laussat, *Memoirs of My Life*, 76.

39. *R. R. Keene and Daniel Clark vs. John Forbes and Thomas Forbes*, docket no. 1465, February 13, 1808, Territory of Orleans Superior Court.

40. Dunbar to Thomas Tunno and John Price, February 1, 1807, *Life, Letters and Papers of William Dunbar*, 351–52, quotes on 351.

41. Chambers, "Slave Trade Merchants of Spanish New Orleans, 1763–1803," 338–39. For Clark's plantation in 1810, see *Population Schedules of the Third Census of the United States, 1810, Louisiana*, reel 10, 16.

42. For Clark's sales of enslaved people see Slave sales, Daniel Clark to Various Buyers, October 2 to October 4, 1787, *Natchez Court Records, 1767–1805*, 44–45. For Clark's early cultivation of cotton see 1792 Natchez census in Mississippi, U.S., State and Territorial Census Collection. Clark's involvement in the building of the first sawtooth cotton gin is discussed in chapter 2 of this book.

43. Chambers, "Slave Trade Merchants of Spanish New Orleans, 1763–1803," 338. For Sauve's plantation in 1810, see *Population Schedules of the Third Census of the United States, 1810, Louisiana*, Reel 10, 286. For Sauve's sugar cultivation, see Laussat, *Memoirs of My Life*, 28. For Sauve being French, see Dunbar to Jefferson, October 15, 1804, *The Territorial Papers of the United States*, vol. 9, *The Territory of Orleans*, 305.

44. Leglaunec, "Slave Migrations in Spanish and Early American Louisiana," 209.

45. James Leonard to Robert Smith, July 14, 1807, Letters Received by the Secretary of the Navy from Officers Below the Rank of Commander, reel 3. In this letter, Leonard, the commander of naval forces based in New Orleans, reported to Robert Smith about an incident in which a local naval commander and his sailors intervened in the disciplining of an enslaved person by her enslaver. Leonard asserted that one reason why locals had reacted so strongly to the incident was the forthcoming ban on the international slave trade in 1808, which, along with emancipation in the northern states, had led to fears that the national government would pursue a policy of emancipation in the territory. I have found no other example of discontent with the 1808 slave trade ban.

46. Head, "Slave Smuggling by Foreign Privateers."

47. *Territory of Orleans vs. One hundred and fifty three negroes the Cargo of the Ship Alerta,* docket no. 2585, July 24, 1810; *Territory of Orleans vs. One Hundred & Six Negroes,* docket no. 2604, August 24, 1810; *Territory of Orleans vs. Seventy negroes,* docket no. 2610, August 30, 1810; *Territory of Orleans vs. Five slaves imported in the armed vessel L'Epine,* docket no. 2613, September 1, 1810, Territory of Orleans Superior Court. Thomas Ingersoll has found similar cases in Federal District Court. Ingersoll, "The Slave Trade and the Ethnic Diversity of Louisiana's Slave Community," 160–61.

48. Docket nos. 2579, 2998, and 3248, Territory of Orleans Superior Court. The records for the Chew and Relf smuggling case are dispersed across three different folders in the Territory of Orleans Superior Court records. The most important documents are in *Chew & Relf vs. Theophilo de Millo & Joseph Walden & Joseph Walden and Co.,* docket no. 3248. Docket nos. 2579 and 2998 are unrelated cases that contain documents about this case.

49. Anonymous letter, October 13, 1810, docket no. 3248, Territory of Orleans Superior Court.

50. Head, "Slave Smuggling by Foreign Privateers," 440–41.

51. Information on origins of enslaved people in Louisiana documents drawn from the Louisiana Slave Database.

52. All statistics calculated from the Louisiana Slave Database. When working with origin data from the Louisiana Slave Database, "adult" is defined as fifteen or older.

53. Robin, *Voyage to Louisiana,* 235–36.

54. Harms, *The Diligent,* 352.

55. Robin, *Voyage to Louisiana,* 236.

56. Figures on escapees calculated using data found in the 854 advertisements drawn from the newspapers in the note on fig. 2. All figures on enslaved people in estate inventories calculated using date from the Louisiana Slave Database.

57. Figures calculated using data from the Louisiana Slave Database. The data for this calculation were drawn from all available records in the database.

58. Dessens, *From Saint-Domingue to New Orleans,* 27–29.

59. Claiborne to Lieut. Walsh, May 12, 1809; Claiborne to Robert Smith, May 15, 1809; Claiborne to the Commander at Plaquemine, May 16, 1809; Claiborne to Capt. Many, May 18, 1809; Claiborne to Smith, May 20, 1809; Claiborne to Many, May 22, 1809; Claiborne to Many, June 3, 1809; and Robertson to Smith, July 8, *Official Letter Books of W. C. C. Claiborne, 1801–1816,* 4:351, 354–55, 358–59, 363–67, 378–80. Also see Dessens, *From Saint-Domingue to New Orleans,* 41–45.

60. "An Act for the remission of certain penalties and forfeitures, and for other purposes," *Public Statutes at Large of the United States of America from the Organization of the Government in 1789, to March 3, 1845,* 2:549–50.

61. Dessens, *From Saint-Domingue to New Orleans,* 29.

62. Mather to Claiborne, August 7, 1809, Claiborne, *Official Letter Books of W. C. C. Claiborne,* 4:404–9.

63. Lachance, "Repercussions of the Haitian Revolution in Louisiana," 209–30; Dessens, *From Saint-Domingue to New Orleans,* 32.

64. All figures calculated using data from the Louisiana Slave Database.

65. Dessens, *From Saint-Domingue to New Orleans,* chapter 3 for importance of the refugees in New Orleans.

66. Dessens, *From Saint-Domingue to New Orleans,* 81. Dessens argues that skilled enslaved Saint-Dominguans were important to the development of the sugar industry. This is certainly possible, perhaps even likely. However, I have found no contemporary evidence for this. This is in marked contrast to the clear importance of white Saint-Domingue refugees to the development of the sugar industry.

67. Tadman, *Speculators and Slaves,* 42–44. Tadman estimates that between 33 percent and 50 percent of enslaved people moved to the region were traded between 1790 and 1820, meaning that between 50 percent and 67 percent moved with a settler. As Tadman points out, these numbers are crude estimates.

68. Hall, *Africans in Colonial Louisiana,* 283.

69. This is reminiscent of O'Malley's portrayal of the intercolonial trade in *Final Passages* (i.e., early disorganization giving way to a more organized trade later) with the major difference that the internal slave trade organized much more quickly.

70. Act 4, Slave Sale, John Hardeman to Illegible; Act 5, Slave Sale, John Hardeman to John Burbin; Act 7, Slave Sale, John Hardeman to Simon Allen, May 21, 1804, *Iberville La. Conveyances, 1770–1900,* part 12, *Original Acts, May 1804–February 1808,* vol. A8 & 9.

71. Cramer, *The Navigator,* 295.

72. Rothman, *The Ledger and the Chain,* 9–13, 46–47.

73. Tadman, *Speculators and Slaves,* 21.

74. James McIntosh to Winthrop Sargent, October 4, 1801, Winthrop Sargent Papers, reel 6.

75. Slave sales between December 9, 1817, and January 29, 1818, and between October 22, 1818, and February 5, 1819, Edward J. Gay Family Papers.

76. Levina Erwin to Jane Craighead, April 10, 1818, Edward J. Gay Family Papers.

77. For Joseph Erwin's plantation in 1810, see *Population Schedules of the Third Census of the United States, 1810, Louisiana,* reel 10, 167. For Erwin's plantation in 1820, see *Population Schedules of the Fourth Census of the United States, 1820, Louisiana,* reel 31, 72.

78. Hillen and Wedenstrandt, "For Sale," *Louisiana Courier,* June 28, 1809.

79. "For Sale," *Louisiana Courier,* January 6, 1809. See Lawrence Powell, *The Accidental City,* 329, for John Clay's probable relationship to Henry Clay.

80. The Morgan ring was not even the only group moving enslaved people out of New Jersey. Hartog, *The Trouble with Minna,* 69–74, 78–82. Hartog interprets New Jersey law in the early 1800s as reacting to the smuggling of enslaved people out of the state. He also identifies another case of smuggling around the same time the Morgan ring was active.

81. "For the Baltimore Patriot," *Baltimore Patriot,* March 5, 1816.

82. Bell, *Stolen,* 56–61, 197–98, 206–13.

83. See Wilson, *Freedom at Risk* for an overview of kidnapping between the American Revolution and emancipation.

84. David Rees to unknown, July 16, 1820, David Rees Family Papers.

85. See Gudmestad, *A Troublesome Commerce,* 7–33, for the lack of large slave-trading firms prior to the War of 1812.

86. Northup, *Twelve Years a Slave,* quote on 159.

87. See Dunn, *A Tale of Two Plantations,* chapter 7. Dunn argues that enslaved people moved from the Virginia plantation he studied to Alabama by their enslavers likely did not experience the same level of dislocation as did slaves sold into the internal slave trade as they retained the same enslaver, plantation practices, and at least some of their preexisting community. Edward Baptist paints a much grimmer picture in *The Half Has Never Been Told,* chapter 1, but largely ignores enslaved people who migrated with their enslavers.

88. Hodgson, *Letters from North America Written during a Tour in the United States and Canada,* 1:194–95, quote on 194.

89. Ball, *Slavery in the United States,* 68–70, quote on 69.

90. For more on resistance to and dread of the internal slave trade, see Gudmestad, "Slave Resistance, Coffles, and the Debates over Slavery in the Nation's Capital," 78–79.

91. Considering biases in estate inventories (see appendix), the proportion of enslaved Americans in the region producing the runaway slave advertisements (which included areas heavily settled by Anglo-Americans and did not record origins of enslaved people) was almost certainly above 4 percent but unlikely to be anywhere close to 39 percent.

92. J. B. Tounoir, "Runaway Negro," *Louisiana Courier,* March 15, 1809.

93. "Ten Dollars Reward," *Louisiana Courier,* May 5, 1809.

94. I am not the first scholar to note this re-Africanization. Hall, in *Africans in Colonial Louisiana,* noted it for the Pointe Coupee region of Louisiana over the same period. In addition, Kevin Roberts and Thomas Ingersoll find something similar in New Orleans by using baptismal records: Roberts, "Slaves and Slavery in Louisiana," 101–51; Ingersoll, "The Slave Trade and Ethnic Diversity of Louisiana's Slave Community," 133–61.

95. Morgan, *Slave Counterpoint,* 61. By 1800, Morgan estimates that Virginia had a negligible African population. In South Carolina, he estimates Africans as 8 percent of the population. While South Carolina's African population almost certainly saw a rebound in the first decade of the nineteenth century with the reopening of the slave trade, it's not credible that it came anywhere near that of Louisiana as a proportion of the population.

96. For example, while adult enslaved people on the German Coast (just upriver from New Orleans) listed in estate inventories were 66 percent Africans in the 1790s, in Pointe Coupee (just upriver from Baton Rouge) adult enslaved people in estate inventories were 45 percent African in the 1790s. All figures calculated using data from the Louisiana Slave Database.

97. From 1770 to 1820, enslaved adult African men outnumbered enslaved adult African women 2.3 to 1 on Louisiana estates. Over the same period, enslaved adult American men outnumbered enslaved adult American women by 1.1 to 1. All figures calculated using data from the Louisiana Slave Database.

98. All figures calculated from data in *Census for 1820,* 123, and *Urban Statistical Surveys,* 82.

99. The literature on early modern African ethnic identities and how those ethnicities transformed both in Africa and the Americas is immense. A good point of entry is Sidbury and Cañizares-Esguerra, "Mapping Ethnogenesis in the Early Atlantic World" as well as several of the responses to the article. Also see Brown, *Tacky's Revolt,* especially chapter 3; Byrd, "Eboe, Country, Nation, and Gustavas Vassa's Interesting Narrative"; Sweet, "Defying Social Death."

100. Louisiana Slave Database.

101. This finding is in keeping with the current consensus of scholars of the transatlantic slave trade that rejects the older thesis by Sidney Mintz and Richard Price that argued Africans came in groups mingled by ethnicity and, thus, with little ability to re-create African ethnic connections in America, forcing rapid creation of new Creole identities. Mintz and Price, *The Birth of African-American Culture.* This finding is also in keeping with the perception of contemporary observers and later historians of the lower Mississippi valley. See Hall, *Africans in Colonial Louisiana,* chapter 9, and Roberts, "Slaves and Slavery in Louisiana," especially chapter 3. Beyond the lower Mississippi valley, the literature on the issue of creolization is immense. For an overview of the debates over creolization see Sidbury, "Globalization, Creolization, and the Not-So-Peculiar Institution," and the sources in note 99.

102. All figures calculated using data from the Louisiana Slave Database.

103. Lozières, *Second Voyage à Louisiane,* 72–146.

104. This fact is not surprising, as contemporaries and historians have all recognized the Chesapeake as the primary source for people moved as part of the internal slave trade or migrating with enslavers. One historian has estimated that Virginia and Maryland had a net export of approximately 117,000 and 53,000 people, respectively, between 1800 and 1820. The third largest exporting state was North Carolina, with a net export of approximately 14,000 people. Tadman, "The Interregional Slave Trade in the History and Myth-Making of the U.S. South," 120.

105. According to Michael Tadman's estimates, Tennessee and Kentucky were the third and fourth largest net importers of enslaved people during the 1810s, respectively. Tadman, "The Interregional Slave Trade in the History and Myth-Making of the U.S. South," 120. The importance of enslaved people from these states in the lower Mississippi valley suggests that during this period, large numbers of enslaved people were both moving in and out of these states.

106. Morgan, *Slave Counterpoint,* 559–658. All figures in the paragraph calculated from the Louisiana Slave Database.

107. See Pargas, "Slave Crucibles" for a study of the assimilation of people transported to the Deep South via the interstate slave trade that finds a great deal of conflict between migrants and nonmigrants but also, over time, assimilation and accommodation. The dynamics in the lower Mississippi valley in the period covered by this book would often have been infinitely more complicated considering the even greater diversity.

108. "Esclaves Marons" (Escaped Slaves), *Moniteur de la Louisiane,* September 11, 1802.

109. Crawford, *The Mobilian Trade Language;* Drechsel, *Mobilian Jargon.*

110. "Esclaves Marons," *Moniteur de la Louisiane,* September 11, 1802.

111. "Criminal case file no. 202, Territory of Orleans v. Atys, the Negro slave of Mr. A. Harang, 1811," Territory of Orleans City Court (New Orleans).

112. All figures calculated using data found in the 854 advertisements drawn from the newspapers in the note or fig. 2.

113. Montomat, "Run-Away Slave," *Louisiana Courier,* May 20, 1811.

114. "Runaway," *Louisiana Courier,* August 7, 1811.

115. Blas Puche, "City Jail," *Orleans Gazette and Commercial Advertiser,* June 18, 1807.

116. L. Dre. Duparc, "Runaway Slaves," *Louisiana Courier,* December 6, 1816.

117. "Negres Marons" (Runaway Slaves), *Moniteur de la Louisiane,* February 11, 1804.

118. All figures calculated using data found in the 854 advertisements drawn from the newspapers in the note or fig. 2. Other historians have found similar results from studying runaway slave advertisements at other times and places. See Geggus, "On the Eve of

the Haitian Revolution," 126; Johnson, "Runaway Slaves and the Slave Communities in South Carolina," 437; Kelly, *The Voyage of the Slave Ship* Hare, 172–73.

119. Roberts, "Slaves and Slavery in Louisiana," chapter 3.

120. Kars, *Blood on the River,* 87–92, 114–19, 135, 169–70. Kars details conflicts between enslaved rebels in Berbice during a 1763 rebellion, particularly between Creoles and Africans. The situation Kars details is somewhat unique, as the rebels took control over much of the colony for an extended period leading to conflicts over power and governance. Still, Kars's analysis suggests that these conflicts grew out of preexisting tensions.

121. For deeper discussions of cultural formation in the region as well as interactions between different groups see Follett, *The Sugar Masters,* 218–33; Pargas, "Slave Crucibles"; Roberts, "Slaves and Slavery in Louisiana"; Seck, *Bouki Fait Gombo,* chapter 5.

5. Enslavers Triumphant

1. Manuel Andry to Claiborne, January 11, 1811, and January 11, 1811, at ten o'clock p.m., *Louisiana Courier,* January 14, 1811.

2. Rasmussen, *American Uprising,* 127–28.

3. Some scholars have also pointed to international instability, especially the recent influx of Haitian refugees from Cuba and tensions between Spain and the United States over control of West Florida, as important contexts for understanding the rebellion. That broader context is certainly important for fully understanding the German Coast Insurrection, and the discussion here is not meant to be an exhaustive analysis of the revolt. See Buman, "To Kill Whites"; Eric Herschthal, "Slaves, Spaniards, and Subversion in Early Louisiana"; Paquette, "'A Horde of Brigands?'"

4. An American, "To the Editor of the Louisiana Gazette," *Louisiana Gazette,* September 6, 1806; Nathaniel Cox to Gabriel Lewis, November 23, 1806, Nathaniel Cox Papers.

5. Gray, *History of Agriculture in the Southern United States to 1860,* 681–83, 697–98.

6. Pitot, *Observations on the Colony of Louisiana,* 72.

7. Henry Gardiner to Sargent, March 24, 1807, Winthrop Sargent Papers, reel 6.

8. An American, "To the Editor of the Louisiana Gazette," *Louisiana Gazette,* September 6, 1806.

9. Poydras to Claude Poydras, August 25, 1796, "Letterbook of private and commercial correspondence of an indigo and cotton planter," 21.

10. Poydras to De Materre, March 13, 1800, "Letterbook of private and commercial correspondence of an indigo and cotton planter," 74.

11. Poydras to Meullion, September 15, [1800], "Letterbook of private and commercial correspondence of an indigo and cotton planter," 92.

12. Boré, "Culture du sucre sa restauration en 1795 par Mr. Boré habitant," Pierre Clément Laussat Papers.

13. Din, "Empires Too Far."

14. The 1785 figures calculated from Spanish census data in Usner, *Indians, Settlers, and Slaves in a Frontier Exchange Economy,* 114–15. The 1810 figures calculated from 1810 federal census data in *Urban Statistical Surveys,* 82–83. The "West Florida" parishes, which were transitioning from Spanish to American rule after their "revolution" were not tallied in 1810.

15. Lowery, "The Great Migration to the Mississippi Territory," 185–86.

16. The 1785 figures calculated from Spanish census data in Usner, *Indians, Settlers, and Slaves in a Frontier Exchange Economy,* 114–15. The 1810 figures calculated from *Urban Statistical Surveys,* 82–83. The "West Florida" parishes, which were transitioning from Spanish to American rule after their "revolution" were not tallied in 1810.

17. Figures calculated from *Urban Statistical Surveys,* 82–83. Here "adult" is defined as sixteen or older, in keeping with the census categories used to tabulate the white population in 1810 and 1820.

18. Figures calculated from *Census for 1820,* 122–24.

19. See, for example, An American, "To the Editor of the Louisiana Gazette," *Louisiana Gazette,* August 8 and September 6, 1806; An American, "For the Louisiana Gazette," *Louisiana Gazette,* September 19, 1806.

20. Cox to Lewis, September 15, 1809, Nathaniel Cox Papers.

21. Cox to Lewis, November 23, 1806, Nathaniel Cox Papers.

22. Hore Browse Trist to Mary Brown Trist, January 7, March 9, and March 25, 1803, Nicholas Philip Trist Papers; An Emigrant from Maryland, "To the Planters of Maryland and Virginia," *Daily National Intelligencer,* September 5, 1817.

23. The 1785 figures calculated from Spanish census data in Usner, *Indians, Settlers, and Slaves in a Frontier Exchange Economy,* 114–15. The 1810 figures calculated from *Urban Statistical Surveys,* 82–83. The "West Florida" parishes, which were transitioning from Spanish to American rule after their "revolution" were not tallied in 1810.

24. Figures calculated from 1805 and 1810 territorial census schedules in the Mississippi State and Territorial Census Collection and *Census for 1820,* 122.

25. Figures calculated from "General Census of St. Charles Parish 1804"; Conrad, *St. Charles,* 389–407; *Urban Statistical Surveys,* 82; and *Census for 1820,* 123–24.

26. Figures calculated from 1804 territorial census and 1810 and 1820 federal census schedules. "General Census of St. Charles Parish, 1804," Conrad, *St. Charles,* 389–407; *Population Schedules of the Third Census of the United States, 1810, Louisiana,* reel 10, 423–30; and *Population Schedules of the Fourth Census of the United States, 1820, Louisiana,* reel 30, 67–72.

27. Figures calculated from 1805 and 1810 territorial census and 1820 federal census schedules. For Jefferson County's 1805 and 1810 territorial census schedules, see the Mississippi State and Territorial Census Collection and *Population Schedules of the Fourth Census of the United States, 1820, Mississippi,* reel 58, 49–60.

28. Claiborne to Jefferson, July 5, 1806, *Official Letter Books of W. C. C. Claiborne, 1801–1816,* 3:351.

29. Mills to Jackson, May 19, 1807, John Mills Letters.

30. Equiano, *The Interesting Narrative of Olaudah Equiano,* 224.

31. Mills to Jackson, May 19, 1807, John Mills Letters.

32. Equiano, *The Interesting Narrative of Olaudah Equiano,* 225–26.

33. Here I am using the term "resistance" in a simplistic fashion. Rather than worrying about deeper psychological and even revolutionary meanings that have often been assigned to the term (and certainly have validity), I am using resistance as enslaved people's attempts to evade enslavers' labor demands or general hegemony over their lives, typically in ways that both enslaved people and enslavers would have recognized as resistant. The extensive historiography of slave resistance cannot be reprised here. For a recent overview see Egerton, "Slave Resistance."

34. For a comprehensive account of escaped enslaved people in the United States, see Franklin and Schweninger, *Runaway Slaves.*

35. "Esclaves Marons," *Moniteur de la Louisiane,* September 11, 1802.

36. Claud Guillaud, untitled advertisement, *Louisiana Courier,* March 11, 1811.

37. "Criminales de oficio sobre haben hallado muerto àun negro nom de Cola de D. Estevan Bore en el Parque de Arroz de la Habitacion de D. Roberto Avart," (Criminal investigation into the death of a black man named Cola, belonging to Étienne Boré, in the rice field of Robert Avart's plantation) October 3, 1800, no. 3985, Spanish Judicial Records.

38. Pitot, *Observations on the Colony of Louisiana,* 29–30; Watkins to Claiborne, February 2, 1804, *Official Letter Books of W. C. C. Claiborne, 1801–1816,* 2:3–13; Robin, *Voyage to Louisiana,* 245.

39. N. Girod, "Mayoralty of New Orleans," *Louisiana Courier,* November 18, 1812. In this article, the New Orleans city council ordered the *Louisiana Courier* to reprint six articles of the 1808 Black Code as well an ordinance concerning the navigation of "Negroes and Mulattoes" on Lake Pontchartrain. One of the articles republished required enslaved people to obtain permission to leave their plantation.

40. [Berquin-Duvallon], *Travels in Louisiana and the Floridas,* 84, 88.

41. Laussat, *Memoirs of My Life,* 55.

42. Mills to Jackson, May 19, 1807, John Mills Letters.

43. Hall, *Africans in Colonial Louisiana,* 344–74.

44. Pontalba to Chappelles, September 1 and 13, 1796, *The Letters of Joseph X. Pontalba to His Wife,* 267–68, 287–89.

45. For a classic study of how information moved among peoples of African-descent in the Atlantic World, see Scott, *The Common Wind.*

46. "Criminal case file no. 167, Complaint against the Negro Azi, a slave of Joseph, 1810"; "Criminal case file no. 182, Territory of Orleans v. Rose Marie, 1810"; "Criminal case file no. 202, Territory of Orleans v. Atys, the Negro slave of Mr. A. Harang,

1811"; "Criminal case file no. 207, Territory of Orleans v. the Negro slave Andre, 1811," Territory of Orleans City Court (New Orleans). The quotes are from case file no. 207.

47. Isaac Briggs to Jefferson, January 2, 1804; Carter, *The Territorial Papers of the United States,* vol. 9, *The Territory of Orleans, 1803–1812,* 146–49.

48. Laussat, *Memoirs of My Life,* 54.

49. Latrobe, *Impressions Respecting New Orleans,* 17.

50. Mills to Jackson, May 19, 1807, John Mills Letters.

51. Latrobe, *Impressions Respecting New Orleans,* 53–54.

52. Dunbar to Sargent, March 16, 1807, Winthrop Sargent Papers, reel 6.

53. Mills to Jackson, May 19, 1807, John Mills Letters.

54. Din, *Spaniards, Planters, and Slaves,* 158–59.

55. Conrad, *The German Coast,* 65–66.

56. "Court Docket and Plantation Accounts Book, 1810–1823," David Rees Family Papers.

57. See "Black Code, 'An Act Prescribing the rules and conduct to be observed with respect to Negroes and other Slaves of this Territory,'" June 7, 1806, *Acts Passed at the First Session of the First Legislature of the Territory of Orleans,* 150–91; "A Law for the regulation of Slaves," March 30, 1799, *Sargent's Code,* 44–48. The former formally reenacted many of the ameliorative features of the Spanish slave code (excepting limitations on discipline and the *coartación,* or the right to self-purchase) but tellingly removed penalties for noncompliant enslavers, turning them essentially into suggestions. The latter placed almost no limitations on enslaver power.

58. Din, *Spaniards, Planters, and Slaves,* i–xiv, 35–46. The theme that the Spanish attempted to balance enslaved people versus enslavers for imperial ends runs throughout the book.

59. Johnson, *Slavery's Metropolis,* 134–36, 146, 149–50. Johnson points out that enslavers did not always appreciate the punishment of the people they enslaved, especially if it involved incarceration and the loss of their labor.

60. See Brown, *Tacky's Revolt;* Burnard, *Mastery, Tyranny, and Desire;* Dunn, *A Tale of Two Plantations* for works that look at the brutal world of slavery in Jamaica.

61. Hodgson, *Letters from North America Written during a Tour in the United States and Canada,* 1:24–26, 41, 43–46, quote on 24.

62. Hodgson, *Letters from North America Written during a Tour in the United States and Canada,* 1:184–96, quotes on 190.

63. [Berquin-Duvallon], *Travels in Louisiana and the Floridas,* 63–64, 91–92; and Montulé, *Travels in America,* 89–90. Also see Samuel Hambleton to David Porter, January 25, 1811, and Porter to Hambleton, February 23, 1811, The Papers of David Porter for the distaste US Navy officers based in New Orleans had developed for the "characteristic barbarity" of the "depraved" planters.

64. See Latrobe, *Impressions Respecting New Orleans,* 53, and [Berquin-Duvallon], *Travels in Louisiana and the Floridas,* 63–64, 91–92, for two writers who identified Creole culture as the cause of mistreatment.

65. Mills to Jackson, May 19, 1807, John Mills Letters.

66. Mills to Jackson, May 19, 1807, John Mills Letters.

67. This interpretation of the region's slavery coincides with Baptist's interpretation of slavery in the "Old Southwest," in *The Half Has Never Been Told.*

68. The discussion of the German Coast Insurrection presented here is not intended to be comprehensive. Other works have explored the rebellion in detail. The most complete work on the 1811 uprising is Rasmussen, *American Uprising.* Rasmussen's work is a popularizing account of the revolt and hence lacks some academic rigor. More rigorous recent analyses of the revolt can be found in Buman, "To Kill Whites," and Paquette, "'A Horde of Brigands?'" Also see Baptist, *The Half Has Never Been Told,* 57–64; Buman, "Historiographical Examinations of the 1811 Slave Insurrection"; Ford, *Deliver Us from Evil,* 130–36; Rodriguez, "Rebellion on the River Road"; Rothman, *Slave Country,* 106–17. For the records of the trials held in St. Charles Parish see no. 2, "Interrogatoire Procès et Jugement des nègres arrêtés pour cause l'insurection" (Interrogation, Trial, and Judgment of the blacks arrested for insurrection), January 13, 1811, and no. 17, "Interrogatoire et Jugement renda contre la nègre Jupiter appartenant à Manuel Andry" (Interrogation and Judgment rendered against the black man Jupiter belonging to Manuel Landry), February 20, 1811, *St. Charles Parish, La., Original Acts, misc. court records, 1741–1899,* part 17, *1810–1811.* English abstracts in Conrad, *The German Coast,* 100–102, 106. For the records of the trials in New Orleans see criminal case files number 184–95, Territory of Orleans City Court (New Orleans).

69. The runaway slave advertisement is quoted in Thrasher, *On to New Orleans!* 166; Rasmussen, *American Uprising,* 74, 83–87, 105–7, 124–25. It is unclear whether Deslondes was a Louisiana Creole or from St. Domingue. See Baptist, *The Half Has Never Been Told,* 17–18.

70. No. 17, "Interrogatoire et Jugement renda contre la nègre Jupiter appartenant à Manuel Andry," February 20, 1811, *St. Charles Parish, La., Original Acts, misc. court records, 1741–1899,* part 17, *1810–1811.*

71. "Insurrection in Orleans," *Columbian,* February 21, 1811.

72. Ten of 887 enslaved people listed in German Coast estate inventories in the 1810s were listed as being from St. Domingue. Louisiana Slave Database.

73. "Insurrection in Orleans," *Columbian,* February 21, 1811. This letter claimed that the leader was "a free mulatto from St. Domingo."

74. See, for example, Brown, *Tacky's Revolt;* Kars, *Blood on the River.*

75. See, for example, Wayne, *Death of an Overseer.*

76. A similar argument is made in Hoffer, *Cry Liberty,* about the Stono Revolt in colonial South Carolina. Hoffer argues the rebellion could have begun as a

confrontation between enslaved people who broke into a store to rob it and whites who were unexpectedly present in the store that then escalated into a rebellion when the enslaved people killed the whites.

77. Quoted in Ferrer, *Freedom's Mirror*, 217.

78. Fessenden, "How a Nearly Successful Slave Revolt was Intentionally Lost to History."

79. Wade Hampton to Secretary of War William Eustis, January 16, 1811, *Territorial Papers of the United States*, vol. 9, *The Territory of Orleans*, 917.

80. Claiborne to Secretary of State Robert Smith, January 14, 1811, *Official Letter Books of W. C. C. Claiborne, 1801–1816*, 5:100.

81. Claiborne to militia colonels and parish judges, January 10, 1811, *Official Letter Books of W. C. C. Claiborne, 1801–1816*, 5:96.

82. Hampton to Eustis, January 16, 1811, *Territorial Papers of the United States*, vol. 9, *The Territory of Orleans*, 917–18.

83. Andry to Claiborne, January 11, 1811, and January 11, 1811, at ten o'clock p.m., *Louisiana Courier*, January 14, 1811.

84. Many Africans who were enslaved and sold into the slave trade were prisoners of war. See, for example, Thornton, *Africa and Africans in the Making of the Atlantic World*, chapter 4.

85. Figures calculated from *Urban Statistical Surveys*, 82–83.

86. "Insurrection in Orleans," *Columbian*, February 21, 1811.

87. The death toll was reported as two whites, Andry's son and the planter François Trépagnier. For the latter see Rasmussen, *American Uprising*, 109. Neither was killed in the battle on January 10.

88. Andry to Claiborne, January 11, 1811, and January 11, 1811, at ten o'clock p.m., *Louisiana Courier*, January 14, 1811.

89. "Insurrection in Orleans," *Columbian*, February 21, 1811.

90. Hambleton to Porter, January 25, 1811, Papers of David Porter.

91. No. 2, "Interrogatoire Procès et Jugement des nègres arrêtés pour cause l'insurection," January 13, 1811, *St. Charles Parish, La., Original Acts, misc. court records, 1741–1899*, part 17, *1810–1811*. Slaveholdings from original 1810 federal census schedules available in *Population Schedules of the Third Census of the United States, 1810, Louisiana*, reel 10, 427, 430.

92. The 1800 investigation into the murder of Cola, a man enslaved by Étienne Boré, was 312 pages long. "Criminales de oficio sobre haben hallado muerto àun negro nom de Cola de D. Estevan Bore en el Parque de Arroz de la Habitacion de D. Roberto Avart," October 3, 1800, No. 3985, Spanish Judicial Records. The St. Charles Parish investigation of the German Coast Insurrection was only twenty pages long.

93. No. 2, "Interrogatoire Procès et Jugement des nègres arrêtés pour cause l'insurection," January 13, 1811, *St. Charles Parish, La., Original Acts, misc. court*

records, 1741–1899, Part 17, 1810–1811. English translation from Conrad, *The German Coast,* 102.

94. For the records of the trials in New Orleans see criminal case files number 184–95, Territory of Orleans City Court (New Orleans). The quote is from case file no. 187. The man executed by firing squad is case file no. 193. The exonerated man is case file no. 195.

95. *Constitution or Form of Government of the State of Louisiana,* 30.

96. *Constitution or Form of Government of the State of Louisiana,* 30.

97. Martin, *The History of Louisiana,* 349.

98. "Resolution," February 5, 1811, *Acts Passed at the Second Session of the Third Legislature of the Territory of Orleans,* 196–97.

99. No. 18, "Déclaration de diverse habitants en faveur des nègres qui se sont comportér avec selle dans l'insurrection du 9 Janvier present année" (Depositions of various inhabitants in favor of the blacks who acted against the insurrection on January 9 of the present year), *St. Charles Parish, La., Original Acts, misc. court records, 1741–1899,* part 17, *1810–1811.* English abstracts available in Conrad, *The German Coast,* 106–7.

100. P. B. St. Martin, "Parish Court, Parish St. Charles," *Louisiana Courier,* February 4, 1811.

101. Answer of the House, no date, *Official Letter Books of W. C. C. Claiborne,* 5:130.

102. Claiborne to the Territory of Orleans Legislature, January 29, 1811, *Official Letter Books of W. C. C. Claiborne,* 5:123–24.

103. "An Act Supplementary to 'An Act regulating and governing the Militia of the territory of Orleans,'" April 29, 1811, *Acts Passed at the Second Session of the Third Legislature of the Territory of Orleans,* 148–65.

104. Eustis to Claiborne, April 25, 1811, Carter, *The Territorial Papers of the United States,* vol. 9, *The Territory of Orleans,* 931.

105. "An Act Concerning the police of slaves in certain cases and for other purposes," *Acts Passed at the First Session of the Second Legislature of the State of Louisiana,* 30–35. The new law required that all plantations had to keep at least one white adult male in residence per thirty enslaved people.

106. No. 57, "Inventaire des biens de la Succession de feu Augustin Meuillon" (Inventory of the goods of the succession of Augustin Meullion), October 5, 1810; no. 4, "Vente Judiciare des biens de la succession de feu Augustin Meuillon" (Judicial Sale of the goods of the succession of Augustin Meullion), January 28, 1811; no. 22, "Vente à l'encan des Bêtes à cornes et trois Esclaves de la succession de feu Louis Augustin Meuillon" (Auction of the horned livestock and three slaves of the succession of Louis Augustin Meullion), March 9, 1811, *St. Charles Parish, La., Original Acts, misc. court records, 1741–1899,* part 17, *1810–1811.* The comment about the "brigands" damaging the house appears at the beginning of the sale on

January 28, 1811. English abstracts available in Conrad, *The German Coast*, 95–97, 102–4, 110.

107. Hampton to Eustis, January 19, 1811, Letters Received by the Secretary of War Registered Series, reel 37.

108. Christopher Fitzsimons to Hampton, March 15, April 26, June 11, and June 15, 1811, *Family Letters of the Three Wade Hamptons*, 14–18.

109. Joseph Vidal to Stephen Minor, March 24, 1811, William J. Minor and Family Papers.

110. "Sugar and Molasses," *Niles' Weekly Register*, September 5, 1829. For Wade Hampton's plantation in 1820, see *Population Schedules of the Fourth Census of the United States, 1820, Louisiana*, reel 30, 6.

111. Bernhard, Duke of Saxe-Weimer Eisenach, *Travels through North America*, 81.

Conclusion

1. Meeting, August 16, 1800, *Records and Deliberations of the Cabildo*, vol. 4, book 3, 213, reel 91–16.

2. Another conspiracy scare occurred on the German Coast around Christmas of 1811, less than a year after the original revolt. Claiborne called on the local militia to prepare in case the scare was real and to perform regular patrols and enforce the slave code. However, he claimed that he believed the fears "to be unfounded." Claiborne to Major McRae, no date; Claiborne to Adelard Fortier, December 24, 1811; Claiborne to Andry, December 24, 1811; Claiborne to Mather, December 24, 1811; Claiborne to the Secretary of the Navy Hamilton, December 26, 1811, Claiborne, *Official Letter Books of W. C. C. Claiborne, 1801–1816*, 6:16–18, 20–22.

3. Rodriguez, "Always 'En Garde'"; Johnson, *Slavery's Metropolis*, chapter 5.

4. The classic statement of the concept of the second slavery comes from Tomich, *Through the Prism of Slavery*, 56–71. In addition, see Tomich and Zeuske, "The Second Slavery"; Tomich, "The Second Slavery and World Capitalism"; Kaye, "The Second Slavery."

5. See Johnson, "On Agency," for an excellent discussion of the issue of agency in slavery historiography.

6. Chaplin, *An Anxious Pursuit*, chapter 8; Chaplin, "Creating a Cotton South in Georgia and South Carolina"; Klein, *Unification of a Slave State*, chapter 8; Lakwete, *Inventing the Cotton Gin*, chapter 3; Rothman, *Slave Country*.

7. See Ferrer, *Freedom's Mirror*, for the strikingly similar story of Cuba's sugar revolution.

8. A similar point is made in Tomich et al., *Reconstructing the Landscapes of Slavery*, 147–48, about the three plantation zones studied being "formed through complex global-local interactions."

9. Robin, *Voyage to Louisiana*, 107.

10. Briggs to Jefferson, January 2, 1804; Carter, *The Territorial Papers of the United States*, vol. 9, *The Territory of Orleans*, 148.

Appendix

1. These conclusions arise from analysis of data in the Louisiana Slave Database. The practice of recording the origins of slaves was common in Spanish America at least from the mid-1500s. See Wheat, *Atlantic Africa and the Spanish Caribbean*, chapter 2.

2. This tradition of meticulous record keeping was a feature of Spanish colonialism. See Burns, *Into the Archives*.

3. Louisiana Slave Database.

4. Statistics calculated from the Louisiana Slave Database.

5. Statistics calculated from the Louisiana Slave Database.

6. The literature on early modern African ethnic identities and how those ethnicities transformed both in Africa and the Americas is immense. See chapter 4, notes 99 and 101.

7. Statistics calculated from the Louisiana Slave Database.

BIBLIOGRAPHY

Manuscript Sources

Barnes-Willis Family Papers, 1783–1840. Dolph Briscoe Center for American History, University of Texas at Austin.

Boucry Family Papers. MSs 790, 800. Louisiana and Lower Mississippi Valley Collections, Louisiana State University Libraries, Baton Rouge.

Nathaniel Cox Papers. Record group 34. George Smith Collection. Louisiana State Museum, New Orleans.

Dispatches from US Consuls in New Orleans, 1798–1807. General Records of the Department of State. Record Group 59. Microfilm, National Archives Building, College Park, Maryland.

Armand Duplantier Letters. MS 4914. Louisiana and Lower Mississippi Valley Collections, Louisiana State University Libraries, Baton Rouge.

Edward J. Gay Family Papers, 1797–1921. MS 1295. Louisiana and Lower Mississippi Valley Collection, Louisiana State University Libraries, Baton Rouge.

Iberville La. Conveyances, 1770–1900, part 12, *Original Acts, May 1804–February 1808, vol. A8 & 9.* Microfilm, City Archives and Special Collections, New Orleans Public Library, New Orleans.

Pierre Clément Laussat Papers. MS 125. Historic New Orleans Collection, New Orleans.

"Letterbook of private and commercial correspondence of an indigo and cotton planter (Julien Poydras), 1794–1800, Pointe Coupée Parish, Louisiana." Record goup 98. Louisiana State Museum. Microfilm. *Records of ante-bellum southern plantations from the Revolution through the Civil War, Series H, Selections from the Howard-Tilton Memorial Library, Tulane University, and the Louisiana State Museum Archives.* Edited by Kenneth Stampp. Frederick, MD: University Publications of America, 1988. Reel 1.

Letters Received by the Secretary of the Navy from Officers Below the Rank of Commander, 1802–1884. Naval Records Collection of the Office of Naval Records and Library. Record group 45. Microfilm, National Archives Building, Washington, DC.

Letters Received by the Secretary of War Registered Series, 1801–1870. Records of the Office of the Secretary of War. Record group 107. Microfilm, National Archives Building, Washington, DC.

John Mills Letters, 1795, 1807. MS 1375. Louisiana and Lower Mississippi Valley Collections, Louisiana State University Libraries, Baton Rouge.

William J. Minor and Family Papers. MSs 519, 594. Louisiana and Lower Mississippi Valley Collections, Louisiana State University Libraries, Baton Rouge.

Mississippi, US, State and Territorial Census Collection, 1792–1866. Ancestry.com.

New Orleans Notarial Archives. Research Center and Historical Documents, New Orleans.

Population Schedules of the Fifth Census of the United States, 1830, Louisiana. Microfilm, Washington, DC, National Archives and Records, General Services Administration, 1944.

Population Schedules of the Fourth Census of the United States, 1820, Louisiana. Microfilm, Washington, DC, National Archives and Records, General Services Administration, 1958.

Population Schedules of the Fourth Census of the United States, 1820, Mississippi. Microfilm, Washington, DC, National Archives and Records, General Services Administration, 1959.

Population Schedules of the Third Census of the United States, 1810, Louisiana. Microfilm. Washington, DC, National Archives and Records, General Services Administration, 1958.

The Papers of David Porter, 1799–1899. Library of Congress, Washington, DC.

Provincial and Territorial Records. Natchez Trace Collection. Dolph Briscoe Center for American History, University of Texas at Austin.

David Rees Family Papers. Louisiana Research Collection. Howard-Tilton Memorial Library, Tulane University, New Orleans.

Santo Domingo Papers and Cuban Papers. Archive of the Indies. Microfilm, Historic New Orleans Collection, New Orleans.

Winthrop Sargent Papers. Microfilm, Massachusetts Historical Society, Boston.

Spanish Judicial Records, Record group 2. Louisiana State Museum, New Orleans.

St. Charles Parish, La., Original Acts, misc. court records, 1741–1899, parts 10–11, *1792–1795, 1796–1798.* Microfilm, City Archives and Special Collections, New Orleans Public Library, New Orleans.

St. Charles Parish, La., Original Acts, misc. court records, 1741–1899, part 17, *1810–1811.* Microfilm, City Archives and Special Collections, New Orleans Public Library, New Orleans.

Territory of Orleans City Court (New Orleans). Louisiana Purchase Bicentennial Collection. Louisiana Digital Library. https://louisianadigitallibrary.org/.

Territory of Orleans Superior Court. City Archives and Special Collections, New Orleans Public Library, New Orleans.

The Nicholas Philip Trist Papers. #2104. Southern Historical Collection. Wilson Library, University of North Carolina at Chapel Hill.

John Minor Wisdom Collection (John McDonogh series), 1801–1864. Howard-Tilton Memorial Library, Tulane University. Microfilm. *Records of ante-bellum southern plantations from the Revolution through the Civil War.* Series H, *Selections from the Howard-Tilton Memorial Library, Tulane University, and the Louisiana State Museum Archives.* Edited by Kenneth Stampp. Frederick, MD: University Publications of America, 1988. Reel 12.

Online Databases

Louisiana Slave Database. Built by Gwendolyn Midlo Hall. https://www.ibiblio.org/laslave/introduction.php.

Trans-Atlantic Slave Trade Database. http://www.slavevoyages.org/voyage/search.

Periodicals

Ami de Lois (New Orleans)
The Baltimore Patriot
Bangor Weekly Register
Baton Rouge Gazette
City of Washington Gazette
Columbian (New York)
Commercial Advertiser (New Orleans)
Daily Advertiser (New York)
Daily National Intelligencer (Washington, DC)
Frankfort Argus
Genius of Liberty (Leesburg, VA)
Independent Gazetteer (Philadelphia)
Louisiana Advertiser (New Orleans)
Louisiana Courier (New Orleans)
Louisiana Gazette (New Orleans)
Louisiana Herald (Alexandria)
Louisiana Rambler (Alexandria)
Mississippi Herald and Natchez City Gazette (Natchez)
Moniteur de la Louisiane (New Orleans)
Newburyport Herald
New England Palladium & Commercial Advertiser (Boston)
New Orleans Daily Chronicle
New Orleans Price Current and Commercial Intelligencer
New-York Daily Advertiser
New-York Spectator
Niles' Weekly Register (Baltimore)

Orleans Gazette (New Orleans)
Orleans Gazette and Commercial Advertiser (New Orleans)
St. Francisville Timepiece (St. Francisville, LA)
The Telegraphe, General Advertiser (New Orleans)
The Union (New Orleans)

Published Sources

Acts Passed at the First Session of the First Legislature of the Territory of Orleans. New Orleans: Bradford and Anderson, 1807.

Acts Passed at the First Session of the Second Legislature of the State of Louisiana. New Orleans: Peter K. Wagner, 1815.

Acts Passed at the First Session of the Sixth General Assembly of the Mississippi Territory. Natchez: John Shaw, 1810.

Acts Passed at the First Session of the Third Legislature of the Territory of Orleans. New Orleans: Thierry and Dacqueny, 1810.

Acts Passed by the Second General Assembly of the Mississippi Territory during Their Second Session. Natchez: Andrew Marschalk, 1808.

Acts Passed at the Second Session of the Third Legislature of the State of Louisiana. New Orleans: J. C. de St. Romes, 1818.

Acts Passed at the Second Session of the Third Legislature of the Territory of Orleans. New Orleans: Thierry, 1811.

Acts Passed by the Second General Assembly of the Mississippi Territory during Their Second Session. Natchez: 1804.

Adelman, Jeremy, and Stephen Aron. "From Borderlands to Borders: Empires, Nation-States, and the Peoples in between in North American History." *American Historical Review* 104, no. 3 (June 1999): 814–41.

Agriculture of the United States in 1860; Compiled from the Original Returns of the Eighth Census. Washington, DC: Government Printing Office, 1864.

Archives of the Spanish Government of West Florida: Vols. 1–19. Edited and translated by The Survey of Federal Archives, Louisiana Division, Works Progress Administration. New Orleans: Survey of the Federal Archives, 1937–1940.

Arthur, Brian W. *The Nature of Technology: What It Is and How It Evolves.* New York: Free Press, 2009.

Ball, Charles. *Slavery in the United States: A Narrative of the Life and Adventures of Charles Ball, a Black Man.* New York: John S. Taylor, 1837.

Baptist, Edward. *Creating an Old South: Middle Florida's Plantation Frontier before the Civil War.* Chapel Hill: University of North Carolina Press, 2002.

———. *The Half Has Never Been Told: Slavery and the Making of American Capitalism.* New York: Basic Books, 2014.

———. "Towards a Political Economy of Slave Labor: Hands, Whipping-Machines, and Modern Power." In *Slavery's Capitalism: A New History of*

American Economic Development, edited by Sven Beckert and Seth Rockman, 31–61. Philadelphia: University of Pennsylvania Press, 2011.

———. "Toxic Debt, Liar Loans, Collateralized and Securitized Human Beings, and the Panic of 1837." In *Capitalism Takes Command: The Social Transformation of Nineteenth-Century America,* edited by Michael Zakim and Gary Kornblith, 69–92. Chicago: University of Chicago Press, 2012.

Barnes, L. Diane, Brian Schoen, and Frank Towers, eds. *The Old South's Modern Worlds: Slavery, Region, and Nation in the Age of Progress.* New York: Oxford University Press, 2011.

Beckert, Sven. *Empire of Cotton: A Global History.* New York: Knopf, 2014.

Beckert, Sven, and Seth Rockman, eds. *Slavery's Capitalism: A New History of American Economic Development.* Philadelphia: University of Pennsylvania Press, 2011.

Bell, Richard. *Stolen: Five Free Boys Kidnapped into Slavery and Their Astonishing Odyssey Home.* New York: Simon and Schuster, 2019.

Berlin, Ira. *Many Thousands Gone: The First Two Centuries of Slavery in North America.* Cambridge, MA: Harvard University Press, 1998.

Bernhard, Duke of Saxe-Weimer Eisenach. *Travels through North America: During the Years 1825 and 1826.* Vol. 2. Philadelphia: Carey, Lea, and Carey, 1828.

[Berquin-Duvallon]. *Travels in Louisiana and the Floridas, in the Year, 1802: Giving a Correct Picture of Those Countries.* Translated by John Davis. New York: I. Riley, 1806.

Berquist, Emily. "Early Anti-Slavery Sentiment in the Spanish Atlantic World, 1765–1817." *Slavery and Abolition* 31, no. 2 (June 2010): 181–205.

Bouligny, Francisco. *Louisiana in 1776: A Memoria of Francisco Bouligny.* Translated by Gilbert Din. New Orleans: Jack Holmes, 1977.

Brown, Vincent. *Tacky's Revolt: The Story of an Atlantic Slave War.* Cambridge, MA: Harvard University Press, 2020.

Buman, Nathan. "Historiographical Examinations of the 1811 Slave Insurrection." *Louisiana History* 53, no. 3 (Summer 2012): 318–37.

———. "To Kill Whites: The 1811 Louisiana Slave Insurrection." Master's thesis. Louisiana State University, 2009.

Burnard, Trevor. *Mastery, Tyranny, and Desire: Thomas Thistlewood and His Slaves in the Anglo-Jamaican World.* Chapel Hill: University of North Carolina Press, 2004.

———. *Planters, Merchants, and Slaves: Plantation Societies in British America, 1650–1820.* Chicago: University of Chicago Press, 2015.

Burns, Kathryn. *Into the Archives: Writing and Power in Colonial Peru.* Durham, NC: Duke University Press, 2010.

Byrd, Alexander X. "Eboe, Country, Nation, and Gustavas Vassa's Interesting Narrative." *William and Mary Quarterly* 63, no. 1 (January 2006): 123–48.

Carondelet, Francisco Luis Héctor. *Circulaire, Adressée par le Gouvernement à Tous les Habitans* (Circular, Addressed by the Government to All Inhabitants). New Orleans, 1794.

———. "Military Report on Louisiana and West Florida." In *Louisiana under the Rule of Spain, France, and the United States, 1785–1807: Social, Economic, and Political Conditions of the Territory Represented in the Louisiana Purchase as Portrayed in Hitherto Unpublished Contemporary Accounts by Dr. Paul Alliot And Various Spanish, French, English and American Officials,* Vol. 1, edited and translated by James Alexander Robertson, 291–346. Cleveland: Arthur H. Clark, 1911.

Carter, Clarence Edwin, comp. and ed. *The Territorial Papers of the United States.* Vol. 5, *The Territory of Mississippi, 1798–1817.* Washington, DC: Government Printing Office, 1937.

———, comp. and ed. *The Territorial Papers of the United States.* Vol. 9, *The Territory of Orleans, 1803–1812.* Washington, DC: Government Printing Office, 1940.

Cauthen, Charles Edward, ed. *Family Letters of the Three Wade Hamptons.* Columbia: University of South Carolina Press, 1953.

Census for 1820. Washington: Gales and Seaton, 1821.

Chaillot, Jane B. "Clark, Daniel." In Dictionary of Louisiana Biography, Louisiana Historical Association. https://www.lahistory.org/resources/dictionary -louisiana-biography/dictionary-louisiana-biography-c/.

Chambers, Douglas. "Slave Trade Merchants of Spanish New Orleans, 1763–1803: Clarifying the Colonial Slave Trade to Louisiana in Atlantic Perspective." *Atlantic Studies* 5, no. 3 (2008): 335–46.

Chaplin, Joyce. *An Anxious Pursuit: Agricultural Innovation and Modernity in the Lower South, 1730–1815.* Chapel Hill: University of North Carolina Press, 1993.

———. "Creating a Cotton South in Georgia and South Carolina, 1760–1815." *Journal of Southern History* 57, no. 2 (May 1991): 171–200.

Claiborne, J. F. H. *Mississippi as a Province, Territory and State with Biographical Notices of Eminent Citizens.* Vol. 1. Jackson, MS: Power and Barksdale, 1880.

Claiborne, William C. C. *Official Letter Books of W. C. C. Claiborne, 1801–1816.* Vols. 1–6. Edited by Dunbar Rowland. Jackson, MS: State Department of Archives and History, 1917.

Clark, John G. *New Orleans, 1718–1812: An Economic History.* Baton Rouge: Louisiana State University Press, 1970.

Clavin, Matthew. *The Battle of Negro Fort: The Rise and Fall of a Fugitive Slave Community.* New York: New York University Press, 2019.

Clegg, John. "Capitalism and Slavery." *Critical Historical Studies* 2, no. 2 (September 2015): 381–404.

Collot, Victor. *Voyage dans l'Amérique Septentrionale.* Vol. 2, *Travel to North America.* Paris: Arthus Bertrand, 1826.

Conrad, Glenn R. *The German Coast: Abstracts of the Civil Records of St. Charles and St. John the Baptist Parishes, 1804–1812*. Lafayette: University of Southwestern Louisiana, 1981.

———. *St. Charles: Abstracts of the Civil Records of St. Charles Parish, 1700–1803*. Lafayette: University of Southwestern Louisiana, 1974.

Constitution or Form of Government of the State of Louisiana. New Orleans: Jo. Bar. Baird, 1812.

Cramer, Zadok. *The Navigator*. Pittsburgh: Cramer, Spear and Eichbaum, 1811.

Crawford, James. *The Mobilian Trade Language*. Knoxville: University of Tennessee Press, 1978.

Dart, Elizabeth Kilbourne. "Bradford, David." *Dictionary of Louisiana Biography*, Louisiana Historical Association. https://www.lahistory.org/resources /dictionary-louisiana-biography/dictionary-louisiana-biography-b/.

———. "O'Connor, John." *Dictionary of Louisiana Biography*, Louisiana Historical Association. https://www.lahistory.org/resources/dictionary-louisiana -biography/dictionary-louisiana-biography-o/.

Dawdy, Shannon Lee. *Building the Devil's Empire: French Colonial New Orleans*. Chicago: University of Chicago Press, 2008.

Dessens, Nathalie. *From Saint-Domingue to New Orleans: Migration and Influences*. Gainesville: University Press of Florida, 2010.

Deyle, Steven. *Carry Me Back: The Domestic Slave Trade in American Life*. New York: Oxford University Press, 2005.

Din, Gilbert. "Carondelet, the Cabildo, and Slaves: Louisiana in 1795." *Louisiana History* 31, no. 1 (Winter 1997): 5–28.

———. "Empires Too Far: The Demographic Limitations of Three Imperial Powers in the Eighteenth-Century Mississippi Valley." *Louisiana History* 50, no. 3 (Summer 2009): 261–92.

———. *The New Orleans Cabildo: Colonial Louisiana's First City Government, 1769–1803*. Baton Rouge: Louisiana State University Press, 1996.

———. *Spaniards, Planters, and Slaves: The Spanish Regulation of Slavery in Louisiana, 1763–1803*. College Station: Texas A&M University Press, 1999.

Drechsel, Emmanuel J. *Mobilian Jargon: Linguistic and Sociohistorical Aspects of a Native American Pidgin*. New York: Oxford University Press, 1997.

Dunbar, Rowland, ed. *Life, Letters and Papers of William Dunbar of Elgin, Morayshire, Scotland, and Natchez, Mississippi: Pioneer Scientist of the Southern United States*. Jackson: Press of the Mississippi Historical Society, 1930.

Dunn, Robert. *A Tale of Two Plantations: Slave Life and Labor in Jamaica and Virginia*. Cambridge: Harvard University Press, 2014.

Dupre, Daniel. *Transforming the Cotton Frontier: Madison County, Alabama, 1800–1840*. Baton Rouge: Louisiana State University Press, 1997.

Egerton, Douglas. "Slave Resistance." In *The Oxford Handbook of Slavery in the Americas,* edited by Mark Smith and Robert Paquette, 447–64. New York: Oxford University Press, 2010.

Equiano, Olaudah. *The Interesting Narrative of Olaudah Equiano, or Gustavus Vass, the African. Written by Himself.* Vol. 1. London: Author, 1789.

Faber, Eberhard. *Building the Land of Dreams: New Orleans and the Transformation of Early America.* Princeton, NJ: Princeton University Press, 2015.

Falola, Toyin. *The African Diaspora: Slavery, Modernity, and Globalization.* Rochester, NY: University of Rochester Press, 2014.

Fehrenbacher, Don. *The Slaveholding Republic: An Account of the United States Government's Relations to Slavery.* New York: Oxford University Press, 2001.

Ferrer, Ada. *Freedom's Mirror: Cuba and Haiti in the Age of Revolution.* New York: Cambridge University Press, 2014.

Fessenden, Marissa. "How a Nearly Successful Slave Revolt Was Intentionally Lost to History." *Smithsonian Magazine,* January 8, 2016. https://www.smithsonianmag.com/smart-news/its-anniversary-1811-louisiana-slave-revolt-180957760/.

Finkelman, Paul. *Slavery and the Founders: Race and Liberty in the Age of Jefferson.* 3rd ed. New York: Taylor and Francis, 2014.

Follett, Richard. "'Lives of Living Death': The Reproductive Lives of Slave Women in the Cane World of Louisiana." *Slavery and Abolition* 26, no. 2 (August 2005): 289–304.

———. *The Sugar Masters: Planters and Slaves in Louisiana Cane World, 1820–1860.* Baton Rouge: Louisiana State University Press, 2007.

Follett, Richard, Sven Beckert, Peter Coclanis, and Barbara Hahn. *Plantation Kingdom: The American South and Its Global Commodities.* Baltimore: Johns Hopkins University Press, 2016.

Ford, Lacy K. *Deliver Us from Evil: The Slavery Question in the Old South.* New York: Oxford University Press, 2009.

Fort, Karen Gerhardt Britton. *Bale o'Cotton: The Mechanical Art of Cotton Ginning.* College Station: Texas A&M University Press, 1992.

Franklin, John Hope, and Loren Schweninger. *Runaway Slaves: Rebels on the Plantation.* New York: Oxford University Press, 1999.

Freehling, William W. *The Reintegration of American History: Slavery and the Civil War.* New York: Oxford University Press, 1994.

———. *The Road to Disunion.* Vol. 1, *Secessionists at Bay.* New York: Oxford University Press, 1990.

Gayarré, Charles. *History of Louisiana.* Vol. 3, *The Spanish Domination.* New York: William J. Middleton, 1867.

Geggus, David. "On the Eve of the Haitian Revolution: Slave Runaways in Saint Domingue in the Year 1790." *Slavery and Abolition* 6, no. 3 (1985): 112–28.

Gomez, Michael. *Reversing Sail, A History of the African Diaspora*. New York: Cambridge University Press, 2005.

Gray, Lewis. *History of Agriculture in the Southern United States to 1860*. New York: Peter Smith, 1958.

Greene, Jack P., ed. *Exclusionary Empire: English Liberty Overseas, 1600–1900*. New York: Cambridge University Press, 2010.

Gudmestad, Robert. "Slave Resistance, Coffles, and Debates over Slavery in the Nation's Capital." In *The Chattel Principle: Internal Slave Trades in the Americas*, edited by Walter Johnson, 72–90. New Haven, CT: Yale University Press, 2004.

———. *A Troublesome Commerce: The Transformation of the Internal Slave Trade*. Baton Rouge: Louisiana State University Press, 2003.

Hall, Gwendolyn Midlo. *Africans in Colonial Louisiana: The Development of Afro-Creole Culture in the Eighteenth Century*. Baton Rouge: Louisiana State University Press, 1992.

———. *Slavery and African Ethnicities in the Americas: Restoring the Links*. Chapel Hill: University of North Carolina Press, 2005.

Hall, James. "A Brief History of the Mississippi Territory." *Publications of the Mississippi Historical Society* 9 (1909): 539–76.

Hammond, John Craig. *Slavery, Freedom, and Expansion in the Early American West*. Charlottesville: University of Virginia Press, 2007.

———. "Slavery, Settlement, and Empire: The Expansions and Growth of Slavery in the Interior of the North American Continent, 1770–1820." *Journal of the Early American Republic* 32, no. 2 (Summer 2012): 175–206.

Hanger, Kimberly. "Conflicting Loyalties: The French Revolution and Free People of Color in Spanish New Orleans." *Louisiana History* 34, no. 1 (Winter 1999): 5–33.

Harms, Robert. *The Diligent: A Voyage through the Worlds of the Slave Trade*. New York: Basic Books, 2002.

Hartog, Hendrik. *The Trouble with Minna: A Case of Slavery and Emancipation in the Antebellum North*. Chapel Hill: University of North Carolina Press, 2018.

Haynes, Robert V. *The Mississippi Territory and the Southwest Frontier, 1795–1817*. Lexington: University Press of Kentucky, 2010.

Head, David. "Slave Smuggling by Foreign Privateers: The Illegal Slave Trade and the Geopolitics of the Early Republic." *Journal of the Early Republic* 33, no. 3 (Fall 2013): 433–62.

Herschthal, Eric. "Slaves, Spaniards, and Subversion in Early Louisiana: The Persistent Fears of Black Revolt and Spanish Collusion in Territorial Louisiana, 1803–1812." *Journal of the Early Republic* 36, no. 2 (Summer 2016): 283–311.

Heywood, Linda, and John Thornton. *Central Africans, Atlantic Creoles, and the Foundation of the Americas, 1585–1660*. New York: Cambridge University Press, 2007.

Higman, B. W. *Slave Populations of the British Caribbean, 1807–1834*. Baltimore: Johns Hopkins University Press, 1984.

Hodgson, Adam. *Letters from North America Written during a Tour in the United States and Canada*. Vol. 1. London: Hurst, Robinson and A. Constable, 1824.

Hoffer, Peter. *Cry Liberty: The Great Stono River Slave Rebellion in 1739*. Oxford: Oxford University Press, 2010.

Holmes, Jack. "Cotton Gins in the Spanish Natchez District, 1795–1800." *Journal of Mississippi History* 31, no. 3 (August 1969): 159–71.

———. "Indigo in Colonial Louisiana and the Floridas." *Louisiana History* 8, no. 4 (Autumn 1967): 329–49.

Ingersoll, Thomas. *Mammon and Manon in Early New Orleans: The First Slave Society in the Deep South, 1718–1819*. Knoxville: University of Tennessee Press, 1999.

———. "The Slave Trade and the Ethnic Diversity of Louisiana's Slave Community." *Louisiana History* 37, no. 2 (Spring 1996): 133–61.

Johnson, Jessica Marie. *Wicked Flesh: Black Women, Intimacy, and Freedom in the Atlantic World*. Philadelphia: University of Pennsylvania Press, 2020.

Johnson, Michael. "Denmark Vesey and His Co-Conspirators." *William and Mary Quarterly* 58, no. 4 (October 2001): 915–76.

———. "Runaway Slaves and the Slave Communities in South Carolina, 1799 to 1830." *William and Mary Quarterly* 38, no. 3 (July 1981): 418–41.

Johnson, Rashauna. *Slavery's Metropolis: Unfree Labor in New Orleans during the Age of Revolutions*. New York: Cambridge University Press, 2016.

Johnson, Walter. "On Agency." *Journal of Social History* 37, no. 1 (Fall 2003): 113–24.

———. *River of Dark Dreams: Slavery and Empire in the Cotton Kingdom*. Cambridge, MA: Harvard University Pres, 2013.

Kars, Marjoreine. *Blood on the River: A Chronicle of Mutiny and Freedom on the Wild Coast*. New York: New Press, 2020.

Kaye, Anthony. "The Second Slavery: Modernity in the Nineteenth-Century South and Atlantic World." *Journal of Southern History* 75, no.3 (Summer 2009): 627–50.

Kelly, Sean. *The Voyage of the Slave Ship* Hare: *A Journey into Captivity from Sierra Leone to South Carolina*. Chapel Hill: University of North Carolina Press, 2016.

Klein, Rachel. *Unification of a Slave State: The Rise of the Planter Class in the South Carolina Backcountry, 1760–1808*. Chapel Hill: University of North Carolina Press, 1990.

Krichtal, Alexey. "Liverpool and the Raw Cotton Trade: A Study of the Port and Its Merchant Community, 1770–1815." Master's thesis, Victoria University of Wellington, 2013.

Lachance, Paul. "Repercussions of the Haitian Revolution in Louisiana." In *The Impact of the Haitian Revolution in the Atlantic World*, edited by David P. Geggus, 209–30. Columbia: University of South Carolina Press, 2001.

Lakwete, Angela. *Inventing the Cotton Gin: Machine and Myth in Antebellum America*. Baltimore: Johns Hopkins University Press, 2003.

Landers, Jane. *Black Society in Spanish Florida*. Urbana: University of Illinois Press, 1999.

Latrobe, Benjamin. *Impressions Respecting New Orleans: Diary and Sketches, 1818–1820*. Edited by Samuel Wilson Jr. New York: Columbia University Press, 1951.

Laussat, Pierre Clément de. *Memoirs of My Life: to My Son during the Year 1803 and After, Which I Spent in Public Service in Louisiana as Commissioner of the French Government for the Retrocession to France of that Colony and for Its Transfer to the United States*. Translated by Agnes-Josephine Pastwa and edited by Robert Bush. Baton Rouge: Louisiana State University Press, 1978.

Leglaunec, Jean-Pierre. "Notes and Documents: A Directory of Ships with Slave Cargoes, Louisiana, 1772–1808." *Louisiana History* 46, no. 2 (Spring 2005): 211–30.

———. "Slave Migrations in Spanish and Early American Louisiana: New Series and New Estimates." *Louisiana History* 46, no. 2 (Spring 2005): 185–209.

Libby, David. *Slavery and Frontier Mississippi, 1720–1835*. Jackson: University Press of Mississippi, 2004.

Liljegren, Ernest. "Jacobinism in Spanish Louisiana, 1792–1797." *Louisiana Historical Quarterly* 22, no. 1 (January 1939): 47–97.

Lowery, Charles. "The Great Migration to the Mississippi Territory, 1798–1819." *Journal of Mississippi History* 30 (August 1968): 173–92.

Lozières, Baudry des. *Second Voyage à Louisiane, Faisant Suite au Premier de l'Auteur de 1794 à 1798* (Second Voyage to Louisiana Following the Author's First from 1794 to 1798). Paris: Chez Charles, 1803.

Malone, Ann Paton. *Sweet Chariot: Slave Family and Household Structure in Nineteenth-Century Louisiana*. Chapel Hill: University of North Carolina Press, 1992.

Martin, Bonnie. "Slavery's Invisible Engine: Mortgaging Human Property." *Journal of Southern History* 76, no. 4 (November 2010): 817–66.

Martin, Francois-Xavier. *The History of Louisiana: From the Earliest Period*. New Orleans: James A. Gresham, 1881 [1827–1829].

McBee, M. W., comp. *The Natchez Court Records, 1767–1805: Abstracts of Early Records*. Baltimore: Genealogical Publishing, 1979.

McClellan, James E. III, and Harold Dorn. *Science and Technology in World History: An Introduction*. 3rd ed. Baltimore: Johns Hopkins University Press, 2015.

McMillin, James. *The Final Victims: Foreign Slave Trade to North America, 1783–1810.* Columbia: University of South Carolina Press, 2004.

Memorial presented by the inhabitants of Louisiana to the Congress of the United States, in Senate and House of Representatives, Convened, Translated from the French. Washington, DC: Samuel H. Smith, 1804.

Mintz, Sidney. "Enduring Substances, Trying Theories: The Caribbean Region as Oikoumene." *Journal of the Royal Anthropological Institute* 2, no. 2 (June 1996): 289–311.

———. *Sweetness and Power: The Place of Sugar in Modern History.* New York: Penguin Books, 1985.

Mintz, Sidney, and Richard Price. *The Birth of African-American Culture: An Anthropological Perspective.* Boston: Beacon, 1992.

Montulé, Édouard de. *Travels in America, 1816–1817.* Vol. 9. Indian University Publications, Social Science Series. Translated by Edward Seeber. Bloomington: Indiana University Press, 1950.

Moore, John Hebron. *Agriculture in Ante-Bellum Mississippi.* Columbia, SC: University of South Carolina Press, 2010.

———. *The Emergence of the Cotton Kingdom in the Old Southwest: Mississippi, 1770–1860.* Baton Rouge: Louisiana State University Press, 1988.

Morgan, Philip. *Slave Counterpoint: Black Culture in the Eighteenth-Century Chesapeake and Lowcountry.* Chapel Hill: University of North Carolina Press, 1998.

Narrett, David. *Adventurism and Empire: The Struggle for Mastery in the Louisiana–Florida Borderlands, 1762–1803.* Chapel Hill: University of North Carolina Press, 2015.

Northup, Solomon. *Twelve Years a Slave: Narrative of Solomon Northup, a Citizen of New-York, Kidnapped in Washington City in 1841, and Rescued in 1853, From a Cotton Plantation near the Red River, in Louisiana.* Auburn, New York: Derby and Miller, 1853.

Olmstead, Alan, and Paul Rhode. *Creating Abundance: Biological Innovation and American Agricultural Development.* New York: Cambridge University Press, 2008.

O'Malley, Gregory E. *Final Passages: The Intercolonial Slave Trade of British America, 1619–1807.* Chapel Hill: University of North Carolina Press, 2014.

Ordinance Establishing the Louisiana Bank. New Orleans: J. Lyon, 1804.

Paquette, Robert L. "'A Horde of Brigands?' The Great Louisiana Slave Revolt of 1811 Reconsidered." *Historical Reflections* 35, no. 1 (Spring 2009): 72–96.

Pargas, Damien Alan. "In the Fields of a 'Strange Land': Enslaved Newcomers and the Adjustment to Cotton Cultivation in the Antebellum South." *Slavery and Abolition* 34, no. 4 (2013): 562–78.

———. "Slave Crucibles: Interstate Migrants and Social Assimilation in the Antebellum South." *Slavery and Abolition* 36, no. 1 (2015): 26–39.

Pitot, James. *Observations on the Colony of Louisiana from 1796 to 1802.* Translated by Henry Pitot. Baton Rouge: Louisiana State University Press, 1979.

Pontalba, Joseph Xavier Delfau, baron de. *The Letters of Joseph X. Pontalba to His Wife, 1796.* Translated by Henri Delvile de Sinclair. Survey of Federal Archives in Louisiana, 1939.

Population of the United States in 1860; Compiled from the Original Returns of the Eighth Census. Washington, DC: Government Printing Office, 1864.

Portuondo, Maria M. "Plantation Factories: Science and Technology in Late-Eighteenth-Century Cuba." *Technology and Culture* 44, no. 2 (April 2003): 231–57.

Powell, Lawrence. *The Accidental City: Improvising New Orleans.* Cambridge, MA: Harvard University Press, 2012.

The Public Statutes at Large of the United States of America from the Organization of the Government in 1789, to March 3, 1845. Vols. 1–2. Boston: Charles C. Little and James Brown, 1845.

Rasmussen, Daniel. *American Uprising: The Untold Story of America's Largest Slave Revolt.* New York: Harper-Collins Publishers, 2011.

Recopilacion de Leyes de los Reynos de las Indias (Recapitulation of the Laws of the Kings of the Indies). Madrid: Viuda de D. Joaquin Ibarra, 1791.

Records and Deliberations of the Cabildo, 1769–1803. English translations. Microfilm. New Orleans: City Archives, 1936.

Rehder, John. *Delta Sugar: Louisiana's Vanishing Plantation Landscape.* Baltimore: Johns Hopkins University Press, 1999.

Roberts, Justin. *Slavery and Enlightenment in the British Atlantic, 1750–1807.* New York: Cambridge University Press, 2013.

Roberts, Kevin. "Slaves and Slavery in Louisiana: The Evolution of Atlantic World Identities, 1791–1831." PhD diss., University of Texas at Austin, 2003.

Robin, C. C. *Voyage to Louisiana: An Abridged Translation from the Original French.* Translated by Stuart Landry Jr. Gretna, LA: Pelican, 2000.

Rodriguez, Junius. "Always 'En Garde': The Effects of Slave Insurrection upon the Louisiana Mentality, 1811–1815." *Louisiana History* 33, no. 4 (Autumn 1992): 399–416.

———. "Rebellion on the River Road: The Ideology and Influence of Louisiana's German Coast Insurrection of 1811." In *Antislavery Violence: Sectional, Racial, and Cultural Conflict in Antebellum American,* edited by John R. McKivigan and Stanley Harrold, 65–82. Knoxville: University of Tennessee Press, 1999.

Rothman, Adam. "The Domestication of the Slave Trade in the United States." In *The Chattel Principle: Internal Slave Trades in the Americas,* edited by Walter Johnson, 32–54. New Haven, CT: Yale University Press, 2004.

———. *Slave Country: American Expansion and the Origins of the Deep South.* Cambridge, MA: Harvard University Press, 2005.

Rothman, Joshua. *Flush Times and Fever Dreams: A Story of Capitalism and Slavery in the Age of Jackson.* Athens: University of Georgia Press, 2012.

———. *The Ledger and the Chain: How Domestic Slave Traders Shaped America.* New York: Basic Books, 2021.

Rood, Daniel B. *The Reinvention of Atlantic Slavery: Technology, Labor, Race, and Capitalism in the Greater Caribbean.* New York: Oxford University Press, 2017.

Russell, Sarah. "Cultural Conflicts and Common Interests: The Making of the Sugar Planter Class in Louisiana, 1795–1853." PhD diss. The University of Maryland, 2000.

Sargent's Code: A Collection of the Original Laws of the Mississippi Territory Enacted 1799–1800 by Governor Winthrop Sargent and the Territorial Judges. Jackson, MS: Historical Records Survey, 1939.

Saunt, Claudio. *Unworthy Republic: The Dispossession of Native Americans and the Road to Indian Territory.* New York: W. W. Norton, 2020.

Scott, Julius. *The Common Wind: Afro-American Currents in the Age of the Haitian Revolution.* New York: Verso, 2018.

Seck, Ibrahima. *Bouki Fait Gombo: A History of the Slave Community of Habitation Haydel (Whitney Plantation), Louisiana, 1750–1860.* New Orleans: University of New Orleans Press, 2014.

Shugerman, Jed Handelsman. "The Louisiana Purchase and South Carolina's Reopening of the Slave Trade in 1803." *Journal of the Early Republic* 22, no. 2 (Summer 2002): 263–90.

Sidbury, James. "Globalization, Creolization, and the Not-So-Peculiar Institution." *Journal of Southern History* 73, no. 3 (August 2007): 617–30.

———, and Jorge Cañizares-Esguerra. "Mapping Ethnogenesis in the Early Atlantic World." *William and Mary Quarterly* 68, no. 2 (April 2011): 181–208.

Sitterson, J. Carlyle. *Sugar Country: The Cane Sugar Industry in the South.* Lexington: University of Kentucky Press, 1953.

Sweet, James. "Defying Social Death: The Multiple Configurations of African Slave Family in the Atlantic World." *William and Mary Quarterly* 70, no. 2 (April 2013): 251–72.

———. *Recreating Africa: Culture, Kinship, and Religion in the African-Portuguese World, 1441–1770.* Chapel Hill: University of North Carolina Press, 2003.

Tadman, Michael. "The Demographic Costs of Sugar: Debates on Slave Societies and Natural Increase in the Americas." *American Historical Review* 105, no. 5 (December 2000): 1534–75.

———. "The Interregional Slave Trade in the History and Myth-Making of the U.S. South." In *The Chattel Principle: Internal Slave Trades in the Americas,* edited by Walter Johnson, 117–42. New Haven, CT: Yale University Press, 2004.

———. *Speculators and Slaves: Masters, Traders, and Slaves in the Old South.* Madison: University of Wisconsin Press, 1989.

Thomas, Daniel. "Pre-Whitney Cotton Gins in French Louisiana." *Journal of Southern History* 31, no. 2 (May 1965): 135–48.

Thornton, John. *Africa and Africans in the Making of the Atlantic World, 1400–1800.* 2nd ed. Cambridge: Cambridge University Press, 1998.

Thrasher, Albert. *On to New Orleans! Louisiana's Heroic 1811 Slave Revolt.* 2nd. ed. New Orleans: Cypress, 1996.

Tomich, Dale. "The Second Slavery and World Capitalism: A Perspective for Historical Inquiry." *International Review of Social History* 63, no. 3 (December 2018): 477–501.

———. *Through the Prism of Slavery: Labor, Capital, and World Economy.* New York: Rowman and Littlefield, 2003.

Tomich, Dale, Rafael de Bivar Marquese, Reinaldo Funes Monzote, and Carlos Venegas Fornias. *Reconstructing the Landscapes of Slavery: A Visual History of the Plantation in the Nineteenth-Century Atlantic World.* Chapel Hill: University of North Carolina Press, 2021.

Tomich, Dale, and Michael Zeuske, eds. "The Second Slavery: Mass Slavery, World-Economy and Comparative Microhistories, Part I." *Review: A Journal of the Fernand Braudel Center* 31, no. 2 (2008).

Tomlins, Christopher. *Freedom Bound: Law, Labor, and Civic Identity in Colonizing English America, 1580–1865.* New York: Cambridge University Press, 2010.

Toulmin, Harry, comp. *The Statutes of the Mississippi Territory: Revised and Digested by the Authority of the General Assembly.* Natchez, MS: Samuel Terrel, 1807.

Travis, Jessica Fearrington. "Lafon, Barthélemy." Dictionary of Louisiana Biography, Louisiana Historical Association. https://www.lahistory.org/resources/dictionary-louisiana-biography/dictionary-louisiana-biography-l/.

Urban Statistical Surveys: Aggregate Amount of Each Description of Persons within the United States of America and the Territories in the Year 1810. New York: Arno, 1976.

Usner, Daniel. *American Indians in the Lower Mississippi Valley: Social and Economic Histories.* Lincoln: University of Nebraska Press, 1998.

———. *Indians, Settlers, and Slaves in a Frontier Exchange Economy: The Lower Mississippi Valley before 1783.* Chapel Hill: University of North Carolina Press, 1992.

Vidal, Cécile. *Caribbean New Orleans: Empire, Race, and the Making of a Slave Society.* Chapel Hill: University of North Carolina Press, 2019.

Wailes, B. L. C. *Report on the Agriculture and Geography of Mississippi: Embracing a Sketch of the Social and Natural History of the State.* E. Barkdale, 1854.

Wayne, Michael. *Death of an Overseer: Reopening a Murder Investigation from the Plantation South.* Oxford: Oxford University Press, 2001.

Wheat, David. *Atlantic Africa and the Spanish Caribbean, 1570–1640.* Chapel Hill: University of North Carolina Press, 2016.

Whitaker, Arthur Preston. *The Mississippi Question, 1795–1803: A Study in Trade, Politics, and Diplomacy.* Gloucester, MA: Peter Smith, 1962.

Wilson, Carol. *Freedom at Risk: The Kidnapping of Free Blacks in America, 1780–1865.* Lexington: University of Kentucky Press, 1994.

Wood, Gordon. *Empire of Liberty: A History of the Early Republic, 1789–1815.* Oxford: Oxford University Press, 2009.

Woodward, Ralph Lee, Jr. "Spanish Commercial Policy in Louisiana, 1763–1803." *Louisiana History* 44, no. 2 (Spring 2003): 133–64.

INDEX

Citizens of a Common Intellectual Homeland: The Transatlantic Origins of American Democracy and Nationhood
Armin Mattes

Between Sovereignty and Anarchy: The Politics of Violence in the American Revolutionary Era
Patrick Griffin, Robert G. Ingram, Peter S. Onuf, and Brian Schoen, editors

Patriotism and Piety: Federalist Politics and Religious Struggle in the New American Nation
Jonathan J. Den Hartog

Becoming Men of Some Consequence: Youth and Military Service in the Revolutionary War
John A. Ruddiman

Amelioration and Empire: Progress and Slavery in the Plantation Americas
Christa Dierksheide

Collegiate Republic: Cultivating an Ideal Society in Early America
Margaret Sumner

Era of Experimentation: American Political Practices in the Early Republic
Daniel Peart

Paine and Jefferson in the Age of Revolutions
Simon P. Newman and Peter S. Onuf, editors

Sons of the Father: George Washington and His Protégés
Robert M. S. McDonald, editor

Religious Freedom: Jefferson's Legacy, America's Creed
John Ragosta